Effective Fervent Prayer

Mary Alice Isleib

Mary Alice Isleib Ministries
Minneapolis, Minnesota

DISTRIBUTED BY:
SWORD PUBLICATIONS
P.O. BOX 139
ABERDEEN
SCOTLAND
PHONE/FAX 0224-276639

Unless otherwise indicated, all scriptural quotations are from the New King James Version of the Bible.

Scripture quotations marked *Amplified* are taken from the Amplified Bible. Old Testament copyright © 1965, 1987 by The Zondervan Corporation. The Amplified New Testament copyright © 1958,1987 by The Lockman Foundation. Used by permission.

Effective Fervent Prayer
ISBN 0-9629986-0-5
Copyright © 1991 by
Mary Alice Isleib
P.O. Box 46105
Minneapolis, MN 55446

Published by
Mary Alice Isleib Ministries
P.O. Box 46105
Minneapolis, MN 55446
U.S.A.

2nd printing, 1992

Dedication

This book is dedicated to all of God's people around the world who are a part of the last-day revival that is coming to the earth. This is a generation that will see and do great things for God, reach the nations with the truth of the Gospel, and usher in the return of the Lord Jesus Christ.

Special thanks to my grandparents, Col. and Mrs. F. W. Barnes, who have prayed for me, supported me, and loved me as long as I can remember. Thanks to my parents, who live godly lives and are among my best friends; and thanks to Ivana Bambusch, who spent hours laboring over the manuscript of this book.

Contents

Preface

When I was between seventeen and nineteen years old, something came into my Christian life that would change me forever. It is called the spirit of prayer. I was saved when I was young, but when the revelation of the power of prayer was birthed in me, my life with God experienced a depth and freshness I had never known before.

My purpose in writing this book is to give you a simple and practical understanding of what prayer is and how to pray. For it to become strong in you, you'll have to be a doer of the Word, and a doer of what you read. I encourage you to read this book over and over again so your foundation becomes strong and your faith grows.

My prayer is that the spirit of prayer will come over you, your family, and your church like never before, and you will go out and preach the Gospel and shake the nations with the power of God.

Jesus is coming soon. If we don't pray, who will? There is still much work to do, more ground to break and prepare, more enemies to defeat, battles to win, strongholds to pull down, and more of the plan of God to be birthed in the earth. "Your will be done on earth as it is in heaven."

We are living in a time that is special; it's also a time where the Church will be required to pray as never before. When you understand what prayer is and how it works, you can see great changes in your life and in your city and nation. You can pray! Jesus in you is a great Prayer Warrior — He knows how and what to pray to bring results. He has given you His Word and His Spirit. You are mighty in Him!

The Church holds the keys to God's plan in the earth. Prayer unlocks the door to God's power in your personal life and to deliverance for the nations. The time is now — so pray, pray, pray! Glory be to God!

Mary Alice Isleib
Uppsala, Sweden
June 1991

Effective Fervent Prayer

Chapter 1
What Is Prayer?

The effective, fervent prayer of a righteous man avails much.

James 5:16

The Amplified Bible translates this, "The earnest (heartfelt, continued) prayer of a righteous man makes tremendous power available [dynamic in its working]." What a great promise! God's power is available for us today! It is not locked up in some inaccessible place far from our reach or possibility to obtain.

There is a way for us to experience that power and make it available to our generation. That way is through prayer — through *effective, fervent* prayer. This type of prayer is a generator for the power of God that will change individual lives, cities, and nations.

There is nothing that prayer cannot touch and change. The spiritual answer for people's need is prayer. In fact, we pray because we love people and we love God! Every time we pray, if we do so correctly, God's mighty power is released and made available to bring victory and breakthrough into even seemingly impossible situations.

We thank God for the finished work of Jesus in the cross and the resurrection, because He has paid the price for everything we need. It's all readily available to us in the spirit realm. God is not withholding anything from us! Although some people think God is like a mean old man who holds out promises in front of us, and just as we're about to grab them, He pulls them away, that is not the case. He also is not mad at us or trying to teach us something. We do not need to overcome God's reluctance when we pray. That is not the problem.

When we pray, we are breaking through resistance from the powers of darkness and taking hold of God's willingness to do His plan in the earth. That prayer causes His power to be released on

1

our behalf! God is not against us; He is for us! God's power is in the spiritual world. We can't always see it and sometimes we can't feel it, but it is there nonetheless.

In many cities and nations, it has been withheld for years; not because of God's reluctance to act, but rather, because God's people have lacked the spiritual understanding necessary to break through and use His power to see their prayers answered. In this book you will learn how to pray so God's power is evident and tangible in your life and nation!

We can, for example, liken the spiritual situation to a factory which has the capability to manufacture sweaters. The factory has two parts: one is the place where the sweaters are actually made, the factory itself. The second one is a small store in front of the factory where the finished sweaters are sold in all their styles, colors, and sizes.

The most important part of the factory is not the store, but the work place behind it where they have everything needed to make the sweaters. All the different colors of wool and cotton, all sizes and shapes of buttons — every detail necessary to make sweaters — is there. The sweaters are actually made in the factory work place, but they are *made available* to people in the store. It's in the store that the customers see the finished products and can buy them at a good price.

It would be ridiculous if the factory had a store, but when you walked into the store there were no sweaters available. You'd say, "Where are the sweaters? Don't you make sweaters? You have everything needed in the factory; why aren't there any sweaters here in the store?"

The reason the shelves are empty is because someone hasn't done his job. The sweaters are ready in the factory, but no one stocked the shelves of the store so people can come in and take what they need. They are not readily available.

Someone Must "Pray the Price"

Many times that's the way it is in the spiritual world. We have everything we need in the "factory of heaven." It's all there waiting, but someone has to *"pray* the price" to get it from the factory out to the front where people can come and take what they need.

The prayers of the saints stock the shelves of life! Prayer makes God's power available. We need to stock our shelves with healings, miracles, revival, and the outpouring of the Holy Spirit for this generation.

Everything we need is already paid for and created by the work of the cross. Now we must take hold of it through the heart of faith and the voice of prayer and make God's power available in the earth. That is what we do every time we pray! We release God's power into the earth! You have an active part in the kingdom of God coming to earth as it is in heaven.

Who is going to do this praying? Every believer is called to prayer. It is a *gift* that Jesus has given us. God loves to hear His people pray. He always answers the call of the righteous. There's a sadness in His heart when there is prayerlessness in the earth.

The Bible says in the Book of Revelation that the prayers of the saints, not just anyone's prayers, are like sweet incense burning before God's throne. He *loves* the prayers of His people.

God is waiting for you to rise up and pray. He is longing for you to break through your flesh and the resistance over your prayer life. He is waiting to teach you and help you. Prayer has not been given to governments, earthly institutions or even religious organizations, but to the living Church, the Body of Christ.

If you are a *believer*, you are called to prayer — bold, fervent, regular prayer! I am convinced that prayer is not for a special group! It's for every member in your church. Not just the pastor or the skillful intercessors, but *every* church member. That should be the goal of every local church — all the members as strong, skillful prayer warriors. You can do that! God will help you.

What Is Prayer?

In its simplest definition, prayer is fellowship with God. It is the ability to work with and understand the spiritual world. Prayer is your communion with God, where *you* talk with God and *God* talks with you. It is where you see what the spiritual state of people and situations is. It's powerful, it works, and it is necessary for your Christian life.

Prayer is not just a Bible subject that we study: Prayer is a *lifestyle*. I heard someone say once that prayer is to your spiritual life what breathing is to your natural life. If you stop breathing in the natural, of course we know what's going to happen — you're going to die. *Prayer* is the *breath* of God in your life that keeps your fellowship and walk with Him fresh and alive. It also keeps you free and strong against the plans and strategies of the enemy.

You may not know it, but there is a desire and an ability in your recreated spirit to pray. Your spirit is hungry for prayer. Your flesh may be weak and untrained in spiritual things, and even bound up, but your spirit is hungry to pray. It's hungry to know God and to talk and fellowship with Him. It's hungry to see the devil defeated!

In Zechariah 12:10, the prophet Zechariah prophesies that a spirit of prayer and supplication would be poured out over the house of David. This is literally referring to natural Israel experiencing a last-day visitation from God, but we know in our day that spirit of prayer has been poured out over us, the Church.

The Holy Spirit in you *loves* to pray. He is the spirit of prayer. Prayer, you're going to discover, is one of the most exciting things you'll ever see and do! Yes, it can be hard work at times, but there is a satisfaction and a reward that can only come from prayer in your life.

Our Foundations Are Important

When we consider our prayer life, one of the important things to understand is the foundations upon which prayer is built. The strength of our Christian life and our prayer life is based on the foundational truths from the Word of God that operate in our lives.

The foundations are what make us strong and help us run the race to the end. You are only as strong in spiritual things as your Bible foundation is strong and deep within you. The carnal man can despise foundation because it seems so simple and shallow, but there is no short cut and no substitute for a deep foundation in your life. The foundation for our prayer life is built on three different legs.

The first leg we will examine is *faith* in the God of the Bible. It has been said that prayer changes things, but the fact of the matter is that it is not just prayer that changes things; it's *believing* prayer that changes things. Our prayers are mighty and strong because of our faith in God — not just our faith in our own programs.

4

We *believe* His Word and His character, and it causes a strong spirit of faith to rest upon our lives and prayers. Our prayers are spoken out, not in doubt or uncertainty, but in secure confidence that our God hears and answers us when we pray.

Your life is weak if it is not built on a Bible knowledge of who God is and what He will do. If you think wrong (and most religious and worldly training is at enmity with God), you will believe wrong. When you think right, in line with the Bible, it can become strong faith in your life.

Everything in God's kingdom must be done by faith. In Hebrews 11:6 it says, "But without faith it is impossible to please Him." We can say, then: Without faith in your prayer life, it's impossible to please God. When we pray, we must pray in faith. No matter which prayer we pray, we must pray in *faith*, because without faith it's impossible to please God.

It's not just prayer that moves God. It's not just prayer that moves mountains. It's *believing* prayer. It's knowing who God is, and what He said He will do. Prayer that comes out of a heart of faith is the kind of prayer that changes things.

Let's look at Matthew 7:7-11:

Ask, and it will be given to you; seek, and you will find; knock, and it will be opened to you.

For everyone who asks receives, and he who seeks finds, and to him who knocks it will be opened.

Or what man is there among you who, if his son asks for bread, will give him a stone?

Or if he asks for a fish, will he give him a serpent?

If you then, being evil, know how to give good gifts to your children, how much more will your Father who is in heaven give good things to those who ask Him!

Here we see that an important aspect of believing prayer is found in the word "ask." Asking is so simple, it almost makes our natural mind turn sideways. Jesus said you must ask God your Father. How are we supposed to pray? Ask, seek, knock — and we will find.

One of the first things you must get into your heart is that it *is* God's will for you to ask Him. It is His will for you to pray to Him, and when you ask Him, *He will answer you.* If you will believe it, and act, it will be counted as faith unto you. It is in asking that the prayer door gets opened.

Realize that the Father is longing for you to come to Him and to ask. He loves you, and is waiting for you to ask, to seek, and to knock. It's that simple. Religious tradition, condemnation, and fear keep us out of that door, but the door is wide open. Through the blood of Jesus we go boldly before the throne and ask that we may receive, that our joy might be full.

In verses 9-11, Jesus goes on to talk about our relationship with the Father; that our Father is a good Father who wants to give gifts to His children.

"Well," you say, "why do I have to ask? If He's my Father, doesn't He know what I need?"

Yes, He knows, but when you ask, it shows that you're interested in Him and what He wants to do. It is also a way for you to exercise your faith. God is moved by faith. He doesn't just pour things on people who don't care. He gives them to people who are interested, who want them, who believe for them, and who ask for them. He is not cheap with His blessings.

God is good and overflowing, and sometimes we get things without even asking because He loves us so much, but that's not the way everything comes. He wants us to ask. He wants us to release our faith. He wants us to believe in Him, that He hears us, and that He will give it to us when we pray!

Let's go to John 14:13,14:

> And whatever you ask in My name, that I will do, that the Father may be glorified in the Son.
>
> If you ask anything in My name, I will do it.

These verses are so simple but so important. We can become hypocrites, religious people ourselves, if we just pray as a performance or out of knowledge, and not with faith in our hearts.

In these verses, Jesus is talking about the greater works, and He says that one of the ways the greater works would be done in our lives is through asking in His Name. We pray to the Father in the Name of Jesus by the power of the Holy Spirit.

When we ask in Jesus' Name, it's like He is standing there and putting His signature of agreement on our prayer — when we pray, of course, in line with His Word.

"Whatever you ask in my Name," Jesus says, "I will do it, that the Father may be glorified." Do you believe He will do it? He said He would. When you pray with faith in God, and your prayers are answered, it gives God glory. Weak, defeated, religious prayers don't glorify God! Faith-filled prayers that get results glorify God!

Jesus again is teaching about prayer in John 15:7. "If you abide in Me, and My words abide in you, you will ask what you desire, and it shall be done for you." Notice there are two conditions in this verse: "If you abide (or live) in me" — that's a condition, to live in Him, — "and my words abide (or remain) in you" — that's another condition.

Living in Him and His Word living in you is not some unobtainable state; God would not have put it in His Word for us to do if it were unreachable. You came into Christ by the New Birth, and now He lives in you and you live in Him. You let His Word come into your heart and it begins to abide in you. You walk before Him with all your heart, so this verse is for you. "Ask whatever *you* will, whatever *you* want," He said, "and it will be done for you."

We know, of course, that when we abide in Jesus and His words abide in us, He begins to change our desires. By the power of the Word and by the Holy Spirit, our desires begin to be conformed to the desires of God. Our desires become His desires.

In some areas of life, Jesus simply wants us to have some things because He loves us. "Ask whatever *you* want." Jesus is standing and saying, "What do *you* want?"

God wants us to ask what we desire, not just what He desires, but what *we* desire. Many people don't think God wants them to have what they desire. I'm not talking about desires after the flesh that profit you or make you depend on yourself, but there are some things in your heart that God *approves* of. He even put them there! He wants you to ask for these things in faith.

As you live in Him, and your desires are judged and developed by the Word, you can ask what you desire, and it shall be done for you. That brings glory to God! That's what Jesus said! He wants you to believe it, believe that it will be done, and pray out of the strength of that faith.

God Answers Believing Prayer

In John 16:23,24, we find Jesus again talking about asking.

And in that day you will ask Me nothing. Most assuredly, I say to you, whatever you ask the Father in My name He will give you.

Until now you have asked nothing in My name. Ask, and you will receive, that your joy may be full.

God wants *your* joy to be full. He wants *you* to be satisfied, *you* to be blessed by His will and plan in your life.

How does it happen? Just put the last three scriptures together: ask in My Name believing, with My Word living in you, whatever you want, and you will receive so that your joy might be full. God answers *believing* prayer. He wants you to expect to receive.

"Oh," some people think, "I could never do that — actually *expect* to receive when I pray."

But the Bible says that's exactly how you're supposed to pray — expecting to receive. When you pray the Bible way, you have to expect to receive. Yes, you must pray according to the will of God, but God's will is revealed for us in His Word. It is not that difficult to know God's will. When we pray, we expect to receive. That is faith. Faith pleases and glorifies God, and makes not only God's joy full, but yours, too!

I'm more convinced than ever that God wants us to be with Him like children are with their parents. You know how children are. When they come home from school, they walk into the house like it's theirs — and it *is* their house. They are secure that it's their house. So they walk into the kitchen saying, "Hi, Mom! I'm hungry." And then they whip open the refrigerator door to get what they need. They don't stand there and wonder if they can open it — they just do it. They have confidence in their relationship with their parents. They know and have faith that their parents will give to them and meet their needs.

Another interesting characteristic of children is that they have no problems asking or receiving. Their general nature is a trusting nature. They're so strong in it, it becomes a boldness that is remarkable. They have no hesitation, because they know the giving, loving nature of their parents. Their parents love them and want to give to them.

God wants His children to be like that. He desires them to be so secure in His presence that they come freely to Him in total confidence, knowing that as their Father, He will care for them in every area of their lives. He wants them to have faith that He will give to them and provide for their needs.

God, our Father, *wants* to give to us. He wants us to expect to receive when we ask. Of course we pray out of a heart of love and respect, but God's Word also declares in Hebrews 4:16 that we can go boldly to the throne of grace to receive — not just to hope for something, but to *receive* it.

Look now at First John 5:14,15:

Now this is the confidence that we have in Him, that if we ask anything according to His will, He hears us.

And if we know that He hears us, whatever we ask, we know that we have the petitions that we have asked of him.

This verse has caused confusion in people's minds, because they are not certain what the will of God is. But God has revealed His will to us in His Word. What His Word says *is* His will! To have your prayers answered, you've got to pray according to His will; according to His Word.

We don't pray by what someone else says, by our past experience, by our circumstances, by our religious upbringing, or by our emotional feelings. We pray according to the will of God, revealed in His Word, and by the leading of His Spirit in line with His Word.

Verse 15 then tells us that if we pray according to His will, He hears us, He listens to us, and He gives us what we have asked. It may seem so simple, but it is what God's Word declares. It's God's way — there is no other. God wants us to believe it, and to pray in that expectant spirit of faith. We know that some things take time to work out, but when we pray, we know that we have it when we pray according to His will. It is *believing* prayer that changes things — and it does!

So the first leg, or foundation, for our prayer life is *faith* in God.

The second leg is what I'm going to call *covenant*, or knowing who God is. It is not hard for us to know who God is — *precisely* who He is. We don't have to wonder who He is and what He's like. His Word reveals exactly who He is, exactly what He's like, and exactly what He will do.

In the Old Testament, every time God appeared to a man or woman, He told them who He was, and He made a covenant with them. We also have a covenant with God through the blood of

Jesus. It's important that we bring this into our prayer lives, because our prayers are rooted in who God is and in knowing Him in covenant. When we know who God is, it makes us strong, confident, and secure in prayer. Do you know who the One you are praying to really is? You can!

God Has Revealed Himself Through His Names

In Luke 11, the disciples asked Jesus to teach them to pray, and Jesus responded by giving them several principles for prayer — what we call The Lord's Prayer. As we study covenant, the second leg of our prayer life, we need to pay particular attention to what Jesus said in verse 2: "When you pray, say: "Our Father in heaven, Hallowed be Your name . . . ." The word "hallowed" means to be set apart, to be praised, and to be worshipped. When we come before our Father, we are to praise His Name; to set His Name aside.

God is a covenant God, and He has revealed who He is by the names He has given Himself. His names reveal His character and His nature. Our God is *more* than most people let Him be. God wants to reveal Himself to you in every side of His character. You can *know* your God!

If we don't know Him, His names, His character, or the covenant we have with Him, we can be tricked into believing something that is not true. We can be tricked into believing a lie.

For example, some people believe that God is a force, a cloud, or maybe an old man with a gray beard in the sky waiting to beat you if you do wrong. He is not any of these. He is a covenant God who has revealed who He is in His Word and by His names.

If you carry wrong concepts into prayer, you will have a weak prayer life with few results. If you don't have a revelation that our God is *Jehovah-rapha*, you can believe that He makes people sick — and that's not true. *Jehovah-rapha* has no sickness in Him. Sickness is a result of sin, death, and the fall. Jesus has broken that curse through the cross. God wants you to know His character so you will have faith in Him and know what you're believing, and why you believe it.

It is also important for you to understand that when the covenant was made with you by Jesus' blood, God gave all that He is to you. He is committed to keep the covenant toward you forever!

In the Old Testament, there are twelve covenant names God gave Himself. They reveal who our God is. Remember, He is *the same* yesterday, today, and forever (Hebrews 13:8).

The first name is found in Jeremiah 23:6, where God called Himself *Jehovah-tsidkenu*: the Lord our righteousness, God who is righteous.

One thing we need to understand as we consider this leg of our prayer life is that everything God said He was in the old covenant, Jesus fulfilled in the new. In Jesus, these Old Covenant names are alive and real to us today. Jesus is our righteousness today.

The second name God called Himself, found in Leviticus 20:7,8, is *Jehovah-m'kaddesh*: the Lord God who sanctifies or sets apart. He's still that today: He sets us apart, and He sanctifies us. Jesus is made unto us sanctification, First Corinthians 1:30 tells us.

God is *Jehovah-shalom*: the Lord God of peace. God revealed this name in Judges 6:24. He is our peace today. "My peace I leave with you," Jesus told us. This includes wholeness, harmony, and satisfaction in life. He is *Jehovah-shalom* today — this minute — for you.

The next one is *Jehovah-shammah*: the Lord God who is always there, or the Lord God who is present. Ezekiel 48:35 and Hebrews 13:5 are some scriptures that reveal this to us.

Jesus talked about this when He said that wherever we went, He would always be there — even to the ends of the earth. If you know Him as *Jehovah-shammah*, you *never* have to be lonely. He is the Lord God who is always present, who is *always* there.

The next name is *Jehovah-rapha*: the Lord God who heals, or Jehovah the Healer. This is found in Exodus 15:26 and Psalm 103:3. "I am the Lord God who heals you," He declared. Then Jesus came, and what did He do? He healed all. By His stripes we are healed today.

God also revealed Himself as *Jehovah-jireh*: the Lord God who is my Provider. This literally means in the Hebrew that He is a God whose provision shall be seen. It's found in Genesis 22:14.

God is the One who blesses us in all things: emotionally, financially, socially, spiritually, and morally. He is the One who is our success. He is willing and able to meet every one of our needs. One of the reasons we can pray for finances is because we serve a God who, in the depths of His being, is *Jehovah-jireh*, the One who provides.

Another name God used to reveal Himself is *Jehovah-nissi*. He is the Lord God who is our victory banner. He's our victory, our banner, our deliverer. The scripture reference is Exodus 17:15.

Our Father is a Father of victory. He has only victory in Him. Healing flows through His being. Provision flows through every ounce of His being.

He also called Himself *Jehovah-rohi*: the Lord who is my Shepherd. He is my Shepherd. I don't want because of Him. This is found in Psalm 23:1. He comforts me and leads me in paths of righteousness.

The next name is *Jehovah-adonai*: the Lord God who is Master. We are servants of God. He is the One we obey. He is Master, and there is no other Master in our lives but Him.

He is *El-Elyon*: the Most High God. He said He was the highest. There is none higher than He. He is the *highest*, the Most High God. Psalm 91:1 is the scripture reference.

Elohim is the next name. He is the Lord God who is the Creator. He is the creator of heaven and earth, as revealed in Genesis 1:1,2.

The last name is *El Shaddai*. He is the All-Sufficient One. He is the Almighty One, as He declares in Genesis 49:25.

In these twelve names, God has revealed who He is. He is no more and no less than these names. Remember the scripture we began this section with? "Hallowed, praised be Your name."

Use God's names in your prayer life. For example, say, "I call you today *Jehovah-tsidkenu*, the Lord God who is my righteousness. I praise You as my righteousness today."

Be specific in your prayer life. Use God's names when you pray. They reveal to you who He is, His character, and what He will do because of it. Understanding this is an important foundation for your prayer life. You are praying to the Living God!

Our Position Is One of Victory

The third leg of your prayer life is your position in Christ. Because of this position, we pray boldly and with great confidence. Ephesians 2:6 tells us that we are actually seated in heavenly places with Him. We have a position in the spirit realm, and we pray from that spiritual position — seated with Christ! We don't pray from defeat, circumstances, or because we're under attack. We pray out of our position of who we are in Christ, seated in heavenly places, redeemed by the blood, a child of God; we pray because of what Jesus has done for us!

The Bible says something else about you and your spiritual position in Ephesians 6:10-12:

> **Finally, my brethren, be strong in the Lord and in the power of His might.**
>
> **Put on the whole armor of God, that you may be able to stand against the wiles of the devil.**
>
> **For we do not wrestle against flesh and blood, but against principalities, against powers, against the rulers of the darkness of this age, against spiritual hosts of wickedness in the heavenly places.**

Paul is talking here about being strong in the Lord and knowing how to wrestle against principalities and powers. He's talking about prayer. Your wrestling against these principalities and powers takes place in prayer.

God sees you as a soldier, a strong warrior — a *prayer warrior*. God wants you as His warrior to pray out in the Spirit of God, using the weapons He has given you, from the position you have in the Spirit, and defeat the enemy.

We must realize that we have everything we need to win in Jesus. Even if you don't feel like a warrior, the Word of God says you *are* one in Christ. Take it by faith. Rise up and fight! Rise up and pray, O prayer warrior!

We are seated in heavenly places in Jesus Christ, at the right hand of the Father, far above principalities and powers! We never pray out of thinking we are just part of some religious concept or a religious philosophy.

We don't just pray from earth, trying to get something done, hoping something will happen. We already have a position in the spiritual world with Christ, and we pray from that position with the weapons God has given us.

God wants us to pick up our weapons and fight! We are not praying out of fear or hearing a bad report, but out of the Spirit of God within us, from our position of victory in Christ. As we begin to realize what our position really is, it will cause great confidence and boldness to come into our prayer life.

God has given us a sure foundation for a strong, mature prayer life — faith in God, covenant relationship, and position in Christ. From the strength of this foundation, we are prepared to build the structure of our prayer habits and turn loose effective, fervent prayer to make God's power available in the strength and intensity that our generation and world must have.

Chapter 2
Effective Prayer

In James 5:16, we read, "The effective, fervent prayer of a righteous man avails much." You'll remember from the previous chapter that *prayer* makes God's power available; it releases God's power into the earth.

When we pray, we want to pray powerful prayers; prayers that work. The question is, how do we pray that kind of prayer? Here in James we discover the answer to that question.

Powerful prayer, New Testament prayer, has two Bible ingredients: effectiveness and fervency. "The *effective, fervent* prayer of a righteous man avails much" or, as *The Amplified Bible* says, ". . . makes tremendous power available." These, then, are the two ingredients to powerful prayer: We must pray effectively and with fervency.

When we pray the Bible way, we get powerful prayer results. When I say powerful prayer, what I mean is this: prayer that gets answers. It's that simple: a prayer that gets answers.

If we're going to get results, if we're going to get answers, we must pray God's way. We can't do it according to our tradition, from the past or from our own experience. If we're going to have powerful prayer, we must pray the way the Bible says to. We must pray with effectiveness and fervency.

Before we look at these two ingredients in detail, we need to consider briefly another word that's found in this verse. The Bible says that it is the effective, fervent prayer of a *righteous* person that makes tremendous power available. This means if you are righteous, if you have been washed in the blood of Jesus, then you have the right, the authority, and the privilege to pray powerful prayers.

Who is called to pray? The Bible says that the *righteous* are called to pray. It's for you if you've been born again. God has given this weapon of prayer to righteous people, to see His power in their lives. So one of the qualifications, besides praying effectively and fervently, is righteousness. And we know that righteousness comes through the blood of Jesus.

Strong prayer is not just for a special group or just for the pastor; it's for *every believer*. Every believer, every righteous one, should be a strong prayer warrior. Every believer should know how to pray effectively and fervently.

We Must Know the Rules

Let's begin with the word "effective." When we talk about effectiveness, we're talking about principles, standards, patterns, and rules from the Word. Effectiveness is praying according to *knowledge* that's found in the Word of God and *principle*, the right ingredients to get the right results.

The Word of God is very clear about different kinds of prayer and how we're supposed to pray them. I heard someone say this once about prayer and people's general lack of knowledge concerning how it functions, and it bears repeating: "What most people do, is to take the subject of prayer, put it into a big bag, shake it up real good, throw it all out, and call it prayer." What a good illustration!

That bag full of messy prayer doesn't work because they never studied the right principles. The person who prays this way has never studied the patterns that God gives us in His Word to pray by. We have to pray by those patterns to get results. We have to use the *rules* in the Word of God to get the results we *see* in the Word of God.

We could take this for an example. When I was growing up, I played basketball and also a little soccer. I realized very simply that the rules for basketball were not the same as those for soccer. If I was going to try to play soccer like I was playing basketball, it wouldn't work.

It's so simple, it's almost silly to think about it, but that's what people have done with prayer.

There are many different kinds of prayer in the Bible, just like there are many different kinds of sports; but in prayer, people have not separated the various kinds of prayers to know what they are and how they work. They just put them all together, mixed up all the rules, tried to play the "game" of prayer, and never got any results.

To pray powerful prayer, we must pray effectively, which means we have to know the principles of the different kinds of prayer, how they work, and when to use them.

I want to liken the different kinds of prayer to playing a game of golf. In golf you have a bag which contains all different kinds of clubs. Some are big, heavy woods and others are small, slender metal clubs.

Although they are all used in the same game and they all have the same goal — to get the little ball in the hole — each type of club has a different purpose.

At the beginning of the game, when you're on the "tee," you take one of those big, wooden clubs, because your goal is to drive the ball down the fairway. You're not going to use one of the little clubs yet, because you'd be ineffective if you did. You've got to use the right club in that situation.

You need a huge one to "smack it" down the course. Then, when you get to the green after a successful fairway shot, you'd better not select one of those heavy woods. If you do, you won't get the ball in the hole; you'll put a big hole in the green, and they'll kick you off the course! No, on the green you need a small, metal club to just tap the ball into the hole.

In prayer, it's time for the Church to get the ball into the hole. It's time to get answers! It's time for effective prayer! We must know the different kinds of prayer and which to use in various situations. There are some prayers that are like big clubs in the spirit, and there are other prayers that are like small, metal clubs that just tap the ball into the hole. There are different prayers with different purposes, and they all have their place in our prayer lives.

Let's take another example that will help us understand what prayer is and how it works. Think about the little old lady who's in a church meeting. She's a nice Christian, a good prayer warrior, but she doesn't fully understand spiritual things.

The pastor is giving a strong altar call that day after the message. The Holy Spirit is moving, and all of a sudden this nice lady starts weeping out loud. Everyone gets nervous; no one in the church understands what is happening. The pastor tells the ushers to take care of her.

The lady beside her says, "Oh, honey, it's going to be O.K. Everything's going to be all right."

The lady herself doesn't understand. "Oh, I feel so lost . . . I feel so sad . . . Oooh, so much love . . . Oooh."

The ushers react by taking her out and trying to cast the devil out of her! What's happening to her is that a spirit of prayer has come over her to pray for the lost. Her spirit is being sensitive to the Holy Spirit and sensing the needs of the people.

Sometimes when the Holy Spirit moves, people yield to a wrong spirit, and they shout, mock, or scream in an uncomfortable way, disturbing the service. Maybe they need some deliverance.

You can tell the difference between what spirit it is when you listen in your spirit. In this case, the lady just needs to pray the intercession for the lost through to victory, but no one understands it. They have not learned the principles of effective prayer or how to work with the Holy Spirit.

The Holy Spirit can move over you and you can be just as effective bowing your head and praying quietly as in drawing attention to yourself.

When you are under a real spirit of prayer, you should be careful never to draw attention to yourself. A person who continually is drawing attention to himself or controlling the prayer meeting is most likely praying out of lack of knowledge under the power of the flesh, or even another spirit. The prayer can be very strong, but you can be strong, and flow with the whole movement of the service. Be in the spirit of prayer. Bow your head and pray.

The Holy Spirit was upon this woman to *pray* for those lost people. Sometimes weepings can come over you for lost people, or for people who are backslidden. Maybe God wants you to help stand for the will of the Lord to be done in that particular service. It should take place in the church prayer meetings, but sometimes in a service the Holy Spirit will quicken people to pray. Sometimes the whole church will yield to the spirit of intercession. That's good! We should be open for it.

If the whole service is not going that way, however, bow your head and pray through. You can be just as effective being quiet as being loud. But if the whole service goes that way, let it fly!

If it's too strong, where you can't carry it through effectively by being in the service, get up and go out to a place where you will not distract people and then give over to the spirit of prayer.

However, you can become so skillful that you can blend in and work with the Holy Spirit, who is the spirit of prayer. When you get used to it, you can learn how to work with it so it doesn't overtake you all the time. In order to do this, you must understand what effective prayer is.

The lady in this story didn't understand what was happening to her, and it caused her prayer not to be as effective as it could have been. We must have knowledge and understanding of proper principles to make effective prayer!

Let's look now at Ephesians 6:10-18. Although we'll be studying all these scriptures, we'll give only verse 18 here:

> **Pray at all times (on every occasion in every season) in the Spirit, with all [manner of] prayer and entreaty. To that end keep alert and watch with strong purpose and perseverance, interceding in behalf of all the saints (God's consecrated people).** *(Amplified)*

Paul here is writing to the church at Ephesus from prison. Just imagine what it would have been like for Paul to look up one day at a soldier who was guarding him and have the Holy Spirit say to him, "That's how my people look in the spirit." That's what happened to Paul one day!

The Holy Spirit gave him a revelation of the armor of God, and how we are dressed in the spirit for battle. He wrote here in Ephesians, beginning in verse 10, that we are to be strong in the Lord and that we have been given armor that is mighty in God.

Then in verse 18, he tells us that the armor is not just for protection in our Christian life, but that it is armor to be used in prayer. As we're dressed in the armor of God, we go out in the spirit from our position in Christ and *pray*.

Be Easily Given to Prayer

The first words in Ephesians 6:18 are "praying always." These two words are good and strong, but many people don't understand what it actually means to "pray always."

Does it mean that you walk around all day groaning? Does it mean you walk around the house all day speaking in tongues — even when someone is trying to have a conversation with you? Does it mean you go to your job praying out in tongues and everyone says, *"What* are you *doing?"* To which you respond, "I'm praying always." Is that what it means? No, it does not. *Praying always means to be easily given to prayer.*

It doesn't mean we walk around all day just praying in tongues, although that may be part of it. It means to be *easily given* to prayer, so that we can pray by faith whenever we choose to, and we are also sensitive to when the Holy Spirit moves on us, to yield to Him, and move with Him. It's developing a prayer life and being easily given to the spirit of prayer.

When you're easily given to prayer, you can pray anywhere, at any time, under any circumstance, with anybody, in whatever way the Holy Spirit wants you to pray. This is God's will for every believer.

When we're at our job, we focus our mind on our work, but we're always easily given to prayer. We have developed a prayer attitude and a God-consciousness. When our mind is taken off our work, our hearts and our minds are always aware of the presence of the Holy Spirit and aware of the fellowship with our God through prayer.

Paul knew this very well. One of the marks of his life and ministry was that he spent many hours in prayer. He said, "I thank my God I speak in tongues more than you all" (1 Corinthians 14:18). He prayed all different kinds of prayer, including tongues. Paul knew how to pray, he was easily given to prayer, and he spent much time doing it. He developed strong fellowship with God.

To be able to be easily given to prayer takes knowledge of the Word of God, and it also takes practice, because prayer is a spiritual exercise. Many times when we begin to pray and come into the prayer life, we exercise spiritual muscles that we're not used to exercising, and sometimes it hurts at first, just like it does if you start to train or exercise in the natural.

When you begin to use muscles that you haven't used in many years, those muscles begin to scream, "Oooh! Stop it! Stop!" because they're not used to that kind of activity.

Our spirit loves to pray, but our mind needs to be renewed, and our flesh submitted to the Holy Spirit. The more we practice prayer, the stronger we get and the more easily given to it we become.

"Praying always," the Bible says, "with all prayer in the spirit." That can't mean that all we do when we pray is pray in tongues. What it says is, pray all prayer in the spirit. It doesn't mean pray all prayers in tongues.

For example, you don't pray the Prayer of Faith in tongues. You pray the Prayer of Faith with your understanding; you stand on the promise of God, speak out God's promise, and speak to mountains in the Name of Jesus. Yes, you may pray in tongues, combining tongues with this prayer and do some spiritual warfare, but the majority of the Prayer of Faith is prayed with your understanding.

So praying in the spirit doesn't mean to pray just in tongues. What does it mean, then? It means to pray out of your spirit, aware of the presence of the Holy Spirit. It means to pray all prayer — all the different kinds of prayer — in the presence of the Holy Spirit, in the realm of the spirit, out of your inner man. When you're going to pray the Prayer of Faith, pray it in the presence of the Holy Spirit out of your heart, and you'll be praying in the spirit.

Coming Into the Spirit

To come into the spirit realm, or to be aware of the spiritual realm, begins with your making a choice. For example, choose to think about God and His Word. When you exercise your will, you are giving yourself to the Holy Spirit, and when you think or speak about God in line with His Word, you are training your mind to come into the presence of the Lord.

The more you discipline your mind to follow your spirit and to follow the Bible, the stronger you get, and the easier it is for you to be aware of the spiritual world.

You are in the spirit *positionally*, but practically you have to give yourself, or yield your mind and your body, to what's happening when you are praying. This is not something natural for the human being. You must practice this until it becomes natural for you.

Listen on the inside, and be aware of the Holy Spirit's presence. At first it may seem awkward and strange, but it's strong. It's not spooky; it just means that your whole being is aware of God, and you're praying out of your heart.

You can be in the spirit anywhere, because God is everywhere. You can be in the spirit in your car, in the grocery store, in your house — anywhere. What does it mean? You are more aware of God and the supernatural world than you are of the natural things around you.

It doesn't mean you are strange and you walk around in a little glory cloud with big spooky eyes all day. It doesn't even mean you can't work, or that you must change your tone of voice. That is not being "in the spirit."

Being in the spirit means to be more aware of God, of your inner man, and of the Word than you are of yourself or circumstances. It also means to be aware of the enemy and his plans and attitudes. You are developing a keenness to the spiritual world.

It's very simple. The more you practice and ask the Holy Spirit to help you, the easier it becomes. Really, what you are doing is developing your fellowship with your Father — walking with Him all day. You are gaining experience on how to make your natural, everyday world supernatural!

One of the ways we learn to come into the spirit — and we have to *learn* to come into the spirit — is to *concentrate* on what we're doing. Simple concentration is a good practice to master the spiritual world. I know it sounds simple, but it will help you take hold of your mind when you come into prayer.

For example, think about what you're doing. You are talking to God your Father. Think about what's happening in your heart. As you do, release what's in your heart more and more to the prayer. You'll find you are concentrated on prayer and the spirit world more than you are on anything else.

It's very easy to come into the spirit. Sometimes it takes practice, because we're so used to yielding to and living in the natural realm, but we can retrain ourselves to come into the spiritual realm. It also takes some understanding.

The enemy is resisting your prayer life because there is power there for you and for others. You must press in to break through. As you press through in faith, you will find that chains will break off you, and the more you pray, the stronger you get! It's not a feeling; it's being aware of what God wants to do while we are praying.

Even if you don't feel anything, or even know anything, have faith in what you are doing. As you grow, you will find the Holy Spirit has taught you much about the spirit world.

Concentrate on praying when you pray, and then you'll be in the spirit. You'll be aware of the Holy Spirit's presence, aware of your spirit man, and aware of the spiritual atmosphere around you.

The more you practice, the more you will understand the spiritual world and the stronger you will get. Also, always be sure that you groom your prayer life by Bible reading and regular church attendance. All of these together will help make you a strong, stable prayer warrior.

Now you understand that we pray these different kinds of prayer in the presence of the Holy Spirit, out of our human spirit, being sensitive to God's kingdom and the devil's kingdom, and concentrating on our prayers.

That's the way we should pray in tongues: We should pray in tongues in the spirit. You say, "What does that mean?"

It means that we should pray in tongues, being aware of God, listening in our hearts, listening to what we're praying, and concentrating on prayer. We should see how it feels spiritually with God and in the spiritual world. Listen, look for different climates, and pray!

When you're going to pray in tongues, don't just pray like a machine. Concentrate on your spirit, be aware of God and of the leading of the Holy Spirit, and *give* yourself to praying. That's what it means to pray in the spirit. It makes for good, strong prayer, and that's what God wants for all of us when we pray.

Pray With ALL Prayer

The Bible tells us to pray always with *all* prayer. That means there is more than one kind of prayer in the Word of God. It doesn't say pray always one prayer. It says to pray with *all* prayer — with all types and kinds of prayer.

In this book, we're going to examine many different kinds of prayer found in the Word of God. Each of these prayers has different rules. It's important for us to know the rules so we can pray effectively.

As I noted earlier, however, most people have put all the rules together, all the kinds of prayer together, shaken them up, labeled it "prayer," and then wondered why nothing happened when they prayed! If we are going to get results, we must pray effectively — using the right rules with the right type of prayer.

Although we will in some way be covering each type of prayer later, let me list them for you at this point:

(1) The Prayer of Faith, (2) the Prayer of Dedication, Consecration, and Submission, (3) the Prayer of Casting Our Cares over on the Lord, (4) Group Prayer, (5) the Prayer of Praise, Worship, and Waiting on the Lord, (6) the Prayer of Agreement, (7) the Prayer of Repentance, (8) Intercessory Prayer, (9) Praying in Tongues, (10) the Prayer of Forgiveness and (11) the Prayer of Binding and Loosing, Spiritual Warfare and Authority.

Although each of these kinds of prayer is distinct and separate, we must realize that often several kinds blend together when we are praying. We'll use the Prayer of Intercession for an example. Intercession is praying for others, and praying that God's will would be done on the earth.

When we pray in intercession, often we use praying in tongues, but that doesn't mean that every time we pray in tongues, we're in intercession. This is why it's important for you to understand why we divide these kinds of prayers, because praying in tongues is different from intercession.

Praying in tongues is praying in a supernatural language. You will *use* praying in tongues in intercession, but at the same time, praying in tongues has purposes other than just intercession.

For example, you can pray in tongues and build yourself up, but that's not intercession; it's a different use and purpose for praying in tongues.

So it's important that you understand the differences in these kinds of prayers, and then use them in your prayer life, letting them overlap and work together, but understanding how they function in a general sense.

God wants our prayers to be powerful and effective — even more than we do! He has not kept the ingredients to that kind of prayer a secret. The effective, fervent prayer, He told us, is the one that makes tremendous power available. That's the prayer that gets results!

Thank God, we can pray effective prayers, prayers made according to knowledge and principles, and get powerful results!

In the next chapter, we'll examine the second ingredient to powerful prayer — fervency.

Chapter 3
Fervent Prayer

The effective, fervent prayer of a righteous man avails much.

James 5:16

We have seen that the two ingredients for powerful prayer are effectiveness and fervency. In order to have prayers that avail, prayers that get answers, we must have both of these ingredients in our prayer life. One by itself will not produce the power we need. It is effectiveness and fervency *together* that equal powerful prayer.

In the Book of James we have an example of a man who knew this, and put it into practice. In James 5:17,18 we read:

Elijah was a man with a nature like ours, and he prayed earnestly that it would not rain; and it did not rain on the land for three years and six months.

And he prayed again, and the heaven gave rain, and the earth produced its fruit.

Elijah was a man like we are, and the Bible says he prayed earnestly that it would not rain. The Lord gave him a word about His plan, and Elijah prayed *earnestly* according to that word. The result was that it did not rain for three and a half years. That's powerful prayer!

Then the word came again from the Lord (Elijah had the principle) and he prayed again (he was fervent), and the heaven gave rain, and the land produced crops!

In the original Greek, the word "to pray earnestly" means that Elijah's soul went out in prayer. He gave out of himself in prayer; he gave all he had! He was fervent. He had the word, meaning he had the principle, and he had the Spirit, the fire of God, and the heartfelt energy of a believer behind the word, and it worked, didn't it? Actually, it affected the whole nation! That's what effective, fervent prayer will do.

25

We've seen what effectiveness is: praying according to knowledge in God's Word, the correct rules, and principles; but now let's look at what fervency is. Fervency means to pray with purpose, with serious intention. In the *American Heritage Dictionary*, the word "fervency" means, "having or showing great emotion or warmth, ardent, extremely hot, glowing." It comes from a Latin word meaning "to boil."

To pray with fervency means to pray with intensity. It also means that you give your being to God, and you let Him fill it with divine yearning. Your degree of fervency is directly related to the degree of your spiritual desire.

Are the things that are burning in God's heart, burning in yours? When you pray with fervency, you pray the different kinds of prayer out of your heart, and you pray them strong, with intensity, following and flowing along with the Holy Spirit inside of you.

One of the best ways I can describe fervency to you is with an example of ironing clothes. You've got your clothes on the ironing board, the iron is set right, and it is supposed to work effectively and take out wrinkles. Everything is ready, but when you pick up the iron and try to get the wrinkles out, absolutely nothing happens!

You may work and work. "What is wrong here?" you'd think. "I can't get these wrinkles out. I've got the iron in the right place and the ironing board in the right place, but nothing is happening."

That's actually what a lot of people are doing in their prayer lives. They're praying and praying and praying by the law of the Word, but the wrinkles aren't coming out. Why? Because *the key to make the wrinkles come out, is to turn up the heat!*

When you get the right amount of heat, you don't have to work so hard under the pressure of feeling that you have to perform a religious duty that in some way pleases God. Then the wrinkles start to come out. Yes, there will still be an element of work, but the heat gives the energy and the ability to do the work.

When you put the iron down with the right principles, and the heat comes from the iron, the wrinkles come out. It's a good example of effective, fervent prayer. So what is fervency? It is like turning the iron on. It is getting some *heat* in your prayer.

Give Yourself to the Holy Spirit

You understand fervency more clearly when you understand the Person of the Holy Spirit on the inside of you. The Holy Spirit is a Person. He is real, and because He reveals the heart of God, He has expressions. He is the *expressive* side of God, or the One who manifests the feelings of God.

James 4:5 tells us, "Or do you think that the scripture says in vain, 'The Spirit who dwells in us yearns jealously?'" The Spirit of God who lives in you is jealous for you. That's the way God feels toward you, as expressed by the Spirit. He wants to have a relationship with you.

Fervency is surrendering your feelings or your soul to the feelings of the Holy Spirit. It is allowing Him to express Himself through your mind, your will, and your emotions when you pray.

You're not out of control or an emotional mess in prayer; you're under the control of the Holy Spirit.

You never pass the knowledge or revelation of the Word, but you must be open to pass your own limited experience!

You pray according to knowledge, but there's a side of the Holy Spirit that wants to take hold with you, to work with that knowledge, and to energize that knowledge with the enthusiasm, intensity, fervency, and even the very feelings of God Himself!

When you study the Word of God, you find that the Holy Spirit is many things. We're not supposed to push any side of the manifold wisdom of God down within us, or be afraid of it. Rather, we're to let that fire and that expression come out through our soul and be released in our prayers.

It's not a strange or a spooky way of praying, but if you're not used to it, it can be different at first, because there are times when the Holy Spirit will express Himself through you. For example, He may express Himself as the spirit of might.

This expression is strong, powerful, and forceful. It doesn't feel like a dove; it feels like a lion! Yield to it! As a matter of fact, stir it up! We are to be open to the Spirit of God when we pray. He lives in us! He wants us to initiate the prayer and be aggressive, expressive, and emotional.

I like what I heard an old-time prayer warrior say: "If the Holy Ghost doesn't move me, I move Him!" The more we learn to work with Him, the more we'll learn how He wants to flow through us, and how He wants us to use and work with the attributes He has already put in us.

Sometimes He wants to make different kinds of sounds; sometimes He wants to lead us to say or express certain things; and sometimes we just feel like we should lie flat on our face before God. Most of the time He is waiting for you, and He expects you to jump in and be intense, or hot, in prayer. So do it!

If you are too sophisticated, you will never pray fervently. If you keep waiting for fire, you may never get it. You have it, so stir it up! Pray intensely, and don't let any backslidden Christian pour water on your fire! Ask God for *more fire!*

In prayer we can develop a sensitivity and a working relationship with the Holy Spirit. We learn the principles, but we can't be afraid to stir up the Spirit within, or to surrender to the expression of the Holy Spirit in our prayers.

For example, when you pray the Prayer of Faith, mix fervency with your prayer and let it come out of your spirit with intensity and strength — not just in faith, but in a *spirit* of faith.

The Holy Spirit longs for you to give yourself to Him and to the heart of God He has put within you. He longs for you to flow in whatever expression He desires. Fervency is your mind, will, emotions, and body all going in the same direction in the flow of what is in your inner man.

When you pray, draw on the inner man. Stir yourself to the life of God on the inside. Pray boldly, and then follow the stream of life that keeps coming from God as you pray. Whatever you pray, if you are still, walking, or crying, do it earnestly, seriously, and with all your heart.

There are many different sides to the Holy Spirit's personality, just as there are to yours. We must be open to learn and express them. He is, for example, like a dove. He is gentle. There are times in prayer when His gentleness seems to *flow* behind our prayers. There is a side of the Holy Spirit that is sweet and precious. If we don't understand this, we can despise it, if we prefer a certain feeling or side of the Holy Spirit.

"Well, I like it when it feels this way." "Well, I like it when the gentleness is there." God wants us to like *every* side of the Holy Spirit, and not be picky about which ones we will flow with. But He always wants us to be *strong* in whatever we are doing! (Ephesians 6:10).

When you become involved in spiritual things, especially prayer, you must be open and teach yourself to become sensitive to how the Holy Spirit wants to flow when you pray. I believe He always wants us to pray with strength, even if we're praying quietly. Yes, there is a time to be quiet, but in that time, there should be strength and life that flows from you; not melancholy and heaviness. Strength is based on what is coming out from your inner man and what is released in the atmosphere you create around yourself.

Do you know that you can groan and travail quietly, but *very strongly?* If you're going to be quiet, be quiet with strength and boldness, because the Holy Spirit is *mighty.*

The majority of Christians misunderstand the personality of the Holy Spirit and the nature of the inner man created in the likeness of God. They pray quietly, but not in an atmosphere of strength and intensity in that quietness. Usually it's melancholy and depressing. And most definitely, they react if you pray loudly at all.

Actually, I have found that the best way to be fervent is to begin fervently with full force, from the beginning of the prayer.

There are different levels and expressions of that might, and we're not afraid of them. We're not afraid to pray in strong, loud tongues. We're not afraid to go into groaning, strong groaning in intercession. We're not afraid of it, because we understand the biblical principles behind it and how the Holy Spirit will work with that kind of prayer.

Jesus Is Our Example in Fervent Prayer

Jesus Himself is our example in strong, fervent prayer. Let's look at Hebrews 5:7: "In the days of His flesh [Jesus] offered up definite, . . . petitions . . . and supplications with strong crying and tears." (*Amplified*)

Notice the words "strong crying and tears." *Jesus* prayed with *strong* crying! In the original Greek, it literally gives the idea that there were times in Jesus' prayer life when He shrieked out, screamed, and cried loudly in prayer.

If Jesus could do it when He walked in the flesh, so can we! We can do what Jesus did and cry out to our God with *strong crying.* No, we don't need to have bizarre experiences when we're praying, but we are not afraid to yield to the Holy Spirit and pray strong prayers. You should pray strong prayers regularly!

The nature of the mind is enmity with God (Romans 8:7). The carnal man is naturally more passive to God than active. Do the opposite — be strong! And don't let carnal, backslidden, rebellious Christians take your prayer life away from you.

There's a time to pray quietly, but Jesus' prayer life also had strong and loud prayer in it. It had emotion in it! Jesus, as a man with a fervent heart, and the Holy Spirit, with the emotions of the Father, were working together. It was coming out through His flesh in strong crying and tears. There was strong expression in His prayer life. He prayed with emotion. He was intensely involved in His prayers.

Just like Jesus, *we* are to pray with strong expression and with emotion — not out of the emotions or our soulish realm, but we are to pray with the soul and body cooperating with the spirit man. We are to pray out of the heart, the mind, and the emotions of *God*, as expressed through the Holy Spirit. And where does He live? In *you*, so let what's in you break out!

The Bible says in Romans 8 that the Spirit knows the heart and the mind of the Father. The Holy Spirit longs for you to give yourself to Him. That's the emotion you pray out of. It becomes your emotion, which you then express openly in prayer. That's the fire you pray out of; it's releasing to the Holy Spirit inside you.

Let the expression of God flow out of you. The very nature and goal of the New Testament is to get what's *inside* of you *out*! Let the life of God flow out! That is the spirit in which we pray. Yes, we may feel emotions, and we may move our bodies a little, but intense prayer doesn't *start* from our emotions. It starts deep inside us, where the fire, the intensity, the fervency, and the emotion come from — the emotion of God inside us by the Holy Spirit. We must join with that, yield to Him, and pray that out. As we do, it comes out as *our* emotion.

Now let me explain something about the nature of the God we serve. Isaiah 42:13 says that God is a Warrior. Warriors are strong. The Holy Spirit is a strong Warrior, too. Yes, the Holy Spirit is love, but according to Isaiah 11:2, He is also the spirit of might!

This spirit of might, or strength, is one of the qualities of the Holy Spirit that we need to yield to more, because He often wants to express Himself in this way when we pray. He wants that spirit of might to be behind our prayers.

The spirit of might is an expression of God. It expresses His character as a Warrior. I've never seen a weak, wimpy, defeated warrior. That spirit of might is inside you, and the Holy Spirit wants to express Himself through you in fervency, through the spirit of might behind your prayers.

Now notice the rest of Hebrews 5:7. Jesus prayed with strong crying and tears, "to Him Who was able to save Him from death, and He was heard because of His reverence toward God."

I want you to notice the *heart* that was behind Jesus' prayers. His attitude was an attitude of worship. He wasn't screaming out just to scream out because it was the latest fashion in Christianity. And don't you scream for that reason either!

Praying loudly is a part of our Christian life that we must accept, but we must also practice the heart attitude behind Jesus' prayers. The heart behind His loud prayers was sensitivity and respect for God. That doesn't mean He compromised and prayed religiously; He prayed strong, loud prayers, but the attitude behind it was a heart of worship, sensitivity, integrity, and respect. It gave *substance* to His prayers.

Some people say, "Amen, sister, tell them they have to worship," because they don't want to hear about strong, loud prayer. We take *both*. There are others who say, "Amen! Strong prayer," but there's no sensitivity, no respect.

We take *both* of them. We take strong, loud prayers with expression in the Holy Spirit, out of a spirit of worship and respect; out of a spirit that lives to please God. That's the way Jesus' prayer life was, and that's the way ours is to be also.

So we pray according to knowledge and principle. We pray effectively, and we pray with intensity, purpose, and fire — fervently. The two combined make a prayer that releases God's mighty power to change individuals, cities, and nations. It doesn't take a special person to pray this kind of prayer. *You*, a believer in Jesus Christ, qualify! Prayer — powerful, result-obtaining prayer — is waiting for you! Dare to break out!

Chapter 4
Praying With the Understanding

Paul, writing to the Christians at Ephesus, says in Ephesians 6:18:

> Praying always with all prayer and supplication in the Spirit, being watchful to this end with all perseverance and supplication for all the saints.

We know, of course, that Paul is telling the Ephesians they should develop a Christian lifestyle of praying always with all kinds of prayer.

As we continue our study of effective, fervent prayer in this chapter, we are not going to discuss a different kind of prayer; but rather, a *way* to pray that is included in many of the different kinds of prayer. We are going to discuss Praying With the Understanding.

Throughout the Bible, we see men and women who took it upon themselves to seek God's face and pray. They prayed out of their own understanding, in line with the character and the Word of God — and they saw powerful results! It is important that Praying With the Understanding be well developed in our prayer lives. Spirit-filled believers who use their private prayer language a great deal may not think it important, but it is a powerful tool God has given us to make His power available on the earth today.

Let's start in First Corinthians 14:14,15:

> For if I pray in a tongue, my spirit prays, but my understanding is unfruitful.
>
> What is the result then? I will pray with the spirit, and I will also pray with the understanding. I will sing with the spirit, and I will also sing with the understanding.

In verse 14, Paul is saying, "When I pray in the spirit, my spirit prays, but my mind is unfruitful, or my mind is still. My mind does

33

not have anything to do when I pray in tongues; it is my *spirit* praying. Now I must concentrate on what I'm doing, but really my mind is not actively involved." Paul is describing to us how spiritual things work and how Spirit-filled prayer works.

When Paul makes this statement, he's not saying that praying with the understanding is *better* than speaking in tongues. No, he's explaining what happens when we pray in tongues and how we should be developed in praying in tongues as well as in praying with the understanding.

Use Your Mind in Prayer

Your mind is to play a part in your prayer life! In verse 15 Paul says, "Well, what am I going to do then? I'm going to pray both ways. I'm going to pray in the spirit, or with the spirit, and I'm going to pray with the understanding also." Paul was strong in praying in other tongues, but he also said, "I will pray with my understanding."

Notice there were two well-developed aspects of Paul's prayer life. Paul prayed in tongues — in fact, he says later, "I thank my God I speak with tongues more than you all" (1 Corinthians 14:18). That means the Apostle Paul prayed in tongues a lot! I believe he probably walked around praying in tongues under his breath all the time. But Paul had another side to his prayer life — he also prayed with the understanding.

When you look at the letters (epistles) he wrote to the churches, you will often find a prayer is included that the Holy Spirit had inspired him to pray — a prayer not with tongues, but out of his understanding.

Just as the Holy Spirit quickens your inner man, He also quickens your *mind* to pray. The Holy Spirit *wants* your mind involved in your prayers. Many Charismatic Christians love to pray in tongues, and they should, because tongues is emphasized for us in the New Testament. Yet when you look at the prayer life of many believers, you find that the side of praying with the understanding is weak.

It's easy to pray in tongues: Your spirit prays, and all you have to do is open your mouth and let the words come out. You don't have to think very much, and sometimes that's good. We live much of our life thinking too much. I once heard someone say, "Stop thinking and pray!"

Thank God, there is a way for us to pray without our minds being involved! But we cannot use that as an excuse not to develop the other side — praying with our understanding as well.

The Choice Is Yours

Notice something else Paul said in this verse, "I *will* pray in tongues." He didn't wait for the Holy Spirit to knock him on the head to start him praying in tongues. No, he said, "I will pray in tongues." He had the baptism with the Holy Spirit and he could choose to pray in tongues any time, any place. He said, I *will* pray in tongues." You can say the same thing!

Paul also said, "I will pray with the understanding. I *choose* to pray with my understanding." You don't have to wait for a big Holy Bible to come out of heaven and knock you on the head, or say, "I'm waiting for heavenly words." You don't have to wait for heavenly words! You've got the Author of the Book on the inside of you, the Holy Spirit, and when you use your will to pray with the understanding, He will quicken you, help you, lead you, and honor your words when you pray. He gives you the *choice* to pray.

Because it's so easy to pray in tongues, we're not as developed in praying with the understanding. The problem is, we haven't exercised enough. When we start coming into the prayer life, it's as if we begin using new muscles. It's just like in the natural when you start a new exercise program and you try to lift weights, you use muscles you probably haven't used in years, and it hurts at first. Those muscles aren't accustomed to that exercise.

That's the way many people feel when they pray. They start to pray in tongues, but they haven't used that prayer muscle much before, and it "hurts." They can't get into it, their mind wanders, and after five minutes, they're ready to quit.

It's not because they can't pray. It's not because they don't want to pray, because in the heart of every believer is the desire to pray. Jesus is a prayer warrior, and He lives inside you! It's a lie to believe that you don't like to pray; you *love* to pray!

You either haven't been taught, or haven't practiced enough; that's all. It's the same way with praying with the understanding.

The problem is not that we don't have the "muscle," or ability — we do; we simply have never developed it.

Finally, there comes a time when we've exercised the speaking in tongues "muscle," and we can do it for hours. It's wonderful, it's good, and we should be able to do it, but then someone says, "Let's pray with the understanding."

"Thank you, Jesus. Thank you, Jesus. Hallelujah. Ooh, this hurts. It feels so uncomfortable." The good news is, the more you exercise spiritually, the more you grow spiritually. The more you pray with the understanding, the better you'll get at it.

One simple thing to understand is that praying in the understanding requires more of you than praying in tongues. It requires you to use *your mind* in prayer. It requires you to *think* about what you are praying about.

God gave you your mind to use. He didn't create it to sit there on top of your head like a big pickle! Many people think their mind is their biggest enemy. "If I could just cut my head off, it would help me," they say. But that's not God's will. God's will is for you to renew your mind and then *use* it.

The Bible says many things about your mind. God wants to turn it from being your biggest enemy to being your biggest blessing. Besides that, you need it to exist in life. When it's renewed and starts to think right, according to the Bible, it helps you live in victory. In fact, it's a *key* to living in victory, because you can't believe right if you don't think right!

The reason people's faith level is low is simply because they don't think right about the Bible and spiritual things. They don't think according to the truth as revealed in the Bible, but according to their natural human reasoning or past religious background.

Your mind is important to you as a prayer warrior, for it is to be used when you pray. You are to pray not only in tongues but with the understanding also. Paul was saying here that he would pray with his mind in action. He would pray so that he could be understood.

One translation of First Corinthians 14:14 says, "I will pray with the aid of my intellect." Your mind was created to *help* you in prayer. So as we talk about praying with the understanding, we're talking about praying with the mind in action — using your mental ability in your prayer, using your thinking capacity, or using your known language. God wants you to be strong and well developed in this area of prayer.

Pray the Word

One of the keys to praying with the understanding is to pray the Word of God. We could really say that to pray with the understanding is to pray the Word. It's fun to pray out the scriptures and to train yourself how to pray that way regularly.

Why do we pray the Word? Because God always honors His Word, not just our human thoughts or ideas. Look at First John 5:14,15:

> Now this is the confidence that we have in Him, that if we ask anything according to His will, He hears us.
>
> And if we know that He hears us, whatever we ask, we know that we have the petitions that we have asked of Him.

Our confidence in prayer is that we have asked according to God's will. Of course we know that Jesus is the will of God in action, and Jesus is the Word, so we could say that the Word is the will of God. When we pray the Word, we pray according to His will. That's why we don't always pray the *problem*, we pray the *solution* by praying a scripture, or a Bible principle that is the answer to the problem. The Word of God is where our confidence lies!

God is saying here, in effect, "Do you want Me to hear you?" Of course, we want Him to hear us. It would be *crazy* to pray to a God that doesn't hear us. The Bible says we *know* that God hears us. Why? Because we pray according to His will and His Word. And God always honors His Word. So when we pray with the understanding, we pray with our known language, and we can pray the Word of God. God wants you to grow in this and become strong in praying the Word.

We're ready and eager, so how do we come into this? First, you need to know that it doesn't happen overnight. You have to *practice* praying with the understanding. You have to use your Bible when you pray.

God isn't looking to see how expert you are at praying. He's looking to see your heart and the words that come out of your mouth. He's not looking to see what you're using to help you pray. So take your Bible with you when you pray, and mix faith with it as you pray the scriptures.

Some people think when they start to pray that they have to be able to stand with no Bible and pray fluently, but that is not the case. Take your Bible with you, open it up, and pray it. Put lists of scriptures for certain topics in your Bible.

"Well, I have to close my eyes." Who says? True, sometimes we *do* close our eyes, but we don't always have to close them. Pray the scriptures. Take your Bible into your prayer closet with you.

Pray Out of Your Heart

If you're going to pray about fear, put a list of scriptures about fear in your Bible. Pray out of your heart, use your mind, and speak those scriptures. Don't be like a robot, however, just reciting some memorized or programmed data, hoping something will work. No, you must put your heart with it. Act like you're talking to God — because you are!

Here is a sample prayer: "Father God, your Word says that You have not given me a spirit of fear, but You have given me a spirit of power, and of love, and of a sound mind; so I thank You for it. That is your will for me. I receive it and I declare that I do have a spirit of love and a sound mind in my life, and I praise You for it, Father. I rebuke the spirit of fear. It's not mine, according to this scripture. Fear, get out of my life, in Jesus' Name!"

God will honor His Word in your life and in the situations you're praying for. He is a covenant God, bound to keep His covenant promises with His children. If it seems uncomfortable to you to pray these scriptures, just remember you're exercising a new spiritual muscle.

The more of the Word of God you speak, the more you will get used to it in your mind, and the easier it will become to pray the Word and the promises of God without having to read them directly from your Bible.

Just allow the Word of God to flow from your inner man, right through your mind, and out into the situation. You have to start somewhere, so don't be afraid or ashamed. Just pick up your Bible, your lists of scriptures, your scripture references, and *pray*.

This is how I learned to pray strongly in English. I would walk the floor and pray the Word of God over myself, my family, and my circumstances for about an hour a day. At first I didn't see any changes, but after some time, I began to see the Word of God work in my prayers as I spoke them out regularly and stood on them in faith.

Another thing that happened as I prayed God's Word like this is that the scriptures got deep inside me, and I learned how to talk to God in line with His Word.

Pray Paul's Prayers

The second way to start Praying With the Understanding is to pray Paul's prayers. Go to these prayers and pray them regularly over yourself, your family, and your friends. Make the prayers personal by inserting the name of the person you're praying for or your own name in them, and then pray them.

Some prayers you can use are found in Philippians 1:9-11, Colossians 1:9-12, Ephesians 1:15-23, and Ephesians 3:14-21. As you pray these prayers, you'll get better and better at learning how to Pray With the Understanding.

Another way to practice this is to find a verse that fits your situation, and pray it word by word or phrase by phrase. Let's say, for example, that we're praying about a meeting in the Soviet Union, and we are praying for a strong anointing to be over the meeting and on those who will be preaching.

We go to First Corinthians 2:4 and pray, "that his speech not be with words of man's wisdom, Father, but in the power of the Spirit." (Put your heart in it when you speak this scripture. Realize that you're talking to God. Pray those words. You can pray them over and over again.)

"No, no, not words of man's wisdom. Not man's wisdom for this meeting. We pray in Jesus' Name, not in the wisdom of man, but in the power of the Holy Spirit. Oh yes, yes, yes, according to this verse — the Holy Spirit's power."

Pray in tongues a while if you want to.

Go back and forth. Speak the Word. Read it. Pray with the understanding. Pray in tongues. Speak it out. Pray it out. Praying like this is powerful in your prayer life!

God has a verse in the Bible for every situation you could ever pray for. It may take a little work to find the verse, but once you do, you can pray it over the situation, stand on it in faith, and watch God answer the prayer from that verse. Use your Bible in your prayer life. It's a prayer manual!

Benefits of Praying With the Understanding

Praying With the Understanding does many wonderful things in our lives. The first thing it does is to build up our mind. If praying with tongues builds up our inner man, we can say that praying the Word or praying with the understanding, builds up our mind.

Do you know that your mind needs to be built up? Yes, it does. The mind is the bridge between the spirit man and the natural world. What comes out of your heart, or your spirit, has to go through your mind for you to be able to act on it. When you pray with the Word of God, it has an ability to build up your mind. The Word has supernatural strength in it that edifies your mind.

I've often gone into prayer when I was tired, or my mind was wandering. The body doesn't always feel like praying, and it doesn't always concentrate on prayer. But when I start to speak the Word, it begins to change my mind.

My mind begins to wake up when I hear the Word of God coming from my mouth; especially if I do this out of a heart that loves God, not just because I have to do it from religious duty.

One of the things that helps people to have sound, strong minds is speaking and confessing the Word regularly. The Word of God has a direct effect on the mental capacity of man. Why? Because when you speak in the understanding, you have the natural ability to comprehend what you are saying and doing. Then it's much easier to join your mind to the life in the inner man and to the anointing in the Holy Spirit.

I don't understand tongues with my mind, but my spirit does, and when I pray in tongues, my spirit is built up. My mind, however, does understand this prayer: "Father, I thank You that I'm a new creation in Jesus Christ. I thank You, Father, that old things have passed away and all things have become new. I thank You, Father, and I praise You that the Holy Spirit is inside me. He's my Helper and my Strength." Your mind understands what you are expressing, and it is built up and strengthened.

God wants your spirit *and* your mind to be built up so they can work together. When your mind becomes built up, enlightened, and empowered by truths from God's Word, your mind and your spirit are flowing together and you will see powerful results.

How To Keep Your Vision

A second benefit of Praying With the Understanding is that it can help you keep your mind refreshed in what God has said to you and about you. The Bible says that without a vision, people begin to get off course and perish (Proverbs 29:18). When you pray the Word of God, it reminds you of what you have, who you are, and what the Bible says about God and His ways in your life. You can keep the vision fresh and clear before you.

Praying God's Word reminds you of what God says about the Christian life and His promises. It keeps the will of God ever before your eyes. God frequently said to do this in the Old Covenant.

"Keep the Word before you," He declared. "Keep the vision before you. Keep the sight before you, so you can obey Me and do my Word" (see Joshua 1:8 and Proverbs 4:20,21). One way to keep the vision before you is to see it, speak it, and pray it!

The third thing Praying With the Understanding does is to help you continually release your faith in God. Do you know why? Because when you pray in your known language in line with the Word of God, you have a mental comprehension of what the will of God is. You can release your faith on the promise of God that you understand.

Of course, you can also release your faith when you pray in tongues and believe that it works. But when you pray the Word, it goes to your mind, you can be clear and specific, you can understand it, and you can immediately release your faith and expect results. The Word of God builds up your faith. That's why it's so important to use it in your prayer life.

Another benefit, and this is so good, is that praying with the understanding requires you to *give* of yourself, of your soul man, to God. It makes you give out of your soul, because you have to think about what you're doing. When you have to think, read, and speak the Word, what happens is that you're giving of yourself. Of course, you also give of yourself when you pray in tongues, but it's a different way of giving to God. It does not always require you to be mentally alert.

There's a sacrifice involved when you use your mind to gather scriptures and facts and present them before God when you pray. It's work to pray with the understanding, but once you learn to come into it, it makes your prayer life rich and strong. God loves it when you put Him in remembrance of His Word (Isaiah 43:26). He respects you and honors His Word in your life when you are praying before Him in your understanding!

Old Testament Prayer

Have you ever considered this: In the Old Covenant, God's people never had the opportunity to pray in other tongues. They couldn't, because they weren't baptized with the Holy Spirit. They prayed with the understanding only, and they saw powerful results. They knew how to work with God. They prayed and talked to Him in line with His Word and His character. God honored their prayers, and they saw great answers to prayer.

The Bible gives many examples of Old Testament prayer. The Old Testament is written for our instruction, so today, even under the New Covenant, we can draw from it and apply its principles to our lives. We're under a different covenant — a better covenant with better promises — and we've received the Holy Spirit; but we can look back at the Old Covenant and understand the ways and the character of God with a fresh perspective. After all, He's the same yesterday, today, and forever!

Talking Face to Face With God

When the Word of God talks about people praying in the Old Testament, it reveals things like the fact that Moses talked to God face to face, as a man would talk to his friend (see Exodus 33:11). Moses wasn't even born again as we understand it, but he had a relationship with God. He had boldness to go before the throne of God and talk and pray to the God of heaven and earth. And God responded to him and worked with him like you would with one of your friends.

Men and women in the Old Covenant prayed out of respect for God, and they also prayed from a friendship relationship with Him. Not only did *they* feel they had a friendship with God, but *God* felt He had a friendship with them! God also had great respect for these people because they kept their words and vows to Him. He found people whose heart was after Him, and He counted it as faith in the earth!

Genesis 18 tells about Abraham being the friend of God. God wanted to share what was in His heart with the man Abraham because He knew Abraham's character; He knew that Abraham would command his house to follow the things of God (see Genesis 18:19). Abraham's life was given over to God. God visited him and talked to him as a man would talk to a friend. God shared His secrets with Abraham!

How do you talk to your closest friends? You share what's intimate and important to you with a friend you trust. That's the kind of relationship God had with Old Covenant people of prayer. Abraham was a man whom God trusted with His personal thoughts and ways.

The Bible says in Genesis 18:17, "And the Lord said, 'Shall I hide from Abraham what I am doing?'" God was not going to hide His plans from Abraham. He wanted someone to reveal His plan to, and He knew if He talked to Abraham — if Abraham knew about the situation — he would respond positively to God's will. God looks for such people in the earth even today with whom He can have that kind of relationship. Yes, there are many who are in relationship with Him through the New Birth, but God longs for those with whom He can have intimate fellowship like He had with Abraham. I want God to feel that way about me — and so should you!

If God knows we know about His plan and the working of His plan in the earth, I want His reaction to be, "She knows about the situation, so she's going to talk to Me about it. She's going to work with my detailed plans and ideas on this to see my will fulfilled. She knows Me and I have been watching her — I know her. I have a friend in her."

God didn't hide what He was going to do from Abraham, and He knew that Abraham would respond from his heart and converse with Him about the situation.

Now look at Abraham talking with God in Genesis 18:22-24: "Then the men turned away from there and went toward Sodom, but Abraham still stood before the Lord." As everyone else went away, Abraham remained in the presence of God to commune with Him.

And Abraham came near and said, "Would You also destroy the righteous with the wicked?

"Suppose there were fifty righteous within the city; would You also destroy the place and not spare it for the fifty righteous that were in it?"

Abraham began talking to God with his understanding in the kind of prayer called intercession; prayer made on behalf of someone else and for the fulfillment of God's plans in the earth. He was standing in the gap for the people in the city of Sodom. More will be said in a later chapter about the Prayer of Intercession, but for now I simply want to emphasize the fact that he was praying *with his understanding* on behalf of these people.

As he continued praying, Abraham made a tremendous statement in verse 27, where he said, "Indeed now, I . . . have taken it upon myself to speak to the Lord." Abraham took it upon himself to speak to the Lord about this very serious situation. Prayer was part of his lifestyle. I have decided in my prayer life to be like Abraham; I'm going to take it upon myself to speak to the Lord about His will and plan in the earth.

The rest of the story tells how Abraham talked to God about the city. Each time he asked God to spare it for a lesser number of righteous — and each time God responded to the request of the man of faith and integrity in the earth. The city *did not* deserve to be spared from God's righteous wrath, but God said He would do what Abraham asked! How bold Abraham was to talk with God like this. God wanted to destroy the city. Abraham's faith as expressed in bold prayer spared his family, and perhaps it could have saved the whole city!

Having God As Our Friend in Prayer

If this was possible in the Old Covenant, it is possible for us. God is the same yesterday, today, and forever (Hebrews 13:8). You and I can become intimate friends with God. In the New Covenant, we're His children, but we can develop such a deep personal fellowship with Him, and He can enjoy the same closeness with us, that even though He's our Father, Master, and Lord, He can be our friend as well. God can be your close friend in and through prayer!

You can have a talking relationship with Him where He reveals His heart to you, and you open your heart to Him. There's respect, integrity, and communion between you and God, and He gives powerful and amazing answers to prayer, because you have developed that kind of relationship with Him.

The Bible gives many examples of Old Covenant men and women who were dedicated to God and held deep convictions. They gave their lives, time, interests — and most of all, their inward parts — to God. They wanted all of Him! They were seeking after God with all their hearts. They wanted to know how God felt and thought.

They knew how to work with God. Not only did they truly love Him, but they also respected Him. They had a relationship that went beyond a casual friendship. It was on a level where they respected God and lived for Him. God respected them and responded to them!

We have the blood of Jesus and the Holy Spirit today, and any believer can live at a high level in the spirit realm with Him. We can go before God today like people did in the Old Covenant. But who will dare to do so? Who will dare today to stand before a just and holy God and plead with boldness? Who will dare to know God in such an intimate way? He who has clean hands and a pure heart (Psalm 24:4). He who will dare to be honest, clean, and on fire before Him! He who will dare to live and die for Him! The man or woman who is wholehearted for Him! That one will talk to God face to face!

What did God say about someone like David? "There's a man who is after my heart." When you find someone who is after your heart, you share what's in your heart with him, and he's going to be free to share with you.

Those are the kind of people those Old Covenant prayer warriors were. They were people of sacrifice. They knew God. They had a deep, personal relationship with Him. They knew the presence of God, and they were willing to adjust their lives to the standards and ways of that presence!

Think of Joshua. He was one of the few who was in the tabernacle with Moses. Joshua was in the presence of God. He knew the presence of God. He knew God — the God of holiness and fire! You can't help but know God when you spend time in His presence, because in His presence is everything He is. Joshua had a living experience with the glory of God! It *changed* him.

Now look at what happened in Joshua 10. We see Joshua come to an intense situation where he needed to pray. He needed to talk with the God of miracles, and the only ability he had in prayer was with his understanding. In verses 12 and 13 we read, "Then Joshua spoke to the Lord." Isn't that simple? But that's what prayer is, speaking directly — face to face and heart to heart — with the Living God. The result was — a miracle!

Then Joshua spoke to the Lord, in the day when the Lord delivered up the Amorites before the children of Israel, and he said in the sight of Israel: "Sun, stand still over Gibeon; And Moon, in the Valley of Aijalon."

So the sun stood still, And the moon stopped.

Notice this: Joshua spoke to God in the sight of all the children of Israel. Everyone heard him talk to God. Don't be afraid to talk to God in front of people. Don't be afraid to talk to God in front of your husband, your wife, or your children. There are times when it's just you and God, but here Joshua stood up boldly before all of them.

It took faith and humility before God and man for Joshua to stand there and pray such a thing. Can you imagine it? They were losing the battle. It took faith to stand there and speak out, "Sun, moon, stand still!" But God heard Joshua. God knew the voice and the heart of that man. He had worked with Joshua before. Joshua was His friend — someone He trusted. God respected the man Joshua.

Joshua talked to God, and look what happened in verse 14: "And there has been no day like that before it or after it, that the Lord heeded the voice of a man."

It takes speaking to God out of a pure, tried, and bold heart that knows Him and is willing to do anything for Him. Joshua's prayer was powerful and precious in God's sight. Although his words were simple, human words prayed out of Joshua's understanding, they caused a miracle to be done that affected the entire nation!

Start praying with your understanding and praying the Word like never before!

Chapter 5
The Prayer of Faith

For assuredly, I say to you, whoever says to this mountain, 'Be removed and be cast into the sea,' and does not doubt in his heart, but believes that those things he says will come to pass, he will have whatever he says.

Therefore I say to you, whatever things you ask when you pray, believe that you receive them, and you will have them.

Mark 11:23,24

We know that faith is involved and released in every kind of prayer, yet there is a specific type of prayer called the Prayer of Faith. This prayer is specifically used when we pray for our own needs. It has nothing to do with praying for other people. It is when we pray about our own personal needs and the needs of our families.

In Mark 11, Jesus was teaching the disciples about how to have their own needs met by using the God-kind of faith. That's what the Prayer of Faith is all about!

We are God's children. He loves us and has everything for us that we need. Now we must tap into the full supply of the grace and ability of God through the Prayer of Faith.

The Prayer of Faith is based on asking and receiving according to the promises of God in His Word. It has its foundation in everything Jesus has already done for us through the cross and the resurrection.

Every promise in the Bible belongs to us and can be received in our lives by praying this prayer. It is important for you to understand this, because the Bible-kind of life is a life of faith.

"The just shall live by faith" (Romans 1:17). This prayer is an intricate part of your relationship with God and living in victory and success. The Bible talks so much about faith, I feel that many believers' problems are a direct result of their ignorance or neglect to speak to their mountain and to stand with purpose and conviction on the promise of God in faith.

This must be done as soon as the need arises. Your success in life requires a quick response to the Word of God. So let this prayer sink deep into your spirit and mind, and start practicing it now!

You Must Hear the Word of God

There are several steps involved in the Prayer of Faith. I want to go over these steps with you in a systematic way so you have a clear understanding of what Jesus said here. Then, when you mix faith from your heart with these principles, you will see results.

The first step is to hear the truth. We must *hear* the promises of God. We must hear the Gospel, because it is God's power to those who believe it.

When Jesus walked on the earth, the reason the people could release their faith was because they first heard what Jesus was saying. They heard the truth and then they knew *how* to believe.

Hearing is vitally important to the Prayer of Faith, because faith comes by *hearing* the Word of God, the Bible tells us in Romans 10:17. We must hear, not just for someone else, but for ourselves. We must hear it ourselves from the Word of God and then allow the revelation of that truth to explode in our hearts.

A good example of this is found in Mark 5:25-28:

Now a certain woman had a flow of blood for twelve years,

and had suffered many things from many physicians. She had spent all that she had and was no better, but rather grew worse.

When she heard about Jesus, she came behind Him in the crowd and touched His garment;

for she said, "If only I may touch His clothes, I shall be made well."

This woman was in a desperate situation; all of her money had gone to her doctors, yet she was getting worse.

Notice, however, the first words of verse 27: "When she heard about Jesus, ..." She *heard* about Jesus. She heard about the healings and the miracles. When she heard about the great things Jesus was doing, it began to move her toward Him. She began to reach out to Him.

The way she did this was with her mouth. She said, "If I can only touch His clothes." She began to release her faith. She *heard*, she *spoke*, she *received*. It all was part of her faith beginning to move and operate. We know, of course, that she did reach out and touch His clothes and was totally healed, but what was the first step to her healing? She *heard*.

We hear the promise of God, meditate on it, plant it in our hearts, and then *faith* will start to come regarding that need.

You have the right to whatever Jesus has done for you and whatever promises there are in the Bible. We are His children! As you hear it and meditate on it, faith comes into you, and that very faith is what you can release when you pray for that promise to be manifested in your lives.

I have found the best way to hear the Word is to read it out loud to myself and to concentrate when I read. There is a promise in the Bible for every need you might have. Get a concordance and find a verse on healing, deliverance, or whatever your situation calls for. Ask the Holy Spirit to help you and lead you to a verse. He will! All you need is one verse to make your own, and the power of the Gospel can operate in your life if you believe that verse!

Receiving the Promise

The second step is to receive the promise. When the woman in Mark 5 heard about Jesus, she had a choice to make. She could have said, "Well, He'll never come my way. I don't know. Oh, I'm sick." But that's not the way she responded; she *heard* and then she *received*. What does it mean to receive? It means to take it, or pull it to yourself. Take it like a hungry dog grabs a bone! If someone is going to give you a gift, when you receive it, you take it to yourself. That's what it means to receive.

The *American Heritage Dictionary* defines "receive" as "to meet with, experience, to welcome, to admit, to perceive mentally, to partake in." All of that is a part of your will. When you hear the promise, dare to make it personal. Accept it for yourself, and participate in it with all your being.

When I was growing up and playing basketball, we had to practice receiving the pass so that when the ball came, we would be ready to catch it. My coach taught me to be open to catch the pass. When the ball came toward me, I had to go to the ball and pull it into my body. I'd line myself up with the ball, and when it came, I didn't step away from it. No, when the ball came toward me, I'd step *to* it and receive it to myself. That's the same way it is with the promises of God! After you hear the promise, step *to* it and *receive* it with all your heart!

There are many different enemies that keep people from receiving God's promises: wrong thinking about the Bible, a wrong concept about God and His chastening, or unrighteousness thinking like, "Well, I'm not worthy . . . ." But you *are* worthy of *all* the promises of God, because you're His child.

Jesus has made you worthy with His blood. He wants you to receive the promises and to draw them to yourself so much that you make them personal.

In the first chapter of Ephesians, for example, it says we have been blessed with all spiritual blessings in Christ Jesus. Make it very personal, and dare to say in the devil's face, in religion's face, and in your circumstance's face, "I have received all spiritual blessings in Christ Jesus."

It will break religious chains off you when you dare to take it for yourself and make it personal. That's what God wants you to do. *Take* it for yourself. Step into the ball and *receive* the pass. Step into the promise and *receive* it as a child freely receives from a parent. *Dare* to receive it without fear or hesitation!

Take the Promise by Force

Blind Bartimaeus is a good example of a man who took a promise from God by force. In Mark 10, we see that he was sitting by the side of the road begging, and he *heard* some good news.

Look at what verse 47 says: "And when he heard that it was Jesus of Nazareth, he began to cry out and say, 'Jesus, Son of David, have mercy on me!'" He *heard* about Jesus and immediately chose to *receive* what Jesus had.

The voice of faith began to come out of him. He began to cry out, "Jesus, have mercy on *me*! You are for *me*!" That's how radical he was. He was so bold and aggressive that all the religious people around him got nervous, and like a lot of religious people do, they began to warn him, "You'd better not cry out so loudly. Be quiet!"

It's interesting to note that people will use sophisticated and acceptable words as a mask for their own unbelief.

Bartimaeus' crying here out of a pure heart was exposing the rebellion that was in the people around him. He was going for God. The others acted like they were, but they were really worshipping themselves, as they seemed offended at Bartimaeus' faith-filled actions.

Jesus never rebukes your crying out to Him when it's from your heart! Pay the price of faith, and cry out! Don't let religious, backslidden Christians stop you. Bartimaeus didn't! He kept his faith toward Jesus and cried out all the more for Him. He didn't just cry out a little; it says he cried out a lot! And through his cry he was saying, "I receive! I want *You*! I worship You! Jesus, You're for *me*! What You promised is for *me*!" And he received it.

We saw that when the woman with the issue of blood received the Word, she began to *say*, "If I can only touch Him!" Even when it looked impossible with all the people around Jesus, her faith spoke! We've seen how Bartimaeus received it; he began to cry out for it and draw it over himself. What did they do? They *heard*; then they *received*.

Believe It's True — For You!

The next step in the Prayer of Faith is to believe. It's one thing to receive, but then you must combine your faith with it. When you receive it to yourself, *believe* that it's true.

When I give these steps, I'm not saying you have to follow them exactly, step by step, because they all work together; but realize that one of the most vital steps *is* believing.

This is the point that Jesus was bringing people to all the time: He wanted them to believe. He said to the woman with the issue of blood, "*Your* faith, not my faith — what *you believed* — healed you." Blind Bartimaeus was healed, and it wasn't because of Jesus' faith; it was because of *his* faith. It was what *he believed*.

When we pray, we must believe. There are many people asking many things, but they don't believe a word they're saying. What does Mark 11 say? "Whatever you ask for in prayer, believe that it is granted to you."

"Well," someone says, "what am I supposed to believe?" Believe that when you pray, what you are saying is true, regardless of the contrary circumstances, and you will have your request.

"Oh, I can't do that. I don't have it. I can't *see* it or *feel* it." That's why you're praying the Prayer of *Faith*! In the finished work of Christ, you have it. It's only in the natural that you don't. So how do you get it into the natural? By the Prayer of Faith. Believe that what you ask, and what you say, is going to happen when you pray. Hear the promise. Receive it. Then *believe* it. Believe it's for *you* — today, right now!

Ask God For What You Want

Asking is the next part of the Prayer of Faith. Mark 11:22-24 says:

So Jesus . . . said to them, "Have faith in God.

"For assuredly, I say to you, whoever says to this mountain, 'Be removed and be cast into the sea,' and does not doubt in his heart, but believes that those things he says will come to pass, he will have whatever he says.

"Therefore I say to you, whatever things you ask when you pray, believe that you receive them and you will have them."

Part of praying the Prayer of Faith is speaking to the mountain. Is it a mountain of financial need? Is it a mountain of sickness? Is it a mountain of depression? What kind of mountain is it? Jesus told us to release our faith by speaking to it.

What are you going to say to your mountain? You're going to speak the Word of God to it, because you have a promise that's *greater* than that circumstance. You have a promise from your Father, so start speaking to the circumstance in Jesus' Name! It seems a bit strange to the natural man and to every human impulse to speak to circumstances and to ordinary earthly things, but Jesus your Lord said to do it! Trust Him, and start commanding the mountain to go into the sea! In fact, shout at it! Get God's ear and heart and scare the devil!

Let's continue with verse 24: "I say to you," because you're a believer, a child of God, "whatever things you ask . . . ." God wants you to *ask* Him for what you want.

Jesus knew that Bartimaeus needed to receive his sight; it was obvious that he was blind. So why did Jesus ask him what he wanted? Because asking causes us to be specific and it is a way for us to release our faith!

Jesus wants you to be specific, like a child is when he says he's hungry. Mothers usually respond with, "Well, what do you want?" Tell Jesus what you want! When asked, Bartimaeus specifically said, "That I may receive my sight." James 4:2 says, "You do not have because you do not ask." That's simple, isn't it? You do not have because you fail to ask.

This is a part of the Prayer of Faith that can be difficult for people if they're in unbelief, or have received wrong teaching. It's also difficult for them if they are afraid that God might not give it to them, or that it would be prideful to ask. God wants us to ask and to be as specific as possible in our requests. If you need money for your rent, tell Him how much you need and ask Him for it. "O God, I hope You will give me the money." No, that's not the Prayer of Faith; that's unbelief.

Here's the proper way to pray: "Father, in the Name of Jesus, I thank You that I have heard the promise that You will supply all of my needs (Philippians 4:19). You are my Provider. You are Jehovah-jirah to me. Father, I ask You for the finances, for the $500 I need for my rent this month. I thank You for it. I ask for it because You are Jehovah-jirah, and You said you would supply all of my needs. I believe that I have everything I need in Jesus Christ. I ask in faith, I believe, and I receive it now in Jesus' Name.

"I *command* that financial mountain to fall into the sea in Jesus' Name. I *command* poverty to *go* from me in Jesus' Name. I refuse to accept lack, poverty, or any other thing except my need met. I stand on the promise of God and I thank You, Jesus, for victory. In Jesus' Name I have it *now* as I pray in faith. And I thank You for it in the Name of Jesus." The Bible calls *that* the Prayer of Faith.

Refuse To Accept Anything But Victory

The last step is to stand. Don't settle for anything except victory. Don't settle for anything except total, complete breakthrough. This last part, of thanksgiving and standing, can be one of the most important parts of this prayer.

When you prayed, you believed that you had it, but you don't have it, so what are you going to do until you get it? Thank God for it and stand. Worship and praise are very important to the Prayer of Faith, because we pray, believe, and receive before we actually see the answer come to pass. That's why it's called the Prayer of *Faith*.

When you pray this prayer, you must be *convinced* in your spirit that you have released your faith. Meditation on the promise for some time before you pray will help convince you. Until it becomes real on the inside of you, and the Holy Spirit causes it to explode, keep reading and muttering it to yourself regularly. This is your confession *unto* faith. It won't be long until you will be ready to make the confession of faith, or pray a confident Prayer of Faith. You should not pray this prayer casually; for that matter, no prayer should be prayed casually.

"Well, I think I've released my faith." No, pray the Prayer of Faith with boldness and confidence that you have prayed about the situation, God has heard you, and you have released your faith.

You don't have to pray again and again. You can pray *once*, release your faith, and know you have it. The continuing part of the Prayer of Faith is the standing, the thanking, the rejoicing, and the refusing to accept anything else until the answer comes. Stand!

By faith *and* patience you must inherit the promises (Hebrews 6:12). Be willing to stand for days and even weeks! Jesus has heard you and your faith is working. Let it work! Don't panic. *Stand* and stand. How long? Until you see it. Like a dog on a bone, don't give up!

Everyone must pay the price of faith. You can, too! Jesus said you could and He doesn't lie! The circumstances may prevail, but keep standing, because they have to change when faith is released from your heart! When the circumstances scream at you, you can say back, "Thank You, Jesus, for my victory!"

I remember hearing a story of a woman who had a growth on her hand. She was so determined for that thing to go, she told the Lord, "I'm going to have my husband pray for this." So before they went to bed that night, he laid his hand over on hers and prayed, "I curse this growth in Jesus' Name." He wasn't excited about it; he was tired and wanted to sleep, but she released her faith. She went out into the living room and said, "Now, Lord, I believe when my husband prayed, this growth had to go, and I'm going to dance in this living room until it falls off."

She started dancing because she believed when she prayed, it worked by the Holy Spirit. She danced and danced, and sometime later she looked down at her hands, and the growth had gone away! I like her determination!

No, it doesn't always happen that fast. Sometimes it's a long stand; but I tell you, *God* honors your faith, and it will happen. The circumstances have to change, according to the Word of God.

Even if the circumstances still exist, we walk in rest, peace, and assurance when we release our faith. We walk in joy and thanksgiving. We keep standing on the Word of God in faith.

We say, "The Word is true. It's mine now. My faith is on it. I'm standing. I believe and I *refuse* to accept anything else, in Jesus' Name. Thank God for my miracle! Thank God, my need is met! I don't know where it's coming from, I don't know how it's coming, but it's mine. I have it now. No matter how long it takes, I stand on the Word of God, in Jesus' Name. Praise You, Father, it's *mine*! Hallelujah!"

Remember, when the circumstances scream, you scream back, "Hallelujah, it's mine!" When the sickness screams at you, scream back with praise that you're healed. When those bills scream at you, go home, put them on the floor, and dance on top of them. When that depression screams at you, "Oh, you're so lonely and so attacked," say, "No, I'm not! I'm full of the praise of my God!" and hit it right in the face with praise.

Keep believing. Keep releasing thanksgiving and joy. Sometimes in the middle of a battle, one of the hardest things to do is to praise God, yet that's where the victory is! People will laugh at you, mock you, persecute you, and think you're crazy, but you are not. You are biblical and supernatural! It's *your* faith that pleases God (Hebrews 11:6). So stop pleasing people, and please God! God is with you!

Hear the promise, receive it, believe it, ask for it, and then stand, thanking and praising God until the answer comes. You will see that everything God has said to you is true. Victory and breakthrough can be yours in every area of your life. Use what God has given you: Pray the Prayer of Faith.

Chapter 6
The Prayer of Dedication, Consecration, and Submission

The Prayer of Dedication, Consecration, and Submission is a strong prayer that deals with our willingness and obedience to fulfill God's plan in our lives. It is not a prayer for others; it deals with our own personal dedication and submission to the will of God.

Although this prayer is strong, it has been greatly misunderstood and misused over the years, resulting in confusion, weakness, and ineffectiveness in believers' prayer lives. However, when we understand this prayer and how it operates, it will cause the strength and grace of God to abound, helping us to carry through every detail of God's plan with joyous victory.

We'll begin in Mark 14. Jesus is in the Garden of Gethsemane with His disciples, praying. The Holy Spirit, who is the spirit of prayer, began to come over Him. In verse 33 we see that Jesus ". . . began to be struck with terror and amazement and deeply troubled and depressed" (*Amplified*). As the spirit of prayer came over Him, there was a *deep yearning*, a troubling, in a sense, coming from within Jesus.

Verses 34 and 35 tell us that Jesus said to His disciples:

My soul is exceedingly sad (overwhelmed with grief) so that it almost kills Me! Remain here and keep awake and be watching.

And going a little farther, He fell on the ground and kept praying that if it were possible the . . . hour might pass from Him. (*Amplified*)

What hour was Jesus referring to? The hour of His death, the confrontation of the cross. Of course, everything He did was in preparation for the cross, but now the actual fulfillment of that obedience was before Him. He was feeling the weight, responsibility, and intensity of that hour. In front of Him was obedience that would change the destiny of mankind. Jesus was experiencing its necessity and impact.

He was also feeling His own inability and weakness to fulfill the will of God. Sometimes we think it was easy for Jesus to go to the cross, but it was *not* easy in His humanity. Jesus was one hundred percent God, but He was also one hundred percent man. As a man, it would be traumatic to think about going to the cross! Just imagine if it were *you* facing that cross. Being the Son of God, it *was* easy, but being a *man* He had to crucify and die to His flesh.

Jesus' words and actions reveal the struggle that was going on within Him. He knew He was going to the cross, but He wanted it to pass from Him. There was a conflict within Him between the desire of His flesh and mind and His desire to fulfill the will of His Father. But as Jesus continued to pray, we see that He totally dedicated Himself to obey God's plan regardless of the cost, and this dedication won an eternal victory for mankind.

If It Be Your Will

Jesus continues His prayer in verse 36:

> Abba, Father, all things are possible for You. Take this cup away from Me; nevertheless, not what I will, but what You will.

The last part of this verse has caused more confusion in the area of prayer than almost any other phrase in the Bible, because people have thought, "Well, Jesus prayed, 'If it be they will,' so I should pray this way also." Therefore, they include those words in all their prayers!

Yet these words make their prayers ineffective. "Father, if it be your will to heal me, then heal me" is not a scriptural prayer, because it *is* God's will to heal. He has already done it in Christ. Healing is included in the redemptive work of salvation.

In this situation, the Prayer of Faith (see Chapter 5), not the Prayer of Dedication, Consecration, and Submission, should be used. In the Prayer of Faith we don't have to say, "If it be your will," because we already *know* what God's will is from the revelation of His Word and character. When we pray in line with God's Word, we don't have to add to every prayer, "If it be your will," because God's Word and promises are His will.

On the other hand, Jesus *did* pray this way, so we can't throw it out altogether and say, "Well, we know what the will of God is, so we don't need this kind of prayer anymore." It's still here in the Word of God, and we need to understand it.

There *is* a time to pray, "If it be your will." That time is in a time of dedication and obedience in your life, when God is revealing His heart, plan, and ways to you and showing you the way you should walk.

This type of prayer should be a general prayer and attitude of our hearts. "Father, my life belongs to You. My life is dedicated to You. Not what I want, but what You want." God is a good God; He is our Father, but He also requires us to listen and to obey Him. This is where the Prayer of Dedication, Consecration, and Submission fits in. It fits into obedience in your life. "Father, whatever You want me to do, I'll do. Wherever You want me to go, I'll go."

When you know what to do, and you are strengthened to do it, don't pray, "If it be your will" anymore — simply obey! So there is to be, in a general sense, a spirit of dedication over our lives. In order to maintain this, we need to add this kind of prayer to our prayer life.

I often pray this way: "Father, today I belong to You. My life is not my own. I live to obey You. I love to obey You. Not my will, not the will of man, or of the flesh, or of the devil, but *your* will is what I desire. Father, not what I will, but what *You* will."

God requires this spirit of dedication in His people. That doesn't mean we sit around all day, saying, "God, what is your will? Should I wear green today, or should I wear purple?" There are many decisions that we make ourselves, but in a general sense, our heart must be open to the Lord, to do His will, to obey Him, and to change when He requires us to change. The way we express that is through the Prayer of Dedication, Consecration, and Submission.

Simple Obedience Is What God Wants

There is also a specific side to this prayer. There are times in our lives when God asks us to do certain detailed and specific things. It is more than just a general dedication of our lives. It is a specific thing that God is requiring of us. Although our mind and flesh may want to go another direction, or experience great weakness or rebellion, we know in our inner man, in our heart, by the Holy Spirit, that there is something God is asking us to do. We are dealing with a specific area in our lives, like Jesus was that night in Gethsemane. He was consecrating Himself to obey the Father's will concerning the cross through the Prayer of Dedication, Consecration, and Submission.

Since the Prayer of Dedication, Consecration, and Submission deals with obedience, we need to understand that obedience is not based on how big or how small the thing is that God is asking us to do. Obedience is based in simply obeying God.

Many people think, "When God calls me to Africa, I will obey." But if we don't obey *today* to do what God has asked us to do, we won't obey in the future when He asks us to do something else. To God, obedience is simple obedience, whether it's big or small in man's eyes.

Do you know it's as much obedience to obey the Bible as it is to go to Africa? It's as much obedience to rejoice in the Lord always or to pray always as it is to be a missionary to India. When we dedicate ourselves to God, we were dedicating ourselves to obey, whether the thing He asks of us seems big or small.

I remember clearly when God called me into the ministry. I was saved, Spirit filled, in the Word, and loved God. I was studying at the university to be a nurse, but I felt, deep in my heart, that God wanted me to do more with my life. I felt there was a call on my life for full-time work in the Lord's kingdom. I had such a desire to get out of the university and go to Bible school, but I was pulled and hindered by the world, by my own ideas, and by my family.

I thought, "God, I want to go to Bible school, but . . ." Finally one day I was praying and I told the Lord, "This isn't right. I need to get out of here and do what You've put in my heart. But God, what are my parents going to say? What are my friends going to say? O God, there's such a struggle in me! Father, I don't have all the understanding, but not my will, your will be done. If You want me to go into the ministry, to go to Bible school, Father, I will go. I just want You to know that I will go, Lord. I will do what You want me to do. I will go wherever You want me to go. Not my will, but your will be done. O God, not my will, but your will be done."

I prayed this many times, sometimes in agony, with groans from deep within me. God was dealing with me, changing me, and helping me by the power of the Holy Spirit. God's timing and plan became clear for me. As I prayed, the strength and courage of God came into me to do what He had told me to do.

That's what the Prayer of Dedication, Consecration, and Submission if for: God wants you to dedicate yourself to Him, and then the strength and ability to carry through what He's put in your heart to do will come supernaturally.

God Requires Willingness

We have seen that the Prayer of Dedication, Consecration, and Submission deals with obedience at every level and in every area of our lives. It also deals with willingness. God not only requires obedience, He requires willingness as well, and He has given us this type of prayer to put us in a position to have them both worked into our carnal mind, which is often at enmity with God.

Look at what Jesus said in verse 38 of Mark 14:

Keep awake and watch and pray . . . that you may not enter into temptation; the spirit indeed is willing, but the flesh is weak. *(Amplified)*

Jesus was speaking to the disciples about their weak flesh. He had the power and anointing to do so, as He Himself was experiencing a personal, deep dedication to God.

Many people say, "Oh, the flesh is so weak," and then use this scripture as an excuse for disobedience, as a cover for their unwillingness to obey, or as a cover for stubbornness. Yes, the flesh is weak, but Jesus is giving us an example here of how to pray, using the Prayer of Dedication, Consecration, and Submission, so we can receive the grace and strength needed to come through the weak flesh and unwillingness into willingness and obedience.

The Prayer of Dedication, Consecration, and Submission is tied with Philippians 2:12,13:

Therefore, my dear ones, as you have always obeyed . . . so now, not only . . . in my presence but much more because I am absent, work out . . . your own salvation with reverence and awe and trembling . . . .

[Not in your strength] for it is God Who is all the while effectually at work in you . . . both to will and to work for His good pleasure." *(Amplified)*

These two verses show what Christianity really is: You and God working together. Man has his part to fulfill, God has His part, too, and you work together for the will of God to be done in the earth. It says that we are to work out our own salvation, but that it is not to be done in our own strength. We must do our part, and God is going to do His part.

Notice the two things God is doing. He's working in you to *will* and to *do* of His good pleasure. He's creating in you a capacity for willingness and for obedience. Have faith in God working in you.

Every day thank Him for what He's doing! Press into God, dedicate yourself totally to Him, and let Him work in you the strength and ability to obey.

This is exactly what happened to Jesus. As He prayed the Prayer of Dedication, Consecration, and Submission, we're told in Luke 22:43 that an angel came immediately and strengthened Him, and Jesus went to the cross and fulfilled the will of God.

It was in the Prayer of Dedication, Consecration, and Submission that Jesus expressed His willingness to obey the Father's will and received the strength He needed to fulfill it. Thank God for the Prayer of Dedication, Consecration, and Submission!

Now I want you to pray; to dedicate yourself, praying from your heart, to God:

"Father, I pray the Prayer of Dedication, Consecration, and Submission. In every area of my life, I belong to You. Father, I'll go where You want me to go, I'll do what You want me to do. Not my will, but your will be done. Thank You, Father that You work in me both to will and to do of your good pleasure. You have a good plan for my life, a plan of peace and joy.

"Father, what You want and what You desire is what I want; that is what I desire. Not my will, but your will for my life every day, Father. Not my own way, not the way of the flesh, but the way of the Spirit. Father, your will, your plan, your way.

"Father, I dedicate my life to You in every area. You have a plan for me in every area of life. Thank You, Father, for the joy of obedience. I will obey You with *joy*. Father, I want to have the spirit of obedience in my life, not rebellion or pride, not resistance or hard-heartedness, but a soft, sensitive heart that is willing to do *anything*.

"I rebuke rebellion and stubbornness in Jesus' Name. Father, I say before your presence that I am willing to do anything You want me to do. No matter what man says, no matter what the world says, You have found a willing person. You have found an obedient person.

"Father, I will do what You say all the way, just the way You say it, no more and no less, and with joy. Thank You, Father, for the spirit of faith and the spirit of obedience. And Father, thank You that your will *will* be fulfilled in my life to your glory. In Jesus' Name, Amen."

Chapter 7
Casting Our Cares on the Lord

God has made a way for us in the midst of problems, stress, pressure, and great intensity to live practically in the peace and joy of the Holy Spirit. That way is through the Prayer of Casting Our Cares on the Lord.

Although this prayer is not as well known or practiced as some of the other kinds of prayer, it is vital to our life, both naturally and spiritually. It's a type of prayer, I'm convinced, that we need to incorporate much more into our prayer lives.

The purpose of the Prayer of Casting Our Cares on the Lord is twofold. First, so we can stay free from worry, stress, and pressure; and second, so we can walk in our Fatherhood relationship with God and not be pressed down by the cares of this life, or controlled by a spirit of fear.

It is not God's intention for you to be weighted down by the cares of life. The kingdom of God, the Bible says, is righteousness, peace, and joy in the Holy Spirit (Romans 14:17). God wants you to live in peace and joy, not in anxiety, pressure, and heaviness.

It's common for the everyday affairs of life to put weights and burdens on your soul. The result is that you become depressed, heavy in spirit, worried, and distracted, and you try to work things out in the flesh.

If you have strong fear in any area, it can steal your faith, and the devil can use that problem against you, resulting in an ungodly torment in your life. You don't have to respond like this, however. God has made a way for you to deal with every problem and circumstance you fear. It is by the power of the Holy Spirit giving you grace to walk through it and to live in peace and joy, no matter what's happening in your life.

This is God's will for you: He wants you to be carefree and completely free from all fear! That doesn't mean that you don't take responsibility, or that you never work. But there is a place in the Spirit to walk in peace, free from anxieties and cares. It's through this prayer, the Prayer of Casting Our Cares on the Lord, that we can find that place.

The enemy wants to steal your peace and joy. One of the ways he does it is when you take the cares of life upon yourself and try to work them out. It's important that we pray this kind of prayer so we're able to keep our freedom in the Holy Spirit.

In order to flow in the Holy Spirit, you must be free and at peace in your mind. It is often the mental realm that hinders people in spiritual things. Their mind is burdened by cares and pressures, or is plagued with all kinds of fear.

Yes, pressures are real in life. That's why we have the Prayer of Casting Our Cares on the Lord, because pressures are real, life is real, and we need a place where we can go and release the cares over on the Lord.

Some people say, "Well, just go someplace and scream to release your stress." No, it's better to take it by the Holy Spirit, *pray*, and release your cares over on the Lord! It's better to rebuke the spirit of fear in Jesus' Name and command it to go from your life!

Second Timothy 1:7 says, "God has not given us a spirit of fear, but of power and of love and of a sound mind." Rebuke the fear! If you carry the care, you are saying that God isn't big enough to work that problem out in your life. You are afraid of failure. Fear is the opposite of faith. Resist the fear and trust God!

God Is Your Father

The Prayer of Casting Your Cares on the Lord begins with a revelation of the fact that God is your heavenly Father and He loves you. *God is your Father!* He *loves* you as His child. When you're born again, you become a child of God.

The Bible says in First John 3:1,2 that *now* we are children of God — right now at this time we are *His* children. That is where the revelation and freedom come to be able to pray this prayer.

God is your Father, and because He's your Father, He *cares* for you! The Holy Spirit wants that truth to explode in your spirit! God is the best Father you can ever have. What we are learning is how to fellowship with Him in prayer as a Father. Casting your cares on Him is part of that fellowship.

Part of the problem, in addition to people being trained by the world to react to life with fear, is that most people don't have a good biblical picture of God. Because of their own earthly fathers, or because of religious training, they have a distorted view of what He is really like.

Christians need to have their minds renewed by the Word in this area so they realize that God is a *good* God, that He *loves* them, that He's not against them, that He *cares* for them, and that He is their *Father*.

We're not alone or helpless; someone cares for us — our Father in heaven. He will take care of *every* detail in our lives if we simply do it His way, which is by faith, and if we refuse to accept fear in any area. One side of our faith in the Fatherhood of God is praying this prayer, taking the cares of our life and casting them over on Him.

Help for a Worried Generation

First Peter 5:6,7 tells us:

Therefore humble yourselves . . . under the mighty hand of God, that in due time He may exalt you.

Casting the whole of your care [all your anxieties, all your worries, all your concerns, once for all] on Him, for He cares for you affectionately and cares about you watchfully. *(Amplified)*

One of the Bible ways to humble yourself is by casting your cares over on the Lord. Worry is not humility.

"Well, I'm just going to work this out myself" is a statement that can be covered with many masks. It is not humility, but self-will.

What is humility? Casting your cares over on the Lord. This generation is an ego generation, a prideful and do-it-yourself generation. It's a pleasure generation, and it's also a *worry* generation. People are *filled* with fear and worry.

Many think it is their nature to worry. They grow up thinking and being trained that it's *natural* to worry. "I'm just a worrier," they say.

The Bible way for spiritual life, however, is not to worry, but to cast your cares over on the Lord and accept the perfect love of God that drives out fear (First John 4:18)! Anything that is not of faith, the Bible says, is sin (Romans 14:23). Worry is sin! When you and I hold onto the cares of this life and allow them to weigh down on our soul, we're not in total faith.

The Word says that God cares for us; it actually commands us to release every care and every worry over onto Him. He wants to take care of those things for us! Jesus said in Matthew 11:30, "My yoke is easy and My burden is light." We make it hard on ourselves, but the Bible has a way out. Jesus wants to set you free from fear!

Cast Your Cares on the Lord

One of the ways out is through the Prayer of Casting Our Cares on the Lord. Spiritually, we are to be like a fisherman who's throwing, or casting, his line out to catch a fish. That's the way it is when we pray this prayer. We're *casting* our cares on the Lord, just like the fisherman casts his line. We take the anxieties, the worries, and the concerns and *cast* them over on the Lord by faith.

We have to be willing to release them to God, saying, "Father, I give all of my cares to You. I humble myself under your mighty hand, and I cast all of my cares over on you. I *refuse* to accept anxiety. In Jesus' Name, I *refuse* to worry. I release these cares before You, Father. I let go of them in my mind, in Jesus' Name. I put them in your hands, Father. You can *have* them. I leave them with You. Spirit of fear, go from me in Jesus' Name!"

That's exactly the way God wants us to pray when it comes to worries, concerns, and cares. This is God's answer to the world's way of tranquilizers and stress relievers. This is a Bible way to come into peace: Cast your cares over on the Lord.

The Amplified Bible says that when you do it — when you cast your cares over on the Lord — do it once and for all. See them in the hands of the Lord; release them into His hands and then *leave* them there. Leave those cares, anxieties, and worries there with God. Don't take them back!

Sometimes our souls are trained the wrong way; they're trained to keep thinking about our problems. Don't misunderstand; we need to think, but sometimes we think too much!

Quit thinking about the problem. Leave it in the hands of the Lord. He is big enough to take care of it for you. You don't need to run around trying to figure out how to do everything.

God wants you to be at peace and be led by the Holy Spirit in how you respond to the affairs of life. Of course, there are some things you know to do, so *do* them; but there are other things that are weights and cares for you, and those you need to cast over on the Lord. It's in doing that, that you'll receive the strength, grace, and direction needed to do what you're supposed to do in everyday life in peace and joy.]

Are You Pressured?

Let's look at James 5:13: "Is any one among you afflicted?" (*Amplified*). The word "afflicted" here also means "pressured." Is anyone among you pressured? It's not just spiritual pressure from the devil that your Father cares about; He cares about natural things as well; about the natural pressures of this life, and He has given the Holy Spirit to help you.

Everyone has life's circumstances and responsibilities to deal with. We always will; it's how you handle them that counts. You can't go on vacation forever. So what is the person who is pressured supposed to do? Pray! That's what the Bible says. If any of you is pressed, stressed, or frustrated — *pray.*

Sometimes we think, "Oh, what should I do? What should I do? I've got this and this — and then there's that problem. And, oh no! Here comes something else. Oh, what should I do?" We've all been there, haven't we? What are we supposed to do? Stop all that worrying right there and *pray!*

"In Jesus' Name, I am not going to give in to this pressure and stress. I cast my cares over on the Lord. Father, You can have this situation, and You can have that situation. You can have this deadline, and You can have that situation. You can have this deadline, and You can have this bill. You can have them *all.* I cast them all onto You, and I leave them there."

Of course, the Prayer of Casting Your Cares is not a "cure-all," but it is a great help when you pray it in faith. The Lord wants to help you in other areas of your life as well.

For example, the Holy Spirit may deal with you about weakness, whether it be mental, physical, spiritual, or emotional. He also wants to set you free from rebellion that drives you to do things your own way, not His. He wants to deliver you from people who have strong control over your life, which causes pressure on you.

Maybe worry and fear is a spirit that has been in your family for years. Jesus will set you free from all generational ties and curses! There are many areas that the Holy Spirit can show you if you are open and willing to deal with them and get them out of your life. Let Him do it.

67

Do Not Fret!

Another scripture that is important in this area is Philippians 4:6:

Do not fret or have any anxiety about anything, but in every circumstance and in everything, by prayer and petition . . . with thanksgiving, continue to make your wants known to God. *(Amplified)*

"Do not fret or have any anxiety about anything." You might read that and think, "Oh, that is impossible! Is this written for *today*?" Yes, it is written for the 1990s.

"Do not have any anxiety about anything." "Oh, come on, everyone has anxiety about something in his life. People are human, aren't they?" Thank God, that's why we have the Bible! If the Bible says it, it is actually possible for us, human though we be, not to fret or have anxiety about anything.

The carnal, worldly man doesn't understand this. "How can you Christians be so happy?" How *can* we be? Because we know our Father. He cares for us and watches over us affectionately. We cast our cares of Him, and He takes them from us. We know the Holy Spirit who helps us with life, and points to the root of every problem we have. Then He sets us free!

I challenge you to release your faith regarding this verse. Near this verse in my Bible I wrote, "There is no problem with problems." At first it was difficult for my mind and flesh to accept. "Oh no, here's a problem and there's a problem. There's a confrontation here and a problem there. Oh, what am I going to do?"

I'm not going to do anything except cast my cares on the Lord and seek Him for the solution. There is no problem with problems. We know there are problems in life, but there is a way to handle those problems in God.

The first thing we need to do is to get this scripture deep inside of us: "Have no anxiety about anything." That means there's no problem with problems. There's an answer, a way out, and God will show it to us. We trust Him to show us. We have faith for Him to help us!

If we release our faith, cast our care and the pressure of it over on God, and refuse to worry about it, God will do what He said He will do — take care of it and answer the problem! If we hold the care ourselves, we tie the hands of God, because if we try to care for it, He can't. That's why He says, "Don't have anxiety about any-thing."

Have You Talked to God?

"In everything by prayer and . . . thanksgiving, let your requests be made known to God." This verse is clear that you must talk to God about your problems. Sometimes people talk and talk about every angle of their problems with other people, but they don't say one word about them to God! We must talk to *God* about these things.

"Well, doesn't He already know?" Yes, He knows, but He wants us to bring them to Him as our Father, saying, "God, what about this? What do You think?"

Have you told God about the situation? He cares about you. He will talk back to you. Be open for what He says.

The second thing to do is seek God about any unconfronted area in our life. If you have a weakness in being able to handle pressure, ask yourself, "Why do I have that weakness if I can do all things in Christ" (Philippians 4:13)?

Maybe there is a door open in your life where you have allowed the spirit of fear to come in and control you. Maybe there is unforgiveness in you that doesn't allow you the boldness to walk freely in the situation you are facing. Did your rebellion get you into that mess?

These things are not always involved when dealing with the affairs of life, but it is important for you to have your whole heart and mind open to God to deal with the problem.

This is not condemnation; it is holiness and purity working in you which gives you authority in God to handle any problem! If your authority is given to something else, you don't have it to use on your problems, so you must take it back to walk in full freedom.

God's Peace Will Guard You

Talk to God just like you talk to a friend. Then, when you ask Him, making your requests and wants known to Him with thanksgiving, and release your cares, the promise of verse 7 will result:

> And God's peace . . . which transcends all understanding, shall garrison and mount guard over your hearts and minds in Christ Jesus. *(Amplified)*

God's peace, not the peace of the world, for there is no peace in the world, will protect us. That's why we must have this kind of prayer — so God's peace can be ours. His peace, which goes past natural understanding, will *guard* our hearts and our minds.

Where do the attacks hit? Where does the pressure come? Against your mind and your heart. The peace of God will supernaturally guard you. It's the peace of God *because you've prayed*. And it doesn't necessarily mean you prayed five hours either; it may just be "an arrow prayer," a quick prayer that goes to God and can be as simple as a thought: "God, what about this?"

It's surprising, if you just pray, how much peace will come and guard your heart, your mind, and your soul realm. God cares for you. He loves you. He has a good plan for you. But you've got to *talk* to Him, *work* with Him, *cast* your cares over on Him, and *leave* them with Him.

Sometimes it's not just "an arrow prayer," either. Are you willing to lie on the floor for hours and cry out to God to give you the answer? Are you desperate for God to show you mighty things? *Call* on Him (see Jeremiah 33:3). Cry out from your heart, even if it takes time to come into peace.

There are times when we must *seek* the Lord. He will reveal Himself and His plan. Are you serious with God? If you are, He will be serious with you.

Cry Out to God!

A pastor told me a story once that I want to share with you. One of his members was discouraged and was getting ready to leave the church. This member held an important position in society, and it would have been a drastic move for him to leave the church.

The whole city would have thought that maybe the church didn't meet the person's needs, or maybe there really was something wrong with this church that was a little different from all the others in town.

More important, the pastor knew it wasn't God's will for this person to leave the church. The pastor saw that the enemy was trying to draw the church member back into the world. The situation was weighing heavily on the pastor's mind and spirit. He was burdened continually about how to keep the member in the church.

Finally, one day the Lord spoke to him and said, "If you'll pray about this, I'll do a miracle." The pastor thought, "Oh yes, I must pray." So he told his wife, "I'm going to lie on the floor all day Saturday and cry out to God for the answer and the victory in this situation. I'm going to stay there until I get a note of victory, or until I get a peace in my heart that the Lord has worked in this situation."

He did what he said, and on Saturday morning he went in and started to lie down before the Lord to pray. He told me it was a temptation for his flesh to want to go to sleep, but he refused to go to sleep, and he stayed there on the floor, praying in other tongues, crying out to God, and seeking God's face for hours and hours. He didn't take a break for lunch. He kept praying about this one situation and this one person, his relationship to the person, and what God wanted to do in the situation.

It was a care for the pastor, a pressure on him, as a minister. It was also something in the heart of the Holy Spirit; He wanted to have someone pray the situation through!

The pastor prayed until the early evening, just about dinner time. At that point, he felt that everything in his heart, everything in God's heart, and everything pressuring him about this situation was released before the presence of the Lord.

The Lord did a miracle and moved on the church member! He showed the pastor the answer to the problem, and today the church member is a strong Christian and a great testimony to the church and the whole community. This happened because of the prayers of a pastor who was willing to cry out to God to take the care and the situation and make it into a miracle.

God help us to be sensitive! There is a time to cast your cares over on the Lord, and there is a time to cry out for hours. You say, "How do I know the difference?" Be led by the Holy Spirit when you pray about the pressures of life that are weighing you down.

Are You Weighed Down?

"Well, how do I know something's weighing me down?" When it takes up a lot of your time, your energy, and your efforts in your thought life.

There's a special feeling when something becomes a weight: It pulls you down to suck you under and take the life from you.

71

When you feel like you're being sucked under, that's the time to go *up* and cast your cares on the Lord. That's the time to seek His face.

Of course, we work through things, but when those things are sucking us under, it's time to cast them over on the Lord. Whatever's trying to suck you under and take your peace, whatever's trying to take your joy — cast it over on the Lord. Let *Jesus* be the Lord of that situation!

Sometimes we worship our life's circumstances by thinking, planning, and scheming about them. If it steals our peace, we're worshipping the problem, because when we worship Jesus, there's peace. When we allow circumstances to exalt over Jesus, the circumstance is our lord, and there's no peace. You don't need to be condemned if there's no peace in your life; you need to let Jesus take you into that peace through casting your cares over on Him.

Look now at Proverbs 16:3:

Roll your works upon the Lord [commit and trust them wholly to Him; He will cause your thoughts to become agreeable to His will, and] so shall your plans be established and succeed. (*Amplified***)**

What a good promise this is! However, in order to get it, we must do the first part of the verse — commit our works to the Lord. He's ready and waiting for you to do it. Roll your works on Him. Cast your cares on Him. It will cause blessing to come to you and let you *enjoy* life, even if there are problems.

Submit to God in every area, and the problems of life will submit to you! Obey God in every area, and the problems of life will obey you! It's only in God's peace that this can happen, and this peace comes by casting your cares over on Him.

Psalm 55:22 is another powerful verse concerning this: "Cast your burden on the Lord, And He shall sustain you; He shall never permit the righteous to be moved." If we will cast our cares on the Lord, He *will* sustain us! This is also a good way to keep yourself protected *after* you cast your cares over on the Lord, when your flesh or the devil says, "What did you do? That's so stupid. That's not going to work. You're going to take that back."

If you're not careful, your mind will start to worry again, and all the pressure will come back. You must respond, "No, this is my verse. I have cast my cares over on the Lord, and you will not torment me devil, with lies and pressure. This verse is true. My God will sustain me in Jesus' Name." Walk then in peace, because the promise is yours, if you'll believe it.

"He shall never permit the righteous to be moved," the verse continues. We can allow ourselves to be moved, but *He* will never allow us to be moved when we cast our cares over on Him.

Your Father loves you and cares for you. Do you have cares today? God wants you to go to Him, talk to Him, and cast those cares over onto Him; not as a religious act, but as a quality decision, releasing them to Him in faith. You can come into the place of God's peace right now. Commit your cares to the Lord, leave them there, absolutely refuse to take them up again, and God's peace will guard your heart and mind in Christ Jesus.

Resist all fear. You can walk in God's peace and joy. It's up to you. Is any one pressured, stressed, or anxious? Let him pray! Cast your cares on God, and He will sustain you.

Chapter 8

The Prayer of Praise and Worship

"Praying always with all prayer . . . " our text in Ephesians 6:18 says. As we continue looking at the various kinds of prayer, I'd like to teach you about what is called the Prayer of Praise and Worship.

We know that praise and worship are a part of our normal Christian life, but I have included them in the list of prayers simply because prayer, as we learned in Chapter 1, is fellowship with God, and praise and worship are part of that fellowship.

You will find that your praise life and your prayer life are closely tied together. As you incorporate more praise and worship into your prayer time, a new dimension will be added to your fellowship with God.

One of the most important aspects, or purposes, of praise and worship is found in Psalm 100:4, where the Word of God says, "Enter into His gates with thanksgiving, And into His courts with praise." One of the functions of praise in your prayer life is to bring you into the presence of God.

When the Bible speaks of the gates and the courts of God, it is talking about our spiritual position and the ability we have through Christ to come into the presence of a holy God.

Jesus' blood has made a way for us to be able to enter in. How? The veil in the Temple was split apart the day He died on the cross. Now every believer can come before the throne of God as a priest, to minister before the Lord. We use praise to enter into His presence and to come before Him with a joyful heart.

In First Peter 2:5 we discover another purpose of praise in our lives. It says that we,

> ... as living stones, are being built up a spiritual house, a holy priesthood, to offer up spiritual sacrifices acceptable to God through Jesus Christ.

Praise is a way for us to offer spiritual sacrifice as priests before the Lord.

God is still a God who honors sacrifice. In the Old Covenant, He honored the sacrifice with fire. In the New Covenant, He continues to do the same — but now He answers with the fire of the Holy Spirit burning in our lives. In Hebrews 13:15 we read:

> Therefore by Him let us continually offer the sacrifice of praise to God, that is, the fruit of our lips, giving thanks to His name.

Notice it says that we should offer up the sacrifice of praise *continually*. That's why praise is such an important part of our prayer life; it keeps that sacrifice continually before God.

There are many different kinds of praise found in the Bible. In the Old Testament, the Hebrew words for "praise" include a wide variety of expressions. Among them are: to bless God, to praise Him, to give Him praise, and to kneel. They also mean to stretch out your hand, to celebrate Him, and to glorify Him.

Because there are so many different meanings to praise, you don't have to get stuck in just one way of expressing praise to God. Experiment, be led by the Spirit, and stretch yourself in your praise life!

God Inhabits Praise

In the church where I worked in Sweden, we purposed to develop strong worship in the believers. From the beginning, we've encouraged people to be free, happy, loud, bold, and even demonstrative in their praise before the Lord, because we've seen so clearly that God *desires* the praise of His people.

Psalm 22:3 tells us that God actually *inhabits* the praises of His people. Praise causes God to live and dwell with us in a much deeper way than if we didn't live a life of praise before Him.

We've purposed to keep our freedom in praise and worship in the church. We sing, dance, shout, and clap unto the Lord because our hearts are so full of joy and praise! You must *keep* your heart stirred up and full of praise and joy. You must press into praise and worship. You are to praise God with full freedom!

In the first building we were in, the floor would sway during our time of praise, because of our dancing before the Lord. Every time we had a service, white particles of dust from the ceiling fell on the desks of the telephone company that had its offices beneath us.

They would come up and say, "You must not do your exercises in this building." So we calmed ourselves down a little bit, and the pastor began to seek the Lord about it. One day as we were praising God like this, the Lord said these words to him: "I will pay *anything* for people who will praise me wildly like this." What a wonderful word from the Lord!

God is looking for people who will praise Him with all their hearts. That doesn't mean you should cause the people downstairs to have white dust on their desks every day when they come to work, but God loves a believer who includes free, bold, and strong praise in his prayer life. God inhabits — He lives in — that kind of praise!

This kind of prayer not only includes praise; it also includes worship, for it is the Prayer of Praise *and* Worship. We know that in heaven right now, the angels, the hosts of heavenly beings, and the great cloud of witnesses, are doing one thing — they are worshipping the King of kings and the Lord of lords; they are worshipping God. Worship is the occupation of heaven!

When we worship God, we don't worship Him for what He has done; we get more intimate in our fellowship with Him and worship Him for *who He is*. Worship touches the innermost part of God's being. He wants you to worship Him. His heart is toward the earth, looking for worshippers! When you worship, it can bring heaven — the glory of God — down on you!

Praise Is a Choice

In Luke 10 we find a story about Martha and Mary, and what happened one day when Jesus went to visit in their home. Martha was totally occupied with all the work she had to do. She was distracted and attacked and was just so busy. Mary, however, had a heart that caused her to want to sit down at Jesus' feet and worship Him.

When Martha complained about it, Jesus told her, in verses 41 and 42:

Martha, Martha, you are worried and troubled about many things.

77

But one thing is needed, and Mary has chosen that good part, which will not be taken away from her.

Notice that Mary made a choice. You must get this in your heart. Worship is a choice! You *choose* to worship God. It's not natural for human beings to worship God. The spirit of this world is an anti-Christ, or an anti-God spirit, and it is against worship of the true and living God. However, in your inner man there is a heart of worship, because the Holy Spirit draws you to the presence of God to worship Him.

God is your Father, and the Holy Spirit creates a bonding of love between you and Him. But you must make the choice to worship like Mary did. Jesus said that it's necessary and good to worship Him. Mary made the choice. She chose a good thing, and what she got from that choice could never be taken away from her.

You will find as you come into a life of worship that no one can ever take away from you what you receive from God during that intimate relationship with Him. You received it directly from God Himself in the place of worship as you were ministering to Him and knowing and loving Him — not just for what He has done, but for who He is to you.

You come close to God's heart in worship — and He comes close to you. His being and presence start to become a tangible part of your life. Your grow in your awareness of who He is, and He really becomes the most precious, first love of your life.

The Bible says in First Corinthians 3:16,17 that we are the temple of the Holy Spirit; we are a dwelling place for the presence of God. When you worship God from your spirit — from deep in your heart, spirit to spirit — you glorify Him and you get filled with His glory and His presence. There is *nothing* that can replace the Prayer of Praise and Worship in your life.

In John 4:21-24, Jesus tells us that God is a Spirit, and that we must worship Him in spirit and in truth. In these verses Jesus was laying down a law of the kingdom of God: the Law of Worship. Every man, deep inside, is created to worship something. He has a longing to be close to and give himself to a higher being.

The spirit of the world has perverted this longing with humanism. Now man is worshipping with no other knowledge except that he himself is the standard, and everything exists for him and his pleasure. But when you come to Christ, you find that the reason you are created is to worship God — even in your prayer time. Man is created to worship *God*.

Jesus said we're supposed to worship in spirit — that means wholeheartedly, with all our heart — and in truth. We're supposed to tie our knowledge of God into a living relationship, and not just be filled with information. We're to have a living, open, transparent relationship with God, worshipping Him in spirit and in truth.

Worship Involves Giving

In Revelation 1:6, the Word of God says that we have been made kings and priests to God. What a priest does is offer up the sacrifice. Part of the sacrifice we offer is worship. In worship, we are giving something to God. We can worship God by giving our money, time, and so forth. But another part of our worship is when we give an unqualified part of ourselves as obedient servants before Him, stilling our bodies and minds in His presence, singing to Him, loving Him, and listening to Him in that place of worship before His throne.

If you listen to God long enough in the place of worship, you will find the answer you've been seeking. Often people pray and pray, but they don't take the time to listen, wait, worship, and minister to the Lord until their answer comes.

There are many different meanings for the word "worship." One of them is to bow down in expression and in heart, putting down your own thoughts, ideas and self; laying everything down, and being totally consumed with God. It means to physically bow yourself down.

Worship means to fall down flat. It means to give reverence or fear to God. Fear here doesn't mean to be afraid of God, but to give God respect. In the New Testament, the word "worship" also means to kiss and adore God. Worship is a place where we love God and He loves us.

God actually commands us to worship Him. When He gave the Ten Commandments to the children of Israel — and to us, because they are examples for us of how to live before the God of the Bible — He spoke to us about not allowing any other god to be before Him (Exodus 20:3-6).

When we worship Him, we are laying ourselves down and literally saying with an open heart before Him, "I am not allowing any other person or any other thing to have the position of lordship over my life. I am totally yours. Everything belongs to You."

Not only does God command us to worship Him; He also deserves our worship. When Jesus died on the cross, He gave everything He had. Because of what He has done and who He is, the exalted King, He deserves our worship! He deserves all the glory, all the honor, and all the praise in our lives. Everything we are comes from Him, from being in Him, and from knowing Him.

So we worship Him because of the command to worship God, because He deserves our worship, and simply because we love Him. There is no personal fulfillment in life without worshipping God.

People in the world worship their jobs, movie stars, rock stars, or even themselves, but really, in the heart of man, there is no personal fulfillment until we give our worship to our Creator, our God, our first love, the Lord Jesus!

Worship Brings God's Strength

I like what I heard someone say once: People are no stronger than the thing they worship. When you become a worshipper of God, you become truly strong in your life with Him, because He's the strongest One there is! He is the God of heaven and earth! There is none like Him anywhere.

When you become a worshipper and press into the worship life, you will find that the strength of God will flow in you like never before.

Just look at what Isaiah 40:31 says:

But those who wait on the Lord shall renew their strength; They shall mount up with wings like eagles, They shall run and not be weary, They shall walk and not faint.

The word "wait" means "to minister to," and the word "renew" literally means "to exchange." As we worship God, as we minister to Him, there is a divine exchange that takes place. Our human strength is exchanged for the awesome strength of God! In that strength we can rise up in the spiritual world. When we rise up in our own lives as worshippers, strength comes, not just as mere human beings, but as eagles that fly, run, and go with the help of God.

In Isaiah 41:1 the Word of God says:

Keep silence before Me, O coastlands, And let the people renew their strength! Let them come near, then let them speak; Let us come near together for judgment.

Worship in our prayer life is the way we draw near to God and enter into His presence.

In worship, the Holy Spirit woos us deep into the presence of God. As we give our affections, mind, and will to Him in the place of prayer, we find that we experience fruit in our lives from being in His presence. One of them is that many pulls from the world and the flesh are broken. The more we yield ourselves to God in worship, strong worship, the more chains and holds of the world break off us, and our hearts instead are chained to the very heart of God.

Another fruit of worship we will experience is purity and holiness. As you come and bow yourself in the presence of a holy God, you will find that the power of His presence will cleanse you from unrighteousness and sin, and it will work the holiness of God in you. The convicting power of the Holy Spirit will work in your life as never before.

This is why worship is so important to you as a prayer warrior — it helps keep your heart clean and pure before the Lord. Often in worship, God speaks to your heart and ministers to you. The glory of God reveals sin and areas that you must deal with.

As you are in God's presence, a great transformation takes place in your life. The glory of God is there working in you, through you, and upon you — and in that glory there is change. There is a transforming experience that can only take place in the presence of God; that only Jesus coming to you and flowing from you in the ministry of the Holy Spirit can work in your life. The transforming power of the Holy Spirit works and operates in the place of worship.

Not only is there fruit that results from the Prayer of Worship in our lives; there are also different results or manifestations of that worship. You will find that as strong worship works in your life or in your prayer group, God's manifested presence will be a result. God will come on the scene!

You will find at times that the prophetic anointing will come over you, and the prophetic words of the Lord will flow. There may also be times when prophetic prayers will come forth, because the Bible says in Revelation 19:10 that the spirit of prophecy is the spirit of worship. When we worship Jesus, it opens the door for Him to speak to and through us.

We also know that one of the results of worship is that the presence of God comes upon the people, and in His presence there is healing and deliverance. The healing anointing works in your life as you practice times of powerful worship.

Remember, the Prayer of Praise and Worship is not simply a religious duty we have to perform. Worship and praise, as Jesus said in Matthew 15:8,9, must come from our heart. It's better to obey and worship God from our heart than it is to sacrifice.

Some people would rather be "religious" and not offend anyone. They would rather not be too free or bold in expressing themselves. But God would rather that you cut loose and praise Him from your heart!

Begin to worship and praise the Lord from your heart for longer periods of time than you ever have before. Come into this intimate relationship with Him that makes your prayer life strong, clean, and open before Him.

Let's look at Philippians 4:6. Here Paul tells us how we're to finish our prayer time; how we're to end all the different prayers we pray:

> Be anxious for nothing, but in everything by prayer and supplication, with thanksgiving, let your requests be made known to God.

This means that every time we pray, we should, as we make our requests known to God, end that time of prayer with thanksgiving. We are to give thanks to God for the fact that He's heard us and answered our prayer, and also for who He is and what He's done in our lives.

As we do this, we know that we leave the time of prayer in great peace, joy, and satisfaction because we obeyed the Bible and prayed the way the Lord told us to pray. We let every prayer and supplication be made known with thanksgiving in our hearts and mouths before the Lord.

Praise and worship is an important and powerful part of your prayer life. Be sure to include it at the beginning, in the middle, and at the end of your prayer. Set your heart, mind, spirit, and body — every part of your being — on God your Father, on Jesus your Lord, and on the Holy Spirit your Strength, Helper, and the One who is always with you.

Many years ago, the Lord gave me a lesson comparing the differences between the Prayer of Praise and Worship and the Prayer of Intercession. It is included here to help and bless you as you learn and practice all kinds of prayer. It will become even clearer after you study the chapter on intercession.

Intercession	Worship
• Gaps to stand in.	• No gaps — you and the Father.
• You are a conductor.	• You are a communer.
• Stand on what He has done.	• Stand on who He is!
• Come in the boldness of your righteousness.	• Come because of the multitude of mercy, fear, reverence (Psalm 5:7).
• A pouring out.	• A drawing toward.
• The person prayed for is the receiver.	• The Lord is the receiver (minister to the Lord).
• A coming forth of life and wholeness.	• A coming forth of holiness.
• Jesus our example as Intercessor (Hebrews 7:25).	• Jesus our example of loving the Father (John 14:31).

Chapter 9
The Prayer of Agreement

Jesus taught much about prayer when He was walking on the earth. He was a man of prayer Himself, and He said many things about the prayer life as He taught His disciples about the kingdom of God. In Matthew 18:19,20, Jesus said this:

> Again I say to you that if two of you agree on earth concerning anything that they ask, it will be done for them by My Father in heaven.
>
> For where two or three are gathered together in My name, I am there in the midst of them.

These verses of scripture are called the Prayer of Agreement. Jesus said here that if any two persons on earth will agree about whatever they ask, it will be done for them.

The Prayer of Agreement deals with two people praying together. This could be two members of a church, two friends or, even more powerfully, a husband and a wife who are in a covenant and who will agree together about the will of God concerning the situation they are praying for. This could also include three or more persons praying in a spirit of agreement, but I want to be more specific and focus on two persons praying together.

The first thing to consider when you're praying a Prayer of Agreement is the person with whom you are praying. Be sure it's not someone who will agree with you in word only. It's important when you pray this prayer that you find someone who will agree with you in spirit. Find someone who thinks and believes like you do, so you will be in agreement in heart as well as word when you pray.

Jesus said, "If any two of you on earth agree." Notice that all we have to do is to be human beings in this earthly realm, and when we agree together in prayer, a power is released in the heavenly realm to bring about results. The Father is just waiting for us to pray in agreement.

You Must Ask Together

Another important consideration about the Prayer of Agreement that we see from Jesus' words here is that the two who are praying must ask *together* about the situation. You may wish to refer to our teaching in Chapter 5 on the Prayer of Faith, about what God wants to do when we ask, and how we should ask according to His Word and His will.

Remember, when you agree together with someone, Jesus said that you must ask together. I remember times when I've called a friend and said, "Would you agree with me about my rent? I need to pay $500, and my dishwasher just broke down! Will you agree with me that I'll have the money to pay for both?" And my friend would say, "Oh yes, I agree that in Jesus' Name you will have it."

But that is not really a scriptural way to pray this prayer, because the Bible says you two must ask together. So instead of being sloppy with your prayer, agree and ask together, one praying and asking and the other saying, "Yes, Lord, I agree and I ask together with my friend here that it shall be done." When you pray according to the Word of God, Jesus promised that it would be done for you by the Father who is in heaven!

Jesus Is There To Bring It to Pass

Verse 20 tells us that when two or three are gathered together in His Name, He will be in the midst of them. In other words, when we gather together in the Name of Jesus and pray in agreement in His Name, in line with His Word and His will, He is there to bring it to pass.

There is power in agreement! There is no power in disagreement. It is in unity and agreement that the power of God can be released in prayer, and you will see mighty results on behalf of the people you pray for.

I heard a story about a church that was praying about finances for a building they were in the process of constructing. They had been interceding and praying, and many were even fasting for the finances, yet nothing seemed to be happening. The pastor began to seek God and ask, "What shall I do about these finances?" (It's important to seek God on which weapon to use and when!)

A thought came into his mind by the Holy Spirit that reminded him of the Prayer of Agreement. So he went to his wife and said, "If you and I will agree together, from our position as the authority of this church, God will do a miracle and give us the money."

They said a simple prayer asking God for the finances for the new building, for a bank to approve the loan, and for God to do a miracle in the situation. It was a short prayer. They agreed together! Both of them asked for the needed miracle in Jesus' Name, thanked God for the answer — and within two days the breakthrough came!

The church had been praying and fasting for many weeks (and I believe that fasting and prayer were important to prepare the way for the answer), but when the pastor and his wife came together in agreement, led by the Holy Spirit, a bank (after many had refused) offered to loan them the money, and they were able to go forward with the construction. God did a miracle! The Prayer of Agreement was the kind of prayer that was necessary to bring the desired result in this situation.

Be led by the Holy Spirit when you pray, and be sure that the Prayer of Agreement is in your "bag" of weapons. Pull it out and use it when you need it — and God's mighty power will be made available in that situation!

Chapter 10
The Prayer of Repentance

If you confess with your mouth the Lord Jesus and believe in your heart that God has raised Him from the dead, you will be saved.

For with the heart one believes to righteousness, and with the mouth confession is made to salvation.

Romans 10:9,10

In this scripture, we find a foundation for the Prayer of Repentance. It was probably one of the first types of prayer that you prayed to God, except perhaps when you cried out, "God if You're there, help me!"

It is the Prayer of Repentance that got you into the kingdom of God. It was likely the first prayer you ever prayed that brought powerful results in your life. It brought you out of darkness into light — into right relationship with God.

This is the prayer that is prayed at the time of the New Birth when you become saved. Yet the blessing and usefulness of this prayer does not end at salvation. It is a powerful prayer that God intends for us to use all of our Christian lives — not to be saved again, but to keep our hearts and lives clean before God.

The word "repentance" means "to change," and to change because something better is coming. It means to turn and go another direction. Look at what *The Amplified Bible* tells us about repentance in Acts 3:19:

So repent (change your mind and purpose); turn around and return [to God], that your sins may be erased . . . , that times of refreshing (of recovering from the effects of heat, of reviving with fresh air) may come from the presence of the Lord.

A Cornerstone of the Christian Faith

What does repentance mean? To change your mind and purpose. Repentance literally says, "With my whole being I am willing to change this area of my life and go with God's will and plan without compromise or rebellion."

Jesus Himself came declaring a message of repentance. "Repent!" He said, "for the kingdom of God is at hand" (see Mark 1:15). What He was saying was this: *You must change!* Every part of your life must change to receive the kingdom of God. God has a new realm coming, but in order to get into it, you must repent; you must change."

John the Baptist's whole ministry was marked by the words, "Repent! Change! Something better is coming. Get ready." Any way you look at the word "repentance," the word "change" is at its core.

Repentance is also mentioned as a foundational doctrine of our Christian faith. In Hebrews 6:1, the Bible says that in believers' lives there should be a strong foundation laid of repentance from dead works and faith toward God.

There is no salvation unless one comes to the cross, turns to Jesus, and permanently changes the direction of his or her life through faith in His blood. There is no other way to be saved.

Repentance is what establishes you in the family of God and gives you your relationship with Him. When true repentance comes from a heart that has been touched by a need to bow before Jesus and let Him be Lord, and a radical and real change is made, God will always honor it. Repentance is actually a gift from God. When you were unsaved and did not deserve any help, the love of God helped you to turn to Him and be able to change the direction of your life.

God's Goodness Leads Us to Repentance

Acts 17:30 says that all men everywhere must repent. God *commands* men to repent. They must, at some point, pray the prayer of repentance. And, of course, we know that it's the goodness of God that leads men to repentance (Romans 2:4).

God is so good! He wants to *change* the lives of men and women all over the world. He wants to come right into their heart — into the center of their being — show them how good He is, how much He loves them, and what a good plan He has for them. He will also convict them of sin and of their need for a Savior. He wants them to repent for sin, to change, and to turn to Him with all their heart so refreshing and life can come to them.

If we look back at Romans 10:9,10, we find that the principles of the Prayer of Repentance have to do with believing with your heart and confessing with your mouth. At the New Birth, the Holy Spirit reveals who Jesus is to you, and you believe by faith who He is. Then, after you see your need for salvation through the cross and the blood of Jesus, you must confess with your mouth that He is risen from the dead and is Lord.

The faith-filled words you speak at that moment have power in them to change you. Verse 10 reiterates the fact that you must believe in your heart and confess with your mouth, and that doing so will bring salvation into your life.

The Prayer of Repentance doesn't stop after we're born again. That's actually the beginning place of repentance in our lives. Repentance is a gift that's also given to us believers, because the Holy Spirit wants to work with us and change us in every area of our lives as we grow in Christ.

In Revelation chapters 2 and 3, Jesus was speaking to the churches about areas in their work that needed to change. When He spoke to them about changing, He didn't make a suggestion to them, such as, "If you'd like to, or feel like it, you could change this . . ." No, He *commanded* them very strongly to *repent*! They needed to see that what they were doing was wrong in Jesus' eyes, to be pricked in their hearts about those things, and then to cry out to God and to change in those areas.

It's not enough to think about areas where change and repentance are needed. There must actually be a radical change made to keep you on the right track with God and in God's will and plan, not in your will and your plan, which would eventually lead to destruction. The Holy Spirit always wants to show you the ways of God for your life. Where your ways don't match His, He wants you to repent and come into freedom and His best.

Be Willing To Change

The Holy Spirit will be generous with you in any way that you have ever grieved Him, been disobedient to the will of God, or gone on the wrong track in your life. He'll begin to deal with you about things you need to change. But *you* have a part in this — repentance begins with your being open to God for change in your life. Many people aren't open to change. It's human nature to find a pattern and then get stuck in it and not change.

As a matter of fact, that's where a lot of religious and denominational patterns have been developed in the church world today. People have become used to a certain way of doing things, and although the Holy Spirit may want to do it some other way, they're unwilling to change. They can become so locked into that one way of doing things that they become stagnant. There is no freshness in their lives. The Holy Spirit is trying to move another way, but they are unwilling and unable to hear the voice of God. Actually, their hearts have become hard, and they have become unwilling to bow before Jesus.

When God speaks to have that change come about — to deal with that area in your life — there must be a confession of sin; a confession of going the wrong way. When repentance comes, the Holy Spirit's power is released to give you the ability to go the right way in peace and joy with God. God corrects us because He loves us, and He always wants us to be open to change!

There are different degrees of repentance that the Holy Spirit will work in your life. One of them is found in First John 1:9, where the Word of God says:

If we confess our sins, He is faithful and just to forgive us our sins and to cleanse us from all unrighteousness.

Notice again the principle of the heart and the mouth. If the Holy Spirit deals with you about sin — if He pricks your heart about a certain thing or an area where you need to change — then He is also faithful and just to cleanse you, if you confess that sin.

It is very important in your life that you allow this side of the ministry of the Holy Spirit to be real to you. Because God loves you, He will discipline you and show you when you are wrong. Because He loves you, He will always be ready to correct you.

When God deals with you about something that's wrong in your life, or about an area where you've grieved the Holy Spirit, He'll deal with you in your heart. God is not a mean God who will make you suffer, will kill you, or will put sickness on you to teach you something.

You would never do that to your own children, and certainly God will never do it to His. It would be totally out of character for Him! God, however, does deal with us — but He does it in our heart, our conscience, our inner man.

Confess It As Sin

When God begins to deal with us about a sin, or an area that is not right before Him, and we do not respond for whatever reason, we open our hearts to become hard and insensitive. Then, little by little, our heart and soul becomes calloused. If we don't listen and obey what the Spirit of God is saying, we can open the door for the devil to attack us with different types of destruction, disease, and other harmful things.

It is vital that we are open to the Holy Spirit when He speaks to us! And you can *know* when He speaks to you; you don't have to be confused about it when the Holy Spirit shows you something.

My parents always told me clearly when I was right or wrong in my attitudes or actions. I just had to be open to listen and change when they spoke to me. God, your heavenly Father, is the same way. So when you, as a believer, are pricked in your heart, confess that sin. Yes, confess it as *sin!*

When God reveals something to you, what are you to do? Do you push it down and pretend you don't have it, or do you humble yourself and say, "O Father, I *do* have this sin in my life, and I'm so sorry. It's grieving You. I confess it as sin. I turn from it. Father, forgive me and cleanse me."

God shows you how ugly sin is so you will rid yourself of it. There is nothing wrong with seeing how ugly sin is, if you deal with it. Repent. Turn away from it. Turn toward God. Then, as you confess your sin, God is faithful and just to forgive you. Once repentance flows from you, then forgiveness will flow to you, and restoration will begin in that area.

I have often seen in Christian work that people come for help with their problems — and the Lord is willing and eager to help them. But then, as the Holy Spirit gives clear direction in areas that they must be open to change and correct in their lives, they are closed, hard, and insensitive to His dealings with them.

I've found that if people are not open to pray the Prayer of Repentance, God can't help them until they honor Him in that area.

Change will not come in your life until you are willing to repent first in the areas that God is dealing with you about. Often, deliverance doesn't come in the degree that the Holy Spirit wants to bring it, unless repentance is brought forth first.

Remember, repentance is a positive thing. In the past, we have thought that repentance was something negative; that it was something we did only because we had been displeasing to God, and now He no longer likes us or loves us. Or we have thought some calamity might now befall us, and God would test us with it.

But repentance is a powerful force in the spirit realm. Repentance is a *positive* thing! We repent because we love God, and because He loves us and has shown us where we need to be corrected and disciplined in our lives. Repentance brings cleansing and freedom to us. It causes our hearts to begin to be soft and sensitive toward God again, and remain that way.

Godly Sorrow

There are different levels in the Prayer of Repentance. In some areas of our lives where God deals with us, repentance goes as far as Second Corinthians 7:9,10, where the Word of God talks about godly sorrow:

> Now I rejoice, not that you were made sorry, but that your sorrow led to repentance. For you were made sorry in a godly manner, that you might suffer loss from us in nothing.

> For godly sorrow produces repentance to salvation, not to be regretted; but the sorrow of the world produces death.

One of the ways the Holy Spirit will move at times is in the area of godly sorrow. Paul talked to the saints about problems in the church in Corinth. There were many different sins going on in that church. The people were carnal. They had given place to the devil, and Paul commanded them to repent.

In his first letter to the Corinthians, Paul strongly rebuked them by the Holy Spirit, and it moved them to *strong repentance*. They cried out to God in repentance with weepings and tears, truly broken in their hearts for their sin. They changed. They let God deal with them.

Paul says in these verses that he is glad they were moved to repentance, they turned to God, and they felt *grief* before Him for what they were doing.

Our Sin Grieves God!

Some people repent for the wrong reasons. They "repent" out of feeling sorry for themselves, because the sin is ugly, because it has hurt them or made them feel bad, or because they got caught! But when we deal with sin, wrong doing, and carnality, we must understand that our action *grieves* the heart of God.

The ground for the Prayer of Repentance is not just that our action makes us feel bad, but that it has grieved the Holy Spirit. We need to see how we sinned against Him and then pray, "O God, I'm so sorry. I've grieved the Holy Spirit. O God, I'm sorry. Forgive me, Father."

It's true that we're not just sinners saved by grace, but when there is sin, unholiness, unrighteousness, and areas where the enemy has come into our lives and built strongholds, or where we've given over to the works of the flesh, repentance is required for us to be restored back to a right relationship. The repentance that the Corinthian church felt was a strong repentance, for they saw that what they were doing grieved the heart of God.

Verse 10 says that they felt a godly sorrow. They cried out and wept before God because what they were doing was wrong. That godly sorrow and crying out to God produced a repentance in them that brought them forgiveness and deliverance.

Paul goes on to say that worldly sorrow never brings true repentance; it brings death. Worldly sorrow is being sorry, but not seeing sin in the light of something that we've done against God, grieving Him. Worldly sorrow sees life's actions on a merely human level. We excuse what we've done as a human mistake or something of that sort.

But when we understand that sin is direct rebellion against God — that God cannot tolerate sin and unholiness in the lives of His people — and when the Holy Spirit deals with it in that light, then we can cry out to God as our heart is pricked.

Godly Sorrow's Results

So we must confess our sin as sin, repent, and humble ourselves before God, and let the Holy Spirit come over us to help us to change, breaking the yokes of sin and bondage and dealing with those areas in our lives. Then we will find that godly sorrow has produced in us what it did in the Corinthian believers.

For [you can look back now and] observe what this same godly sorrow has done for you and has produced in you: what eagerness and earnest care to explain and clear yourselves . . . what indignation [at the sin], what alarm, what yearning, what zeal [to do justice to all concerned], what readiness to mete out punishment [to the offender]! At every point you have proved yourselves cleared and guiltless in the matter.

2 Corinthians 7:11 *Amplified*

Godly sorrow produces care in us. It produces zeal in us. It produces a point in us where we have cleared ourselves from guilt, shame, and all unrighteousness because of the power repentance brings into our lives.

God will *never* despise or turn away from one who comes to Him whose heart is pricked by the Spirit of God. God will use the Prayer of Repentance for restoration and wholeness in that area of life where He wants to make them free; that area He wants to purify and cleanse.

When you're a person who is quick to repent and confess your sin, and when you're tender and sensitive before God, you show a true spirituality in your life.

Spirituality is a love for truth. Jesus is always speaking truth to us, not because He's mad at us, but because He loves us. It is truth that makes us free. Love is always tied to truth. Jesus will speak truth into the areas of your life where you need it, and if you'll respond to that truth and allow the Holy Spirit to deal with it, it will produce life, strength, and freedom in your life.

Pray the Prayer of Repentance. Let God change you, because something better is coming — purity, freedom, and joy!

Chapter 11
The World of Tongues

> Suddenly there came a sound from heaven like the rushing of a violent tempest blast, and it filled the whole house in which they were sitting.
>
> And there appeared to them tongues resembling fire, which were separated and distributed and which settled on each one of them.
>
> And they were all filled ... with the Holy Spirit and began to speak in other ... languages (tongues), as the Spirit kept giving them clear and loud expression.
>
> Acts 2:2-4 *Amplified*

Here in Acts we have an account of one of the most wonderful events in the history of the Church. Of course, the Bible is full of many significant occurrences, but this is certainly one of the greatest.

What happened on the Day of Pentecost is that ordinary people — people like you and me — began to experience the power of the Holy Spirit in their own personal lives.

Jesus had that power in His ministry, and He had told His disciples it would come to them also. "You will receive power from on high," He had said. "You will receive the Holy Spirit."

This is the account of what took place when that mighty power — the Holy Spirit Himself — was released over them. Suddenly, these ordinary people began to speak in a new language — a heavenly language — which was given to them supernaturally by the Spirit of God. It was wonderful!

The door into the realm of the Holy Spirit, His power, His ways, and the supernatural world of God swung open to them in a new way. What they received is available for us as well. We can also experience the power of the Holy Spirit coming upon us and flowing through us with the manifestation of speaking in a new, heavenly language. We can speak in tongues today!

Actually, by definition, speaking in tongues is a supernatural utterance given by the Holy Spirit in a language never learned by the person speaking. The language is not understood in the mind of the speaker, and it is not usually understood by those who hear it.

Tongues is not a learned expression; you cannot teach yourself to speak in other tongues. The Holy Spirit gives that expression through you.

You *can* speak in tongues as an act of your faith when you receive it as a free gift, and you can be easily given to it. But because the source of the language is the Holy Spirit, every time we speak in tongues, we operate in the supernatural power of God and in the spiritual world. Tongues, in fact, is a door to the supernatural; it opens the world of the spirit to us.

In reality, you could say that in the act of speaking in tongues, there is a whole world of unexplored supernatural adventure waiting for you! There is a *world of tongues*. In this prayer world, there are many different expressions, uses, and experiences from the Word of God that are available to you.

There's so much more to speaking in tongues than we've ever thought. When we speak in tongues and get strong in it, we come into a new world by the Holy Spirit, and it makes the supernatural more tangible to us. In that world are supernatural expressions, gifts, and words that all come from the heart of God.

So it is not just a little, insignificant thing that we do when we speak in tongues. It is not a narrow, limited experience unless we allow it to be that. In the world of tongues, there is a broad place for the Holy Spirit to speak through us supernaturally the heart and the mind of the Father.

Praying in tongues is not a religious duty. Neither is it just being a prayer mill, where you turn a little dial and start speaking like a machine gun. There's more to it than that: It is a relationship with the Holy Spirit. In that relationship, you can become very sensitive to the source of those tongues, the Holy Spirit Himself, and to where and how the tongues are to be used and expressed.

Clear and Loud Expression

Notice that the scripture says the Holy Spirit gave them "clear and loud expression." In the world of tongues, there are clear expressions, different expressions, and loud expressions. God is a God of personality and variety. He expresses His personality through the Holy Spirit.

The Holy Spirit will give you clear and loud expressions when you speak in tongues; specific expressions and utterances that are supernatural, that are divine in their origin and purpose, and that have *different* purposes before God in the spiritual world.

Notice that the Bible says we *speak* in tongues. Speaking in tongues can be compared to speaking a natural language with all the various tones and sounds of that language. It is not just a form of monotone prayer, but a spiritual language and vocabulary that we use to pray with.

When we begin to speak a language in the natural, many different things open to us: experiences and avenues of expression that were formerly closed take on a whole new meaning. This is so with the supernatural as well. When we begin to speak in tongues, many new things and ideas open to us.

In the language of tongues, there will be expression, purpose, and communication in what you are speaking in the spirit world. For example, you will find when you get into the spirit realm that you can be *before* the Lord, but not necessarily speak directly *to* Him, although that's a part of it too.

There is another side, where you can be before Him in the spirit, and speak in tongues by the Holy Spirit as a form of spiritual warfare. You are not speaking to God, and you are not praying against God; you are in the spirit world, before the throne of God.

Away from that place, when you use the language of tongues, you can correctly handle prayer requests and needs in a spiritual way with the help of the Holy Spirit working in and through your prayer language.

You are not speaking directly to the devil in tongues. People sometimes ask, "Does the devil understand tongues?" I don't think the devil understands tongues. The thing he does understand when we speak in tongues is the Holy Spirit and His *power* behind the tongues. The source of the tongues is the Holy Spirit, whether we're speaking directly to God or we're speaking out into the spirit realm, dealing with an enemy.

Whenever you deal with a supernatural energy, God has supernatural weapons to overpower that enemy. Tongues is one of those weapons. The force behind the tongues is the Spirit of God, and He is a weapon! Jesus Himself said that He cast out devils by the Spirit of God (Matthew 12:28). You have the same Holy Spirit within you. Pray in tongues, stir up the gift and weapons of God within you, and use them on your enemies!

Tongues — A Communication Tool

You're going to find that speaking in tongues includes many things. It is your means of communication in the spirit world. In the spirit we can also speak with the understanding (see Chapter 4), but for now we want to focus on the new language and world that the Holy Spirit opened on the Day of Pentecost.

Tongues is the language of the supernatural realm, just like Swedish is the language of Sweden. In the same way that you have to know Swedish to operate efficiently in Sweden, so it is in the spirit world with tongues. Yes, you can make it without being baptized in the Holy Spirit, but it's not God's highest and best for you.

The supernatural world is opened completely for you through the door of being baptized in the Holy Spirit and speaking in tongues. That's what happened on the Day of Pentecost. The Holy Spirit came over them and gave them clear and loud expression — in other tongues!

We read that the Holy Spirit gave them *clear expression*. That means that in the world of tongues you can see a difference between different types of Holy Spirit expressions, just like I have learned new and different sounds and expressions as I have studied the Swedish language.

God is not a robot with a dry, monotone personality. He doesn't mumble. He gives clear and loud expression in His language. Even in the natural, we don't talk in a mumbling monotone with no expression. Every day we have expression and words — and so does the Holy Spirit!

Some people put God in a box and limit their experience in the spirit world. "Well," they say, "you can only pray like *this*, and it can only sound like *this.*" No! There is much room in the spiritual world for speaking the Holy Spirit's words.

Just look at the English language: Do we have only one word and one way to say that word? No, we have different words, and we say them in different ways.

It's the same in the spiritual realm. There are different words and different ways to release them for different purposes. There is clear and distinct expression in the language of tongues. There is room in the spirit realm for a variety of expressions and sounds. Don't be afraid of the fullness of the Holy Spirit!

"I Speak in Tongues More Than You All"

Some people say, when we talk about tongues, "Well, what if we speak in tongues a little bit too much?" How can we speak in tongues too much? Paul said he spoke in tongues more than the entire church at Corinth! That's a lot.

There is no limit on how much we should speak in tongues unless we limit ourselves, or let others limit us. Of course, anything can be abused, but that's no reason not to come into the fullness of life in the spirit and the adventures of the spiritual world. As a matter of fact, God is just waiting for you to dare to experience this in your Christian life!

Paul taught on the supernatural world in his teaching on spiritual gifts in First Corinthians. In the first verse of chapter 12 he says, "Now concerning spiritual gifts, brethren, I do not want you to be ignorant." Paul is saying, "I do not want you to misunderstand the spirit world. I want to teach you now about the spiritual realm and how it works."

He then takes chapters 12, 13, and 14 to explain about the ways the Spirit of God will work, move, and administrate in that sphere. He teaches on the gifts of the Spirit in chapter 13, and in chapter 14 he begins a teaching about speaking in tongues and the spiritual gifts in the local church. You should read First Corinthians 12, 13, and 14 together to get a clear understanding of Paul's message.

One thing needs to be clear here when considering chapter 14: To understand it, it must be taken verse by verse and with the knowledge that Paul is talking about the two ways tongues are manifested by the Holy Spirit.

The first is through the gifts of the Spirit, found in First Corinthians 12: word of wisdom, word of knowledge, prophecy, gifts of healing, working of miracles, special faith, tongues, interpretation of tongues, and discerning of spirits.

These nine gifts of the Spirit come as He, the Spirit, wills. They are demonstrations of God's power to help, to encourage, to set people free, and to bless the church. Included among the gifts of the Spirit are tongues and interpretation of tongues.

No one chooses of his own will to operate the First Corinthians 12 spiritual gift of tongues. No one decides in his mind, "I'm going to give a tongue, you give the interpretation, and it will help the church." You do have to *yield* to the Holy Spirit, but it's a supernatural, spiritual gift that comes as *He* wills.

This spiritual gift of tongues is one of the types of tongues that Paul refers to in First Corinthians 14. It's for public use as a gift given by the Holy Spirit to the church to lift it up as a group and to individually meet the needs of people.

Together, the gift of tongues and interpretation of tongues equals prophecy. Someone speaks in tongues, and that person, or another person, interprets and it blesses the whole church. It's powerful!

In chapter 14, Paul talks only minutely concerning this manifestation of the gift of tongues. In this chapter he teaches primarily on the second way tongues is manifested: the individual believer's tongues (Acts 2).

Not every believer will have the gift of tongues to edify the church as a gift of the Spirit, but *every* believer can speak in tongues as a result of being baptized in the Holy Spirit.

The Holy Spirit will give you a private prayer language for your personal prayer life and your fellowship with God. You can use it anywhere, anytime, as you will.

You need to know that there are these two types of tongues, and that they are different from each other in their operation, manifestation, and uses. One is a manifestation of the nine spiritual gifts found in First Corinthians 12, and one is a private prayer language for every believer, as was given on the Day of Pentecost, to those who will believe and receive it.

Some people say they can't speak in tongues because they don't have the gift, but the reason they say this is because they lack teaching about the difference between the two.

Every Expression Has Significance

So in First Corinthians 14, Paul is teaching about speaking in tongues and the gifts of the Spirit in the Church. In doing so, he reveals more about the private prayer language and the world of other tongues than in any other place in the scriptures.

In verse 10 he says:

> There are, I suppose, all these many [to us unknown] tongues in the world . . . and none is destitute of [its own power of] expression and meaning. *(Amplified)*

Paul is using a natural experience with earthly languages and comparing it with spiritual languages. He says there are languages in the world that we don't understand, but they have their purpose and significance.

In the same way, there is a language in the spirit with different expressions, and each expression has a purpose and a meaning. It has significance. Every time English is spoken, each word has meaning. Likewise, every time you and I speak in tongues, no matter what sound comes out in the prayer, it has *significance* in the spiritual realm.

I may not understand it all with my mind, but it *does* have meaning. Every time we come into the language of the Spirit - every time we speak in tongues — it has meaning in the spirit world, even though we may not understand it with our minds or our experience. It makes natural people look at you like you're strange. They say, *"What* are you doing?" The answer is, "I'm *communicating* and working in the dimension of the spirit. The Holy Spirit is my Helper!"

Let me give you an example of rare experiences I've seen that will help you to understand the world of the spirit and how the language of tongues can operate. When I was in Bible school, a proven and well-known prophetess would sometimes visit our meetings. She'd go up on the platform as she was bidden by the leaders, open her mouth, and heaven came with her. She knew God!

She was so happy and free. To me she seemed a bit wild! She'd get up on the platform and get lost in the spirit. It was *strange* to the natural mind, and I'm not talking about being bizarre, but she would *yield* to the Holy Spirit.

She would make strange noises, yet she wasn't in the flesh. She would laugh, sing, pray in strange-sounding tongues, and just *flow* in the Holy Spirit. I didn't understand it, but if felt so *good* in my spirit. I remember thinking, "I hope she comes regularly to the meetings. I like it when she goes out into the spirit realm. It is so strong! I want to experience that in my life!"

Let God Out of the Box

I'll never forget how a well-respected prophet of God was up on the platform in one service, praying in tongues, and it seemed like he went up into another dimension. He yielded to the Holy Spirit by speaking in tongues.

Then this prophetess went up on the platform with him. They were praying and prophesying, and then they looked at each other and started speaking *in tongues* to each other.

I thought, "*What* are they doing?" She'd speak in tongues and he'd speak back, and she'd speak and then he'd speak. They were talking to each other solely in tongues before God, and what they were saying had purpose for both of them in the work of the Lord.

People could say, "What in the world is that? That's not in the Bible." But it *is* acceptable and biblical in the spirit realm.

They were operating supernaturally before God. They were in the spiritual world; they weren't in the flesh. The anointing was *strong* over the meeting. Before God, in the spirit, they were speaking words in tongues to one another. When you have an understanding of spiritual things, an experience like that doesn't bother you.

I've had similar experiences. There have been times when I was praying and someone suddenly came over to me and began to speak in tongues. I felt they were speaking right into my spirit. Once someone prophesied in English to me and then they spoke in tongues — and in my spirit I knew what they were saying.

The Holy Spirit was working in me through those words. He was giving me something I needed — a supernatural equipping. This person was speaking to me by the Holy Spirit. This doesn't happen all the time, and you can't make a doctrine out of it, but there was significance in that type of expression by the Holy Spirit.

Sometimes people get negative toward the operations of the Holy Spirit and critical toward His vessels when they don't understand His expressions and how you can be before God in the spirit realm, doing spiritual work and communicating in the spirit.

There have also been times when I've been interceding with someone on behalf of God's will for another person when we started praying and speaking out into the spirit. I would speak and they would speak and I would speak and they would speak.

Someone could say, "What are you doing? Are you trying to do that just to make it up?" No, you don't try to make it up. It doesn't happen all the time, but every once in a while it does.

You say, "Well, what were you doing?" Together, we were expressing in prayer the will of God, directed by the Spirit. We were praying as the Holy Spirit led to accomplish the purposes of God, which we don't always understand with our minds.

A World of Wonderful Expressions

It is important for you to understand that in praying in tongues there is a whole world of wonderful expressions that the Holy Spirit desires to open for you in your prayer language.

He makes clear and loud expressions with purpose and meaning behind each word of tongues. In the right place, at the right time, in the right situation, each word has its place by the Spirit of God. The whole world of the spirit realm is open in a new way! It is available to all who are willing to step into it.

Although there *is* such a wonderful world of unexplored supernatural territory in the Holy Spirit baptism, there are people who are not released in the supernatural, who don't speak in tongues, or who are afraid of entering the fullness of the supernatural world.

When I was fifteen, my grandparents talked to me about the baptism with the Holy Spirit. I'd been born again when I was eight, and had grown up in a Christian home, but it was when I was fifteen that they approached me about this subject.

They are godly Charismatic Episcopalians who were filled with the Holy Spirit in the 1960s, when the Charismatic move began to go through the denominational churches in the United States. As long as I could remember, they'd been speaking in tongues — and it was fine for them, but I was too scared of it for myself. I was a sophisticated 15 year old with a strong will, and I was afraid that I'd lose control if I were to speak in tongues.

I didn't want to be strange like all the other Charismatics I knew and walk around speaking in those crazy tongues. I couldn't figure out where tongues came from, and in my mind I thought they sounded a little bit strange. All those thoughts were a cover for my fear. I was desperately protecting my self-life!

But one Sunday night I went to a service where the preacher preached about the power of the Holy Spirit and how He comes over you when you're baptized in the Holy Spirit and speak in tongues. That night I decided I wanted to have this baptism, so I ran down to the front of the church. They laid their hands on me — and absolutely nothing happened!

I was totally afraid to release to the prayer language. I tried with all my heart. I squeezed my eyes tight, and I *tried* to speak in tongues. But my mind was confused, and the fear was hindering me. I didn't know what was waiting on the other side if I spoke in tongues!

This went on for about a year. I tried for a year to speak in tongues, but I never really opened my mouth, so nothing came out.

One night when I was in a Bible study with some of my girlfriends, I felt like there was a huge bubble on the inside of me. I couldn't understand what it was. All I knew was that I had to get it out, or I was going to die!

I wanted to praise God, but all I knew was, "Praise God, praise God, praise God." I would lift my hands and say, "Praise God. Oh, there's more I want to say, but I don't know what it is . . . . Praise You, Jesus. Praise God, praise God." My spirit was reaching out to be released in the Holy Spirit, but my mind was hindering me.

That night I stood up in the middle of the Bible study and commanded everyone to stop. The teacher looked at me with a strange look and said, "What's wrong?"

"I have a bubble on the inside of me," I said, "and if I don't get it out, I'm going to blow up! I think it's the Holy Spirit, and I think I need to speak in tongues *now*!"

They all smiled, because they were praying for me anyway, so they said, "O.K., go ahead. Speak in tongues."

So I stood there, raised my hands, and started *screaming* in tongues. I finally lost control and the Holy Spirit took control! It's one of the best things that's ever happened to me besides being saved. It was *wonderful* to have the *power* of the Holy Spirit released in my life.

Hindrances to Freedom in the Supernatural

One of the things that kept me back from releasing to the Holy Spirit and speaking in tongues was fear. It is this same fear that stops many people from entering the world of tongues. They're afraid of what could be ahead, perhaps because of things they've heard or seen, and that fear holds them back from what they are so longing to receive.

Actually, fear can be their "protection" for not having to surrender the ego life to God. Many people are unable to reach out into full freedom in the Holy Spirit because they are bound in fear and are protecting themselves from unknown things of the spiritual realm. Everything done in the spirit world is done by faith, not by what we see, fear, think, or know!

When you minister to people to receive the baptism of the Holy Spirit, you can help them by being sure that you minister with love, because love breaks down fear. Also, take authority over the spirit of fear, and teach them that there is absolutely nothing to be afraid of. Fear is from the devil!

Another thing that holds people back from being released into the supernatural is their mind and intellect. Not only are they afraid because they don't know exactly what is going to happen, but their human understanding hinders them.

Their spirit is reaching out to be released in the Holy Spirit, but mental bondages, hangups, and strongholds hold them back. It's not in their mental ability, capacity, or understanding to speak in tongues. They don't understand it with their mind, although they try hard to do so.

Tongues is not understood by the mind. As a matter of fact, the Bible says the mind is "unfruitful" when we speak in tongues. It's a wonderful thing to finally get your mind to shut up and shut off when you release to the Holy Spirit.

Many times people are held back by their mind because of a lack of teaching, or wrong teaching. When you minister to them, give them the Word of God so they can understand, be more at peace in their mind, and have faith built into their hearts.

The third thing that holds people back from being released in the supernatural and speaking in other tongues at whatever level the Holy Spirit wants, is cultural and religious traditions.

"We've never done this before. In our church we've never done this. This is beyond our experience." Yes, hallelujah, it *is* beyond our experience!

"I've never experienced this before. It is not in my religious tradition. It is not in my cultural upbringing. We middle-class people are formal and reserved, you know."

No, it is not in your upbringing, but it is in the Spirit of God! You can *break out* of culture and tradition and come into a new freedom in the spirit. Ask God to help you! Then do it, in Jesus' Name.

These three things — fear, mental hindrances, and tradition — hold people back from the realm of the spirit. The Holy Spirit will help you come through them if you, by faith, accept what the Word of God says and receive the gift of the Holy Spirit. It is a free gift to those who will receive it. Thank God, we can come through fear, mental blocks, and traditions into the Holy Spirit and the wonderful world of tongues!

The Holy Spirit Is Our Helper

Romans 8 gives us some important insights into speaking in tongues and the world of the spirit that are available for us. In verses 26 and 27, it says:

> Likewise the Spirit also helps in our weaknesses. For we do not know what we should pray for as we ought, but the Spirit Himself makes intercession for us with groanings which cannot be uttered.

> Now He who searches the hearts knows what the mind of the Spirit is, because He makes intercession for the saints according to the will of God.

The Holy Spirit is our Helper. The original Greek here means that He, the Holy Spirit, "takes hold together with us." If there is a problem that I'm praying about, and I don't know exactly how to pray, I begin to pray in tongues.

As I begin to pray in tongues, I'm taking hold of the problem, whether it's big or small. Whatever it may be, when I don't know how to pray, the Holy Spirit takes hold together with me against that problem.

He cannot take hold unless I've taken hold first, because He's a *Helper*. That is His nature; His character. To get Him to work, you've got to come into Him in line with His character. A helper can't help someone who's not doing anything, because then he wouldn't be a helper.

So as I start to take hold of the problem by speaking with the understanding, but primarily by speaking in tongues, the Holy Spirit literally takes hold of the other side, *together against* that problem with me.

The Holy Spirit takes hold together against the problem with me, and *together* we move it out of the way, or into the will of God. That's part of the Holy Spirit's job. It's one of the things He does when we enter the world of tongues. He helps us in our weakness when we don't know what to pray or say. He pleads on our behalf.

As I pray, the Holy Spirit is working with me, praying through me, and praying for me. I'm the one who has to speak in tongues, who has to yield to Him, but as He takes hold together with me and *He* pleads the case through me, the result is victory!

This, of course, is not the only way to see results in prayer, but we are focusing our attention here on praying in tongues and seeing how the Holy Spirit helps us and works with us as we do so.

You must understand that as you speak in tongues, the Holy Spirit *helps* you. He not only gives you the supernatural language, but He comes to your aid, taking hold of the situation with you and speaking through you.

You are not out in the supernatural world of the spirit by yourself. As you yield to the Holy Spirit, He takes hold of whatever you're speaking or praying about with you. Thank God for the Holy Spirit!

The Holy Spirit is a Helper and an Intercessor. He loves to find gaps, broken parts in the will of God, and bridge them together. The way He does this is through us as we pray. He intercedes for us personally when we pray in tongues, and He also intercedes through us and with us when we take time to pray for others. As an Intercessor, He *knows* how to stand in the gap. He *knows* what the will of God is. After all, He *is* God.

Going Past Our Natural Language

The end of verse 26 tells us how the Holy Spirit intercedes for us. He does it with groanings which cannot be uttered, or that are too deep for utterance.

What that means is this: The Holy Spirit will intercede for us and through us with sounds that are past our natural language; groanings which we cannot speak with natural human words. They're *past* English, Swedish, or Russian; they're *past* the reach of natural language.

There are different kinds of groanings or sounds that the Spirit will speak through us. Speaking in tongues is a simple form of a groaning, because we're not making that sound with our natural language. It is the Holy Spirit speaking through us by our human spirit. We're actually the one speaking, but the Holy Spirit is the One giving the utterance, and what He's speaking is not natural language. It's a groaning that's too deep for our natural speaking.

I have a friend who was ministering in a church in Finland. In one meeting when she began to pray for the church, she started praying in tongues; at least, to *her* it was tongues. She was just shouting out in tongues, but the congregation understood it — for she was speaking Finnish!

She kept saying, "Money, money, money," over and over in the Finnish language. She did not understand it, but they did. We found out later that the church was in a financial crisis.

God needed someone to speak out and pray over that situation. She yielded to Him, and unknown to her natural mind, she prayed in Finnish. The church got encouraged and the victory came through shortly thereafter. This doesn't happen very often, but it's possible in the spirit realm.

I remember one time I was driving through Sweden from city to city, preaching and teaching. One day between meetings as I was lying in the back seat of the car, building myself up praying in the Holy Spirit, one word kept coming out of my mouth. It flowed out of my spirit with an urgency, so I kept speaking it.

The girl who was in the front seat of the car turned around and said to me, "Do you know what you're saying?"

I said, "No."

"In Polish," she said, "you're saying, 'Turn right, turn right, turn right.'"

Now that wasn't for the person driving the car; it was for someone else that the Holy Spirit knew about who needed to make a right turn in his life, or in their situation, or whatever, but He needed me to speak it out in intercessory prayer.

So there are times when we speak in tongues, but the language that comes out is actually a natural language. But remember, this is not a common occurrence. The majority of the time when we speak in tongues, we are speaking the supernatural language of the Spirit of God, unknown not only to the speaker but to the hearers as well.

The Holy Spirit speaks through us with groanings that are too deep for natural speaking; with sounds that are past our natural language. Again, there are different types of these groanings given by the Holy Spirit.

To understand and enter this supernatural world more easily, I divide groanings — those utterances past natural language — into two groups.

The first group is what I will call "simple tongues." It is speaking in tongues with the Holy Spirit baptism. Within this category are different expressions and purposes of your prayer language. We will look at them in the next chapter.

Coming Into the Second Level

Right behind simple tongues is another category of groanings I will call "the second level." This expression is a bit deeper than simple tongues, and it is more of a distinct sound of a groaning than a language; but it is part of the Holy Spirit's vocabulary.

In this second level of groanings are actual groaning sounds, weeping, travail and a loud cry, or a roaring sound, all of which can come from your inner man when you're speaking in the Holy Spirit in this level. (We'll talk about each of these in a later chapter.)

Every believer can be *easily given* to the Holy Spirit to where it's not hard but normal to come into this type of prayer. The Holy Spirit has to begin it inside of you, but the more you practice in prayer, the easier it gets to give over to it.

You don't have to pray in the second level for everything, but there is a place in prayer for these sounds to come out of you to accomplish a specific purpose or result. You learn to work here by experience and practice.

The best way to find the second level in your prayer life is to start in simple tongues, which everyone who is baptized in the Holy Spirit can do. Then, by faith, imagine that there's a well inside of you, and on top there is a bucket that goes down into the well.

The Bible says there's a well of understanding inside us, and a wise man draws it up (Proverbs 20:5). There are springs of life inside you, but you've got to tap into them. Let the Holy Spirit take you down all the way; don't just skim the surface.

You can start by praying in simple tongues; that will put the bucket down into the well. Just see how deep the bucket goes.

Sometimes it's hard to put spiritual things into words, but I believe you can understand this by the help of the Holy Spirit. You can check, test, and see if the second level is open to you at that time. Sometimes when you begin to pray in tongues, it's not open, and the bucket stops at the simple tongues level. That means you've got enough water. But sometimes the bucket goes *way* down into the well. You can, in many instances, judge how far down you're going to let the bucket go.

Take the Water You Need!

Some people put the bucket on the top of the water when the Holy Spirit wants you to let your bucket go all the way down to the bottom of the well and *pull up* as much water with the groaning sounds as is necessary to meet the need you are praying for. The Holy Spirit must take hold with you in groanings of the second level. He is *used* to it. He doesn't mind it. He is not embarrassed by the sound; it's just a different sound and feeling to the human flesh.

If you're not accustomed to this expression of the Holy Spirit, allow yourself to yield to it next time you pray. You will see how it feels, how you can be easily given to it, and how you can learn to work with it. Try it! See if there is a groaning sound just behind the sound of your simple tongues. If it's necessary to pull up a big load of water to meet your prayer need, you can do it by yielding to the Holy Spirit in the second level.

As we consider the world of tongues and its expression through simple tongues and the second level, we need to look at the relationship between tongues and the Prayer of Intercession. Remember, these are two different kinds of prayers.

When we pray for ourselves, we pray both with the understanding and with tongues. So also in intercession, which is praying for others, we do not pray or speak in tongues only; we also pray with our understanding.

Included in intercessory prayer is praying with the under-standing, simple tongues, and second level — groanings. There is a flow you can come into in intercession by the Holy Spirit that will allow you, as you yield to each level of groanings, to flow in and out of the various expressions and sounds. When you work with the Holy Spirit, they come according to what is needed at that moment.

Remember the bucket? Let it drop down, as it were, to the point where the flow of the Holy Spirit is, and yield to it!

A whole, wonderful world is waiting for you. All it takes to step into it, is to do it. God has destined you to help bring change and victory to this world, and one of the ways you can to it is through these supernatural expressions of the Holy Spirit.

So what are you waiting for? Take on the challenge, press into God stronger, and walk through the door into great adventure and satisfaction in the world of tongues.

Chapter 12
Simple Tongues

Speaking about the Day of Pentecost, Acts 2:4 says that the disciples:

> ... were all filled ... with the Holy Spirit and began to speak in other ... languages (tongues), as the Spirit kept giving them clear and loud expression. *(Amplified)*

Like the believers in Acts, we too have been given by the Holy Spirit a spiritual language when we were baptized in the Holy Spirit. We also can speak in other tongues. Though tongues may become very natural to us, it is a supernatural utterance whose source is the Holy Spirit.

As you read in the last chapter, tongues is a language that opens the spiritual world for us. It is a supernatural language in which the Holy Spirit gives clear and loud expression. He uses different words in different ways to accomplish different purposes through our prayers. Each expression of the Holy Spirit has a job to do, and is a clear communication in the spirit world.

We discovered that in the world of tongues there is a beginning level called *simple tongues*. Within this category are five different expressions and purposes that the Holy Spirit gives. Every believer can yield to the Holy Spirit and come into the spiritual realm through praying in simple tongues whenever they want. By an act of your will you can step through the door of the supernatural and participate in these expressions of the Holy Spirit.

Speaking to God

Let's begin in First Corinthians 14:2:

> For he who speaks in a tongue does not speak to men but to God, for no one understands him; however, in the spirit he speaks mysteries.

115

One of the first purposes and expressions of speaking in tongues in the first level is simply to speak to God. My spirit speaks to God, and God understands it. In the spiritual world, I'm speaking mysteries, secrets that He understands, that my spirit understands, and that will be illuminated to my mind later. It doesn't matter whether my mind understands it now or not; my *spirit* longs to communicate with God, and when I pray, my spirit speaks to Him.

Sometimes if you take time to listen to your prayer language, the Holy Spirit will give you the interpretation. You'll have a knowing in your spirit about what you've said to God. You'll know you're saying something to Him about victory, or your spirit is prophesying, or you're speaking to Him about who He is or what He's done, or something similar. Try it.

You don't always have to have the understanding of what you say, but sometimes you'll get it if you will train yourself to listen. Practice. Speak in tongues to God. Then listen on the inside and see if you hear a word, or have just a feeling about what you're praying about.

You don't always have to have an awareness of the interpretation when you pray. Take it to your heart and do what the verse says: speak to God.

I take this so literally that I sometimes tell the Lord, "I'm going to speak to You about this situation in tongues because I don't know how to pray about it." As I begin speaking in tongues, I feel the Holy Spirit in me expressing my heart to God and praying His will through me. Of course, you don't always have to say, "God, I'm praying about this in tongues now," but every once in a while do it on purpose.

Your spirit longs to speak to God, so speak to Him! You don't always have to know what you're praying about. Just pray! Speak to God and then speak to Him some more. It's wonderful to be in the spirit, speaking to God.

It's a blessed experience to come before Him and pray in tongues! Practice: You talk, and then give Him time to talk back. *Prayer is communication!*

I have noticed that a lot of Christians come in, start speaking in tongues like a machine, maybe say, "Hallelujah!" a few times, perhaps pray the Word a little, and then turn around and leave —

and God is saying, "Oh! Just a minute, I wanted to tell you something."

"No, no, not now. I've got to hurry. I'm late for work," and off they go.

They pray what I call lazy prayers — insensitive to the fact they are fellowshipping with God. You don't treat your earthly friends like that. If you did, you wouldn't have any friends. *God* wants fellowship with you. He wants to talk to you face to face as a friend.

That doesn't mean you have to spend five hours saying, "O God, speak to me, God. O God." No, practice listening sometimes after you pray in tongues. You can even listen *while* you're talking. Many times my spirit speaks by the Holy Spirit and at the same time my spirit listens. Speaking but listening. It's called sensitivity — and you can develop it if you practice it on purpose.

Once you start to come into the spirit and train yourself to function there, it's *so* easy to work there, just speaking to God and listening for His response. This is a part of the world of tongues, and it's available for *you*!

Prime the Pump

Jude 20 tells us about a second expression of simple tongues that you'll sense coming from your inner man when you pray in tongues:

> But you, beloved, building yourselves up on your most holy faith, praying in the Holy Spirit.

As a side note here, remember that you don't always have to be consciously aware of what's coming from your spirit. Don't get caught up in your mind, thinking, "Well, how am I praying now? What expression is coming out now?" Take it by faith. Begin to practice. Pray, and you'll start to recognize these different types of flows in the Holy Spirit.

Praying in the Holy Spirit builds up your faith. There is a time when we're praying in tongues that we are literally building a strong spiritual building on the inside of us, brick by brick as it were, building ourselves up in the Holy Spirit.

Like a weight lifter who begins to lift weights and build up his muscles in the natural, you will be built up spiritually if you use what you have and begin to pray in tongues often and regularly.

Practice this expression of simple tongues when you pray. When you do, pray loud and strong! Be bold! Be aware of what you're doing: "I'm building myself up. I'm praying in tongues and building myself up spiritually."

You will find that you *will* be built up. You may not feel anything when you begin; it may seem dry, and you may feel oppressed, but pray in tongues anyway. Build yourself up. Keep lifting the weight, and before you know it, life and strength will be flowing within you.

I walk around my house and pray like this a lot, just building myself up, staying strong in the spirit by praying in tongues.

Another way to look at this expression of the Holy Spirit is by comparing it to priming an old-fashioned pump over a well. Sometimes you must pump and pump until the water begins to flow. Pray in tongues and keep at it until that spiritual water, the water of life, begins to flow within you. The more you pray like this, the stronger and the more built up you will become. Then the way to *stay* strong in the spirit is to continue praying in tongues.

Really, anytime we pray in tongues, we are being built up, but God has also made a way for us to purposefully *choose* to build ourselves up through this expression of the Holy Spirit. When you are built up spiritually, you are strong spiritually. You can break through the attacks of the devil and the pressures in the world praying this way! Pray in tongues! Build yourself up! Be strong and mighty in the Holy Spirit!

Praise the Lord

In Acts chapter 10 we find the third expression of simple tongues. Here we see that tongues can be an expression of praise and joy in the Holy Spirit.

In this chapter, Peter had gone to the house of the Roman centurion, Cornelius, and was preaching the Gospel to the people who had gathered in his home. In verses 44-46 we read:

While Peter was still speaking these words, the Holy Spirit fell on all who were listening to the message.

> And the believers from among the circumcised [the Jews] who came with Peter were surprised and amazed, because the free gift of the Holy Spirit had been bestowed and poured out largely even on the Gentiles.
>
> For they heard them talking in [unknown] tongues . . . and extolling and magnifying God. *(Amplified)*

As these people were speaking in tongues, the main thing that was seen and felt in the spiritual atmosphere around them was the extolling and magnifying of God. There is a side of the Holy Spirit where tongues is an expression of praise.

As I told you in the last chapter, I was afraid to release to the Holy Spirit and speak in tongues, but on the inside I was reaching out to God; longing to praise Him. What I wanted to do most of all was praise God, because saying "Thank You, Jesus," with just natural, human, English words wasn't enough.

Have you ever felt that way? There's *more* for you than just saying, "Thank You, Jesus. I love You, Jesus. Oh, Jesus, I want to praise You in my heart. Praise You, Jesus" in English. That's good, but there is so much *more* in your heart. There is strong, joyful praise in our hearts to God, and it longs to be expressed.

Release the Mighty Stream

As we speak in tongues, that praise, thanksgiving, and worship can be released in a mighty stream to God.

That's what I wanted. I wanted to *praise* Him! And when I was filled with the Holy Spirit, that was the first expression I felt coming through me when I prayed in tongues. With *praise* I stood there in the room that night.

It was so *good* to be free! The glory of God was over me! It was so good to *praise* and give thanks from deep within! It set me free — free from the limitations and chains in my mind. My mind was finally still, but my spirit was *praising* God; and everything within me released in love toward God!

That's what the Jews saw that day. That's what they felt as these people were filled with the Holy Spirit and began to praise and magnify the Living God through speaking in tongues. It was, and *is, wonderful!*

What did Paul say in First Corinthians 14:15? "I will pray with the spirit, and . . . I will sing with the spirit." Not only can we speak and shout praise to God in tongues, but we can also *sing* praise to God in tongues.

In regard to singing, remember this: God is not looking for good singers; He's looking for worshippers. He doesn't care what your voice sounds like; it's the tone of your heart that's most important to Him. If you use the excuse, "I can't sing," you need to change the way you think, change the way you talk, and *sing* in Jesus' Name, because it *pleases* the heart of your Father. He doesn't hear a voice that's out of tune. He hears sweet melody to His ears. So start singing!

In First Corinthians 14:17, Paul says that when we praise in tongues, or when we pray in tongues, one of the things we do is to give thanks well to God. God is pleased and blessed when praise comes out of our hearts in tongues. Of course, He loves it when we praise Him in the understanding, but we can also give thanks well by praising Him in tongues.

Have you ever had this expression of praise come up from your spirit man when something good has happened, and you wanted to say, "Praise God! Hallelujah!" but instead of English, the words came out in a shout of praise in tongues? You gave thanks *well*, the Bible declares, praising Him in tongues.

If this is a new expression for you, start now to praise God by faith and shout to Him for the victory — in tongues! It brings glory to God to let that joy, that praise, and that worship come out of your spirit in tongues. It is an expression the Holy Spirit desires to have operating in your life every day.

Our Lord Is a Warrior

Another expression of simple tongues is what I'm going to call spiritual warfare. Part of the nature of our God is that He is a Warrior (Exodus 15:3). He hates it when His people are attacked, so He has given them mighty spiritual weapons to defeat the enemy! One of those weapons is the Holy Spirit — His works, His gifts, and His power!

Remember now, tongues has its origin in the Holy Spirit. He knows how to disarm the enemy. He is the spirit of might and power. There are times, you'll discover, when your prayer language is used and released as a weapon: right up from your inner man comes loud, bold, strong, "warring" tongues.

In Second Corinthians 10:3, the Bible tells us that we are in a spiritual war and that we have spiritual weapons. If we are in a war, we *need* weapons, and we have them, but we must use them all. The devil wants to take these weapons away from you, because it's only with spiritual weapons that we win the spiritual war. If the devil can keep you in the natural realm, or even limited in the spiritual realm, it's a victory for him.

We have been given many weapons: the Name of Jesus, the blood of Jesus, and so on; but the Holy Spirit Himself is also a weapon: as is the language He gives us. Jesus said He cast out and defeated the devil by the Holy Spirit (see Matthew 12:28).

One of the places where we release our weapons is in prayer. Prayer is a launching pad for spiritual weapons! There are times when we pray in other tongues that it flows from our inner man as a weapon, mighty against the forces of darkness. The tongues flow in the spirit of might — loud, strong, bold, and fast!

When we pray like this, the Holy Spirit is releasing His will, His plan, His power, and His presence against the enemy and his work.

When there are enemies in the spiritual world coming against the work of God (and there are!), the Holy Spirit prays through us against the enemy. Our language is used as a weapon in the spiritual atmosphere, in heavenly places, to press through the darkness, take our authority, and run the devil out! Sometimes he doesn't want to go, but he must! Sometimes he acts like he doesn't hear, so we are loud and authoritative with him in the Holy Spirit's power! Be loud and strong against your enemy! Be aggressive!

Some people say, "But how can you pray that way in other tongues? I thought tongues was just for speaking to God. Are you fighting God?" No, tongues is not just for speaking to God; *tongues* is a language that opens the whole spiritual world to us. We operate in the spirit when we speak in tongues. With it we can speak *to* God, and with it we can also speak *before* God, led by the Spirit, out into the spiritual world.

This may seem foreign to you, but it is not foreign or even strange to the Holy Spirit. He led Samson to kill enemies. Samson was a deliverer, and by the Holy Spirit's power over him, he was used to defeat God's enemies! It's the same Holy Spirit in you today who will lead you to kill spiritual enemies that are already defeated, but sometimes very alive and active. Pray in tongues, led by the Spirit out of your inner man, and be mighty against your enemies! You are a warrior for God!

Pulling Down Strongholds

I remember one time many years ago when I was in an extremely religious church in Australia. They wanted to come into the fullness of the revival and move of the Holy Spirit, but were hindered from doing so. I was standing behind the pulpit one service preaching and teaching, and had glanced down at my notes to prepare for my next statement. When I lifted my eyes to look at the people again, the gifts of the Spirit started to operate and I saw, as in a vision, a demon up on one corner of the church and a second one up in the opposite corner.

You don't always have to *see* demon power; in your recreated spirit you can *sense* the presence of darkness. That's why you can release to this type of prayer by faith, because your inner man is very keen to spiritual climates and knows the devil's work and the presence of darkness. Don't accept it! Take authority and pray against it in Jesus' Name and with the Holy Spirit's help in tongues.

It's not often that I have actually had a vision in the spirit of demon power like that. It was a gift of the Spirit, discerning of spirits, that was operating at that time to help and bless God's people. The spiritual realm was opened for me, and I saw the presence of those two demons. They were like little imps sitting up on the corners of the church, and I could see that they were holding the church in bondage.

When I looked up and saw those two little imps in the spirit, my spirit man reacted to the spiritual activity, and I jumped from behind the pulpit and started *screaming* at them in other tongues — right in the middle of the teaching! I prayed for several minutes. The people were shocked and looked at me like I was crazy, and to the natural eye I was, but the Spirit of the Lord had opened my eyes to the enemy that was holding that church in religious tradition and bondage, and I went out in the spirit and did spiritual warfare.

I had to come up in the heavenlies where the battle was being fought over the church (Ephesians 6:12). I was certainly before God — I was preaching in the anointing — but from that place I went out in battle, praying in strong, loud tongues.

The result? The church broke through into freedom and liberty and changed like they never had before. The people were dancing and shouting because they could feel the victory and the presence of God!

We *can* go out in the spirit and do warfare in other tongues. God has made this available to us. We talk *to* God, and we also talk *before* God in the presence of the Holy Spirit, led by the Holy Spirit Himself speaking through us with His language and His expressions. Don't wait for a vision or a gift of the Spirit. Start now when you are attacked in everyday life! Start making war in the heavenlies over your city and church!

As we saw earlier, the Bible tells us in Exodus 15:3 that our Lord is a warrior. He does not war against people. *People* are never our enemies, even though the devil can use them. We *do* have enemies and we *do* wrestle, but not against people. We wrestle against principalities and powers; against the kingdom of darkness. They operate on earth and in heavenly places, so God gave us supernatural weapons to use against them to win!

The Spirit of Might Is Within You

Paul, in Ephesians 3, praying for the believers in that city, asked that they would be *filled* with the Holy Spirit and all of His might! You have the might of the Lord, who is a warrior, within you. You have the strength of the Lord within you, in your spirit, by the Holy Spirit. When there is an enemy, you and I can release to the Holy Spirit, draw upon His strength, and do battle: wrestle, against that enemy — and win!

There *is* a place in your prayer language for your tongues to be used as a weapon. As the might and the strength of the Holy Spirit flows from your inner man, the Holy Spirit does *battle* in the spiritual world through you. But He needs you to pray!

This is a part of the adventures you have in God when you are filled with the Spirit. God wants you by the Holy Spirit to do battle against the kingdom of darkness — and you *can*, simply by praying in tongues through this expression of the Spirit of God.

Pray like this, for example: "I come against the spirit of the world, the anti-Christ spirit, that is operating in my daughter's school. I *command* you in Jesus' Name to loose your hold over that school," and then start speaking boldly and strong in tongues. Let the Holy Spirit do *battle through you*!

Ephesians 6:17 says that the Word of God is as a sword. From Genesis to Revelation, the Bible is the Word of God; it's the written Word of God. It becomes revelation to us by the Holy Spirit, and then when we speak it out of our mouths, it is like a sword.

When we speak in tongues, those words are also words given by God. They are *God's* words. Remember, it's the Holy Spirit who is the source of tongues. He has given them, and He is God.

Speaking in tongues can become natural and easy for us to speak in, just like our natural language is, but we must always remember that the source of those tongues is the Holy Spirit in us; and that it is by *Him* that our spirit speaks. The Holy Spirit is *God* — and the *Holy Spirit* gave those words. They're your words, but they are inspired by the Holy Spirit.

I don't make up words myself when I speak in tongues. The source is my spirit by the Holy Spirit. The words originate with Him. I have to form the syllables. It's my voice, I yield to the Holy Spirit as an act of my will, I choose to speak, but my understanding is unfruitful.

The Holy Spirit's words become my words! In this way, my prayer words sometimes take the form of a sword in the spirit. Those words in tongues do spiritual warfare in the spirit realm.

There is another side of this expression of tongues in spiritual warfare that relates to the gifts of the Spirit found in First Corinthians 12. In the gifts of the Spirit is a gift called diversities of tongues. Many times when we are praying, we come into this gift. We come into the flow of the Holy Spirit — into the anointing — and in the anointing there are these diversities of tongues. There are different sounds, different types of languages — and some of them are like sounds of war. This is in the spirit of prayer. It's an expression of the Holy Spirit, of the gifts of the Spirit through you, but many times we step over into it when we start praying by faith.

Every believer who's filled with the Holy Spirit has God's words: the written Word and the spoken word. They can by choice pray in tongues, flow in the Spirit on a simple level before God out into the spirit, the Holy Spirit praying through them, and do effective and powerful warfare. It may seem different at first as you begin to pray like this, but it is a supernaturally ordinary expression you have in your prayer vocabulary!

The Holy Spirit was the weapon Jesus used to set those people free. We can pray in tongues strong and fast, yielding to the spirit of might, and by the Holy Spirit break down strongholds and set people free! It's one of the jobs of the Holy Spirit. It's an expression we can share with Him to bring victory and breakthrough!

Speaking Out God's Plan

The fifth expression or purpose in simple tongues is to pray out the will of God. Proverbs 20:5 says:

Counsel in the heart of man is like water in a deep well, but a man of understanding will draw it out. *(Amplified)*

Another translation says that the plans are in the heart of man like water and that a man of understanding draws it out. What a good verse this is to understand, that when we pray in tongues, we are drawing the counsel and plans of God out from within us like water comes out of a well.

The Holy Spirit again is involved here, because Jesus tells us in John 7:37-39 that the Holy Spirit is like a river of living water that flows from our belly. By praying in tongues, we draw out the water; the river begins to flow, and as it does, the counsel and plan of God that's in our spirit is prayed out.

Many times I have said, "Father, I'm not exactly sure what your plan is in this area of my life, so I yield to the Holy Spirit." He knows everything about you and me! "I trust that your plan will be born, and that as the rivers flow out of me, so will your plan and counsel."

Pray in tongues and the plan of God is prayed out of you. You can't see it or feel it, but the Holy Spirit is preparing a way and a path for you to walk on. You don't have to do it eight hours a day, but know and be aware that there is a side to praying in tongues where you can speak out the will of God, and prepare the way so you can supernaturally walk in every detail of the plan of God for your life.

Romans 8:27 tells us that the Holy Spirit makes intercession for us according to the will of God. He makes intercession *through* us for other people, but there are also times when He becomes an Intercessor *for* us personally. Really we're the ones praying, but when we pray in tongues, we can have faith that the Holy Spirit, according to this scripture, is praying out the will of God for that situation. Trust Him to pray God's will out through you. Make a quality decision to do it, and you will see the results.

Take an adventure into the world of tongues. Simple tongues — speaking to God, building ourselves up, expressing praise and worship, entering into spiritual warfare, and praying out the will of God — is for every believer any time. God desires that each of these expressions of the Holy Spirit be a part of our lives. Don't get stuck on just one of them. Don't miss any of them! God will help you and teach you to flow and be comfortable in them all. Let the world of tongues begin to open to you in new ways. Dare to step out into expressions that may not be familiar to you.

Take a Spiritual Walk

Have you ever developed a walking routine where every day you would take the same path? After a while you get to know *exactly* what's on the path. You know where the rocks are, where the trees are, where you have to step a little more carefully — you *know* that path. It's familiar to you, because you've been there many times. You know it, and it feels simple and comfortable to you.

But what happens one day if a friend comes along and says, "Let's go down this new path today?"

"Well, I don't know. I've never been there before. It doesn't look very well marked." You don't really want to go, but because it's your friend asking, you go ahead and go, but you don't enjoy it much.

You don't know where the holes are, and if you're in the forest, you have to push the branches back. You don't know where you're going, and soon you begin to think, "I wish I could go on my normal path. It would be so easy just to do what I always do and go down that path I know."

About half way you say to your friend, "I can't take this anymore. I want to go on the path I know." At the next turn you discover a short cut back to "your" path, and you take it. "Ah, now this is better. It's so easy. I feel good here, and it's a comfortable and secure path."

I have found that in life in the spirit, that's the way some people are. They know the path of praying in tongues to build themselves up. They know that path well. Then the Holy Spirit or their own spirit wants to go down a little different path; down a new expression. Your friend the Holy Spirit may lead you down a new path, or you may simply choose to go down that path yourself in this simple level of tongues.

The Holy Spirit leads you down the path of spiritual warfare — and you start, but, oh — after just a few minutes, you stumble on a rock. You keep going though; you keep speaking in tongues. You keep on that path — and suddenly you get hit in the face by a branch from a tree. "Oh," you think, "I don't *like* this path. It feels so strange!"

You're not used to it. It doesn't feel comfortable. You don't like the resistance you feel, and your flesh is out of shape to handle the work of that path, so you go back to the path you know, and your prayer life is *limited* because of your fear, insecurity, and even laziness. *Stretch* yourself in God! *Make* yourself press into a new expression. *Hang on* like a bulldog through the resistance, and soon that new path will feel just as good, just as comfortable and secure, as the old familiar one. How fun it is to walk with God!

When some people go down that new path, say the path of warfare or the path of worship, they say, "Wow! *This* is exciting! What a thrill! I've never been on a path like this in my life. This is fantastic. What a view on this path! I *love* this path!" And every time they go on a walk in the spirit, they *run* to that new path.

When the Holy Spirit wants to walk down another path, whichever one it may be — maybe the path of praying with the understanding, or of loving God — they don't want to go there. They are, as it were, grabbing the Holy Spirit's arm, or the arm of their own human spirit, and running off the path He wants to go on, back to the one that's so exciting to them. Don't be like that. Walk with the Spirit of God down every path. Keep close to Him, and each path will become a source of blessing and joy in your life.

There can be excesses and extremes in any spiritual truth, but what the Holy Spirit has for us is a sensitivity and a *full* range: every path and every expression in prayer. He wants us to be able to go down *every* path and be *good* at them.

127

The more you pray and work with the Holy Spirit, the more you'll understand, the stronger you will be, and the more sensitive you will become.

These five expressions of simple tongues are waiting and available. *You* can enter the world of tongues in a new way today. Try it! Enjoy it!

Chapter 13
The Second Level — Groanings

As we consider more about the world of tongues and the various expressions of the Holy Spirit within it, let's look briefly at Romans 8:26 again:

> So too the [Holy] Spirit comes to our aid and bears us up in our weakness; for we do not know what prayer to offer nor how to offer it worthily as we ought, but the Spirit Himself goes to meet our supplication and pleads in our behalf with unspeakable yearnings and groanings too deep for utterance. *(Amplified)*

The Holy Spirit our Helper takes hold together with us as we speak and pray in tongues. The way He does this, the Bible says, is with "groanings too deep for utterance."

What that means is that the Holy Spirit prays with expressions that are beyond our natural language and past our articulate, or known, speech. The Bible calls them groanings.

Speaking and praying in simple tongues is one form of a groaning, because when we pray that way, the prayer is created with sounds past our natural, known language. Speaking in tongues is not our own understandable vocabulary; it is a heavenly language. In it, with the Holy Spirit's help, we form syllables and make sounds that are too deep for human utterance and expression.

In the Holy Spirit, in the world or language of tongues, there are different levels and types of groanings. Let me encourage you: Don't let the word "groaning" scare you. It is a biblical word that is used in both the Old and New Testaments.

Because the Word of God is our standard, we must accept this word "groaning" and its spiritual importance in our prayer lives. God must not think the word strange, since He used it and others to reveal a form of scriptural prayer that is powerful and effective when used properly.

In the last chapter, we discussed the first level in the world of tongues — simple tongues. Right behind the expressions in simple tongues there's another level of different expressions that the Holy Spirit has given us in prayer.

I call this type of prayer the second level, or groanings. It's not any greater than praying at the simple tongues level; it's just a different side and depth of prayer in the Holy Spirit, and it accomplishes different purposes in the spirit world. God wants you to be released in it and to have all the expressions included in the groanings as a strong part of your prayer life.

I refer to this prayer as a level, because what you have to do to come into it is to allow the Holy Spirit to lift you up a spiritual step, just like you would go up a flight of stairs in the natural. It's like taking a step from simple tongues to the second level, or groanings.

I believe it is God's will for every Christian to come into the various levels in the expressions of the Holy Spirit, and to come into them easily. However, it doesn't mean you're more spiritual because you can come into this second level.

Everyone who is baptized with the Holy Spirit can pray in simple tongues. Beyond that, the Spirit of God has even more expressions for you to yield to and as you do, you will find they are filled with spiritual adventure.

Yielding Is the Key

Romans 8 states that part of the Holy Spirit's work in our prayer life is to take hold together with us when we pray. In the second level, He takes hold or works in and through us in a different way than He does in simple tongues.

In the various expressions of simple tongues you can pray by faith; you simply choose to pray, and the Holy Spirit takes hold with you and honors your faith as you pray out of your inner man.

In the second level, it's a little different: You cannot just *choose* to pray in the various expressions of this level. The Holy Spirit will gently lead you into this, and you must allow Him to take you to this level and then yield to Him when He does. It is not an act of your will that brings you into groanings; it is as the Holy Spirit wills and gives the initiative.

In simple tongues, you can by an act of *your* will come into any of the five expressions of that level, but with the second level of groanings and sounds in the spirit, the Holy Spirit takes hold first, and you follow.

I have found one thing about the Holy Spirit: He is more willing than we allow Him to be in leading us into the second level. Really, the second level is just one of many types of manifestations of the Holy Spirit in prayer.

Although you cannot choose by an act of your will to come into this type of prayer, you can be *easily given to it* — so easily given to the sounds on this level that they become as natural to you as your expressions in simple tongues. You can, in fact, be so easily given to it and so well trained to enter this level that it almost becomes second nature to you. Why? Because the Holy Spirit lives in you, and He is close and real to you.

The Holy Spirit must be the Source, like He is in the first level; however, in the second level, He willingly takes the gentle initiative. He is willing to manifest this type of prayer; more willing than the Church has allowed Him to be.

If you can, imagine a dividing line between simple tongues and the second level — groanings. It's not a big, heavily guarded, impassable line. It's not too deep, far or hard to cross. There's just a slight difference in the way the Holy Spirit takes hold with us. *He*, not we, initiates prayer in the second level. He lovingly and easily lifts us up the step.

Remember the illustration I used about the bucket in Chapter 11? If the way into the second level is not open — if the Holy Spirit is not taking hold there — we cannot go in. But if the way is open, then we can go in freely and boldly. We yield to Him as He initiates the entrance into this second level of utterance.

The more you know Him, and the more you practice prayer, the easier it is for you to recognize when these types of groanings are within you, and when your spirit is responding to the prayer request with these expressions. You will see that you don't have to wait for a "heavy anointing" to go there; just yield to it. That is the key!

You can be so easily given to the groanings, and so accustomed to working with the Holy Spirit, that it's easy to come into this prayer when the way is open. Just like simple tongues has such wonderful and powerful expressions, the second level is also a natural, intimate, and mighty place to be with the Holy Spirit. Its various expressions, each with significance and function in the spirit world, are clear and loud expressions given by the Holy Spirit to bring change and to establish the will of God in the lives of people, cities, and nations. The Holy Spirit knows best what is required for everything we pray for, so as we yield to Him, He prays the will of God through us!

How Is the Holy Spirit Taking Hold?

Let's begin with an explanation of the different sounds or expressions within this groanings category. The first expression of the second level, I simply call "groanings," because that's exactly what it sounds like.

We've learned that all the various expressions of the Holy Spirit in the world of tongues are forms of groanings in the general sense, because they are all past our natural language and vocabulary; but I call this expression of the second level, "groanings" specifically, because when you pray out of your spirit in this fashion, it literally sounds like a groan as we know it.

If you will listen and feel in your inner man when you pray, you will find that the groanings sound is *right behind* simple tongues. Some people think the anointing to pray this way is deep and heavy, and almost impossible to find, but the Holy Spirit is not so difficult to work with. He is willing to use us!

It's not difficult to find the anointing or the place of groanings in your inner man, and it's not difficult to yield to this utterance. Of course, religious traditions and bondages in our lives can try to hinder us from yielding to the groanings, but once you start praying this way, you will find that this type of prayer can also set you free!

We don't pray with groanings all the time, because God has different equipment and many weapons for us to work with in the spirit world. However, we must be aware of the fact that there is a place where the Holy Spirit wants to take hold with us in groanings, and He wants to do it regularly.

You don't have to wait until you feel a big bomb coming to you from heaven to give over to the groanings. "Oh, here comes something! Bam! Groaning! Oooh . . . Oooh!" No, it's not that way. On the other hand, you can't say, "Well, let's all start groaning." Again, the key is *to yield*.

What you *can* do is start in simple tongues. As you start there, you'll find it's easy to come into the groaning sound and yield to the Holy Spirit as He takes hold with you. Reach deep into your inner man with a "spiritual hand," and see if the Holy Spirit grabs your hand and meets you at that depth with groanings. If the door is open, go in! If it's closed, stay where you are and pray in the simple level.

This is how it works spiritually: The more you learn the ways of the Holy Spirit and give over to His expressions, the easier it becomes for you to recognize them and flow with Him.

What I do when I come into prayer is to search for and ask the Holy Spirit for His road and way in the situation. What I mean by this is that I don't look for a thrilling spiritual adventure; I check within my spirit man for how deep the Spirit wants to go with the particular prayer request I am praying over. Then I go with Him down that road by yielding. I don't ask questions; I just drive the car down the road!

I search in the simple tongues range to find how the Holy Spirit wants to express Himself by identifying which expression is coming from my spirit. Often He is willing and longing to take hold with the second level groanings, but He needs people who will yield to Him in this way.

As you give over more and more to the groanings, it will almost seem like there's no dividing line between the levels of prayer, because you'll become so easily given to flowing in each level.

Remember, we don't have to groan over *everything*; however there are many things the Holy Spirit wants to give birth and life to. There are divine dreams and plans God has deposited in your spirit and also events in line with His eternal will that will come forth into the earth when it is His time to reveal them.

The Holy Spirit is just waiting and longing for someone to pray at this level so He can give life, and break through with His will in that particular situation.

It's *easy* to come into the groanings; especially if you position yourself for it. What is it that you are really longing for deep in your heart? Don't just think of things that you know you *should* be aware of. Dare to think God's thoughts that are within you. What has God placed within you as a desire of His heart for yourself, your church, your city, your nation, or the world? Begin to pray about that area. Often you will find that the longing within you will be expressed in prayer as a groaning.

At other times you will find that the Holy Spirit is longing and yearning for His plans to break through into their proper position and place in the spirit realm. Therefore, you will begin to feel and express His burden and desire as you pray in this level and type of prayer, but you won't be consciously aware of how you're praying or what details you are praying for.

God *wants* you to come in and be able to yield to Him in this place in the spirit realm! It may seem and sound strange, but don't let that stop you. You *can* come to the place where you pray on the simple level — and where you're easily given to the spirit of prayer and to groanings on the second level.

God Hears Groanings

The Old Testament has many examples of people yielding to this type of groaning prayer. One is found in Exodus 2:23-25:

> However, after a long time ... the king of Egypt died; and the Israelites were sighing and groaning because of the bondage. They kept crying, and their cry because of slavery ascended to God.
>
> And God heard their sighing and groaning and [earnestly] remembered His covenant with Abraham, with Isaac, and with Jacob.
>
> God saw the Israelites and took knowledge of them and concerned Himself about them. *(Amplified)*

The children of Israel were under extreme duress, enemy oppression, and bondage — they certainly were not living the life God had intended for them. Because of this, they began to groan and cry out to Him from deep inside!

The Hebrew word used here for groaning means simply "to groan." As they started to cry and groan from deep in their hearts, the Bible says the Lord heard their groanings, sighs, and cries, and it caused Him to remember His covenant.

The next action we see God making is to call and prepare Moses as His spokesman and deliverer for the people. God began immediately to make their deliverance a reality. Even if they didn't see it with their natural eyes yet, God was moving! (see

Exodus 3:7, 8). God hears, and He is moved by the groanings of His people. Groanings bring deliverance!

The heartfelt groaning of a believer is one of God's avenues to bring deliverance, freedom, and life to the one praying, or to the situation you are praying for. Is there an area of your life that is under bondage, duress, or enemy oppression and attack? Groaning in prayer can bring deliverance to you, according to the principles in these verses.

Groanings are not the only way God can bring life and victory, but they are one of the ways. The purpose of groanings is to give birth to the will and plan of God, to bring life that consumes every form of death, to break through and deliver from bondage and enemy oppression, and to set God's will and proper course for life into motion.

Not only did God have plans to rescue them from Egypt and its bondage, but He also declared as He answered their prayer that He would bring them into a land flowing with milk and honey. Their prayers not only brought them deliverance; they set them on the right course and brought them into God's promised place and will. God had a whole new standard of life and victory for His children to walk in, and the groaning prayer helped them to get there!

The Holy Spirit Came Over Them

You may be thinking, "Why could they pray like this in the Old Testament? How could they get into the second level and into groanings? They didn't have the Holy Spirit like I do."

The answer is found in understanding the personality of the Holy Spirit. According to Romans 8:26-28, groaning is in the very nature, heart, and work of the Holy Spirit!

In the Old Covenant, God would come over His children to help them; and when He did, they could groan and cry out from the spirit of prayer He would bring with Him. He is, in fact, the spirit of prayer. Of course, they couldn't pray in the simple tongues level, because they weren't baptized with the Holy Spirit. They had the same Holy Spirit, but the Holy Spirit did *come over* them to accomplish His work in and for them.

The Holy Spirit's work and personality have not changed. He is the same today as He always has been. In the New Covenant, however, He is not just *over* believers — He is *within* them!

We have more variety and fullness in prayer than they ever had, because we have access to the simple tongues level as a result of being baptized in the Holy Spirit. They had the same Holy Spirit, but He was *over* them, not *in* them. The spirit of prayer was available for them to yield to, and He came upon them as they began to cry out. Many received mighty answers to their prayers.

But the Holy Spirit is *in* your life. Just as He led the Israelites into groanings in prayer to bring them a supernatural deliverance, He will also lead you. You don't have to wait for Him to come upon you; He is already within you to help you pray. He will take hold of your weakness with this type of prayer and birth the victory through you!

As you yield to groaning in prayer, He will come, meet your cry and longing, and help bring forth the heart-groaning and cry within you. You are God's child, and as you seek His will and plan in life, the Holy Spirit intercedes for you according to God's will (Romans 8:27). It is *the will* of God for you to allow the Holy Spirit to make intercession for you and through you with groanings!

Life Through Groanings

Another example of this kind of praying in the Old Testament is found in the life of Hannah. In First Samuel 1, Hannah was in the Temple praying, deeply distressed because she wasn't able to bear a son for her husband.

In those days, when a woman couldn't have a son, it was a great disgrace to her. The will of God to bear children was being hindered in Hannah's life because there was bondage and oppression working against her in this area.

In light of this problem and out of her frustration to walk in God's best, Hannah began to seek the Lord and cry out to Him for help. Her cry is described in verses 10, 12, and 13:

> And [Hannah] was in distress of soul, praying to the Lord and weeping bitterly.
>
> And as she continued praying before the Lord, Eli noticed her mouth.
>
> Hannah was speaking in her heart; only her lips moved but her voice was not heard. *(Amplified)*

Hannah was praying with anguish and strong weeping. She was praying so intensely that her lips moved, but there was no sound. The Bible says she was praying strongly, so it is clear that she must have moved to a level where the groanings had gripped her deep within, even if there was no sound. Think about that!

What Hannah was doing is part of the action that is described in the *American Heritage Dictionary* as "a groan," which is defined as, "to voice *a deep, wordless, prolonged* sound expressive of grief."

Hannah was not actually releasing the sound, but it was obvious that her prayer was something unique and strange in appearance, because Eli the priest looked at her and thought she was drunk. When someone is drunk, they are under the influence of another spirit. Hannah was under the influence of a spirit here — the spirit of prayer!

Eli, perplexed, asked her, "How long are you going to be intoxicated?" Her actions seemed strange to him. He didn't understand the prayer she was involved in. As a matter of fact, it was foreign to him.

It is sad to me that many people and leaders in the Church today don't understand groanings in prayer and the *art* of intercession. I pray that we never lose this powerful form of prayer in the Lord's work in our day due to lack of knowledge, misunderstanding in the Body of Christ, or religious tradition and fear of man.

"No," Hannah told Eli, "I'm not drunk. I have a sorrowful spirit, and I was pouring out my heart before the Lord." Eli suddenly understood. He told her, "Go in peace, for what you've prayed for is granted to you." In due time, Hannah had the son she'd longed for, Samuel. He was given birth not only in the natural, but after prayer with groaning had gone forth first! *Groanings produced life!*

Jesus Prepares for a Miracle

A classic example of groaning in prayer is found in John 11. Here we're told the story of what happened when Lazarus, a friend of Jesus, died. When Lazarus became sick, his sisters, Mary and Martha, sent word to Jesus, but He stayed several more days where He was before coming to their city of Bethany.

By the time Jesus arrived, Lazarus was dead and had been in the tomb for four days. Mary and Martha were grieving and confused. Grieving with them were religious people who were not only in unbelief, but they had strong hatred and feelings of mockery toward Jesus as well. Then, too, Lazarus was dead and buried.

By the circumstances and spiritual atmosphere around Lazarus, it looked like nothing more could be done — it was a closed case. Maybe it was enough for Jesus to comfort the sisters and then continue preaching and healing people elsewhere. Everyone would understand. After all, Lazarus *was* already dead.

But Jesus had another thought when He came to town that day. He'd come to change the spiritual atmosphere, fulfill the plan and will of God, and raise Lazarus from death even in adverse conditions! As we will see in this chapter, Jesus began to yield to the Holy Spirit — to the spirit of prayer — and to release mighty spiritual weapons that brought absolute victory and breakthrough into this situation. One of the weapons He used was groanings.

As Jesus approached town, He was met by both sisters in turn, and He began to experience the negative spiritual environment around them and the whole situation. In verse 33, we discover how Jesus responded:

> When Jesus saw her [Mary] sobbing, and the Jews who came with her [also] sobbing, He was deeply moved in spirit and troubled . . . *(Amplified)*

Another translation states that He groaned in the spirit and was troubled.

The Greek word here is *embrimaonai*, which comes from another word, *brimaomai*. These words together graphically display what was happening with Jesus. They mean "to snort with anger, to have indignation on, to sigh with chagrin (which implies being distressed), to groan, and to murmur against" (see *Strong's Concordance*).

It is clear by this definition that Jesus was yielding to the second level of prayer. He was releasing to groanings. There was a great stirring within Him, and from the reaction of the religious leaders it seems as if Jesus was outwardly displaying His inward reaction to the situation. In verse 36, they said, "See how He loved him."

Changing the Spiritual Atmosphere

Why was Jesus groaning? The spiritual atmosphere was not conducive or prepared for the miracle God wanted to do, and there was great resistance toward the plan of God being manifested. The grief, confusion, unbelief, and death needed to be broken through *spiritually* so that life could come to Lazarus *naturally*. Jesus knew it was the groanings that would bring this breakthrough, not another kind of prayer, or He would have prayed differently.

Jesus was deeply troubled, deeply stirred in a spiritual reaction, to what the flesh and the devil were producing in the natural circumstances. Like an animal that snorts when it is angered, so Jesus prayed that day with spirit emotion, angered by what He was experiencing. He was not angry at the people present, but with the forces of darkness manifesting around and through the people and the situation. He *groaned*, the Bible says.

I imagine it looked and sounded strange to those who were gathered around. It would be especially strange when you understand that the *American Heritage Dictionary* defines "a snort" as "a rough, noisy sound made by breathing forcefully through the nostrils." It also means to make an abrupt noise. Imagine that Jesus prayed that way! These people had no idea that powerful weapons of prayer were working, and that something was changing in the spirit world around the situation.

Even believers today have a wrong concept about Jesus and His actions. Religious thinking has forced the Church to believe that Jesus is a meek little creature with long, wavy hair, who never offended anyone. If they really thought about what Jesus did that day, they would probably have thrown Jesus out and labeled Him as a freak who was off the deep end, and definitely *did not* have a ministry. And to take it a step further, they would *never* accept *the method* Jesus used to break down strongholds.

God forbid that the Church reject and replace God's ways, exchanging them for acceptable, man-pleasing Christianity. Let's go with Jesus!

Jesus Sets the Scriptural Standard

We are forced by these scriptures to recognize and admit that Jesus prayed in this fashion. Jesus is not a weak, odd character. He is a powerful Warrior (Exodus 15:3) and the Lion of the Tribe of Judah, who engages His enemies. He always did the will of the Father — so groanings must be somewhere in God's heart and plan.

Jesus was scriptural, and He was setting God's rules and standard for the Christian Church yesterday, today, and forever! It is biblical for modern-day believers who are in Christ to pray with groanings — for Jesus is our example.

It also is clearly scriptural that we pray with groanings publicly, openly, and freely in church life. In this instance, Jesus was not in the back room praying; He was on the street with everyone watching. Yet in some Spirit-filled churches, praying in this fashion is *forbidden* or hidden, because of man's religious ceremony and etiquette, because it is simply unheard of through lack of knowledge, or because people are afraid of the prayer itself, or of its offending someone.

Of course, there can be abuses and extremes with any biblical principle, including groanings, but let's not water down, despise, or cut off what God has given us. He knows we need these weapons to break through the death and darkness in our cities and nations in the last days! Done in the right spirit, and led by the Holy Spirit, groanings can be a blessing for everyone. Jesus revealed the power of groaning prayer, and the result was life from the dead!

Travail

Another expression we encounter in the second level is called travail. The dictionary defines "travail" as "strenuous mental or physical exertion, tribulation, agony or anguish, and the labor of childbearing." Travail in prayer is a dimension where these qualities are working in and through the groaning that is coming from your inner man. Many times it works together with the first expression we saw in this chapter, the actual sound of a groaning.

We can learn more about this in First Kings 18:41-44, where the prophet Elijah is used in a symbolic example of travailing prayer. He has just confronted the prophets of Baal in a mighty and victorious demonstration of God's power, and now he goes to the top of a mountain and prays for the promised rain.

And Elijah said to Ahab, "Go up, eat and drink; for there is the sound of abundance of rain."

So Ahab went up to eat and drink. And Elijah went up to the top of Carmel; then he bowed down on the ground, and put his face between his knees.

140

And said to his servant, "Go up now, look toward the sea." So
he went up and looked, and said, "There is nothing." And seven
times he said, "Go again."

Then it came to pass the seventh time, that he said, "There is a
cloud, as small as a man's hand, rising out of the sea!"

The position Elijah assumed here was the position used by
women in ancient days when they were giving birth to children. He
went up on the top of the mountain, bowed himself down on the
ground before God, which is symbolic of prayer, and the Bible says
he put his face between his knees. He was in a natural birthing
position, which revealed what was taking place in the spiritual
world by his action.

Elijah must have stayed in that position much, as it was after
seven times that his servant actually saw rain. Rain is a symbol for
the Holy Spirit and also has a biblical connection to revival.
Zachariah 10:1 says to ask for rain in the time of the latter rain.
James 5:7 then relates the latter rain to the harvest and the coming
of the Lord! Jesus, the Farmer, is waiting for the fruit of the earth
until it comes up; and it won't come without rain.

We are on the threshold of a great end-time harvest, but the
rain must fall. There should be a hunger in your spirit for spiritual
rain and harvest, and you should act on that hunger with travailing
prayer to bring forth the rain!

A New Testament description of this story is in James 5:17,18,
where it states that Elijah prayed earnestly for rain. How did he
pray? With strong prayer! And notice he did not just pray once, but
seven times. He prayed in intercession, again and again, until the
breakthrough came and the cloud was seen. Travail is a mighty
weapon in the spirit, and when it is articulated in prayer, it will
bring the will of God to birth.

In the Bible, travail is compared to a woman giving birth to a
child. Does this mean men can't pray this way? Of course not! It
is compared to natural childbirth, but it is a spiritual activity for *all*
believers who are open and ready for the Holy Spirit to flow
through them in this fashion.

Travailing prayer's pattern is similar to a woman having a
baby. In the woman, life has been conceived through an intimate
relationship. The life has grown, and now it is time for the baby to
come. There is a yearning at delivery for life to come forth, so there
is a groaning and a travail to give birth. At that time, the woman

shouldn't fight the natural birth process. She shouldn't rebel against her own body; she should work with it to give birth to the baby. Heavy labor is involved, but it is natural for her to give birth.

Yield to the Holy Spirit

In the same way, it is *natural* for your spirit to give birth to God's plans, visions, and dreams. It is natural for the Holy Spirit to want to give life to situations filled with death and bondage. With the groanings and travail there's a bringing forth, and God's life comes into what you are praying for. A spiritual delivery comes from heaven!

God has intended for the Church to be the womb on earth for His heavenly will to be birthed and manifested. As we fellowship with Him through the Word and prayer, God drops the seeds of His will and plan, both personal and universal, deep within us. Over time they grow and come to the place where they are ready to be born.

When the delivery is in progress, the woman works to push the baby out. In this type of prayer, there is a yearning from your inner man for the will of God to break forth. There is a "pushing" work of the Holy Spirit in the sounds and flavor of your utterances and your travail in prayer.

In the natural, a baby does not come with just one little push. It takes work to bring forth a child. It also takes labor in the spirit to bring forth some of the things God wants to give birth to in our own lives and in the lives of others as we intercede. It takes some labor to smash down demonic strongholds and break through the devil's plan for the earth. Then, when the need is prayed through, you are released, just like the mother whose baby has been delivered!

Let me give you some practical advice: In this type of prayer, you don't need to act or look like you're having a baby! You'd be surprised how many strange things people do and then call them "spiritual." I've heard a lot of odd reports about prayer groups.

You don't have to act like you're trying to have a baby; just yield to the Holy Spirit, and give yourself to the groanings which come in the form of labor and agony in prayer. All you have to do is yield to travail. You can groan loudly, and you can groan softly

— but you don't have to do strange things or assume unattractive positions with your body.

There is a positive demonstration of what the Holy Spirit is saying or doing in prayer. For example, when we are in spiritual warfare and praying in warring tongues (see Chapter 12), there are times when we actually use our hands when we pray. We point our index finger as a sign of authority when we rebuke the devil, or we demonstrate breaking through chains and smashing bondages with our hands, according to Psalm 18:34, where David said that in God there is a training of the hands for war! (See also Psalm 144:1.)

Concerning travail, the Word of God says in Jeremiah 30:6 that the prophet looked and saw men with their hands on their loins, crying out in pain as a woman giving birth. Sometimes when we groan and travail in prayer, the natural response that corresponds with the spiritual action is to put the hands on the loins while praying.

You don't *always* have to put your hands on your loins; just flow with the Spirit of God and don't get dependent on soulish or physical actions as you come into this area of prayer. But, as always, be sure to stay free to express what the Holy Spirit is saying and doing through you.

Laboring Prayer!

Isaiah 42:13,14 tells us more about this expression of the Holy Spirit:

> **The Lord will go forth as a mighty man, He will rouse His zealous indignation and vengeance like a warrior; He will cry, yes, He will shout aloud, He will do mightily against His enemies.**
>
> **[Thus says the Lord] I have for a long time held My peace, I have been still and restrained Myself. Now I will cry out like a woman in travail, I will gasp and pant together.** (*Amplified*)

This scripture clearly describes for us that God cries out like a woman in travail. As a born-again Christian, it is the Spirit within you who ushers you into the second level expression of travail — groaning with labor and spiritual anguish. If you'll go with it, the Spirit of the Lord will use your prayer to give birth to spiritual realities.

Sometimes in travail, it really feels like you are going to explode unless you pray and push forth what the Lord is giving. It can also seem that there's much work, fighting, and plowing to be done for the subject you are praying for. So what do you do? You bear down and work with this type of prayer. You pray! Groan! *Travail!* Labor in the Spirit!

Notice this scripture says that the Lord will cry out as a woman in travail; that He will gasp and pant together! How is the Lord going to cry out in travail except it be through us as we yield to this expression of the Holy Spirit and travail in prayer? It also says that God has held His peace and been still for a long time, but now, at history's climax, He is again speaking in and because of the travailing prayers of His people!

The *King James Version* of this verse is clear about how travailing prayer is also a weapon to pull down demonic strongholds: ". . . I will destroy and devour." The Hebrew word for "destroy" means "to punish, revenge, and quarrel." Through travailing prayer, we ward off spiritual darkness and attack the powers of hell that have been unleashed against the Body of Christ to hinder it from fulfilling the high calling of God.

There's No Birth Without It

In Isaiah 66:7-9 we read:

> Before [Zion] travailed, she gave birth; before her pain came upon her, she was delivered of a male child.
>
> Who has heard of such a thing? Who has seen such things? Shall a land be born in one day? Or shall a nation be brought forth in a moment? For as soon as Zion was in labor, she brought forth her children.
>
> Shall I bring to the [moment of] birth and not cause to bring forth? says the Lord. Shall I Who causes to bring forth shut the womb? says your God. *(Amplified)*

When these verses are read together, it is clear that it is *impossible* for Zion, which spiritually represents the Church - the dwelling place of God in the New Covenant - to give birth before she travails. There *must be* travail to give birth. Who has ever heard of such a thing? Can you really give birth without a travail? Of course not!

When we do, we produce spiritually weak, sick, and immature babies. The travail comes when the baby is ready; babies born before travail are premature and need life support, or they will die.

Many spiritual babies have died because man has tried to produce them before travail.

There must be groaning, and there must be travail. You can't give birth to a strong baby without them! In some cases, there will be no *life* without them; only death and abortion of the plan of God. Of course, as in the other prayers, travail is neither the only way to pray nor a "cure-all." God wants to teach us travail so we may walk in the benefits and fruit of travail.

This type of prayer should have an important place in our lives. The Holy Spirit desires to plant the plan of God within the Body of Christ through the Word and worship, and then give birth to it through the Church, but those secrets will not come forth until labor and travail have been made. They must be given birth first in the spirit; then they can manifest in the natural.

"Shall a land be born in one day? Or a nation be brought forth in one moment?" No, humanly it's impossible. But as soon as Zion travails — *as soon as* we begin to travail in prayer — our children will be brought forth; not our natural children, but our spiritual children — the family of God, the holy nation! Revival will visit people worldwide!

Revival will be born in our nations not just in one day, but in many days and with many kinds of prayer, including travail. That's how the Spirit of God will give the nations spiritual birth and life. That's how the power of the enemy will be broken.

We must stand up, use our authority, and fight the way the Holy Spirit wants to fight through us with *weapons* that are mighty and powerful to pull down every demonic stronghold and break every curse. The labor and travail must come, and therefore God's life — life from heaven in every area — can spring forth!

Who Aborts God's Dreams?

I like what the Spirit of God says in verse 9: "Shall I bring it to the moment of birth and not cause to bring forth?" God by His Spirit has been planting visions, callings, and dreams in your life, in the Church, and in the nations for revival — and He is going to bring it forth! That's one reason why the spirit of prayer is over us. God does not start something and then abruptly stop it. He doesn't abort "spiritual babies" He has created. It's the Church that becomes spiritual abortionists when we don't pray.

When the baby is ready to come into the earth, or into the full plan of God, all God needs is someone who will yield to the Holy Spirit and labor, travail, and give birth to it. The womb will not be shut, for God never shuts the womb; but man can shut that spiritual womb through unbelief, fear, lack of prayer, not understanding life in the Spirit, and so forth.

There are plans and prophecies that God is bringing forth today, and we can be used in prayer to give birth and to labor in the Spirit to see the will of God made known, both in our own lives and for others.

In Jeremiah 30:6 , it says:

> Ask now and see whether a man can give birth to a child? Why then do I see every man with his hands on his loins like a woman in labor? Why are all faces turned pale? (*Amplified*)

At this time, there was trembling and fear throughout the land of Judah, for the people were suffering bondage and oppression. But the Spirit of God said in verse 8:

> I will break [the oppressor's] yoke from off your neck, and I will burst your bonds; and strangers will no more make (you) slaves. (*Amplified*)

The promise of freedom had been given, but it was not fully manifested yet. So why were their men standing like women in labor, with their hands over their loins? There was still bondage; there wasn't full freedom, or a complete fulfillment of what God had said. There was something more that needed to come forth; oppression that needed to be broken, and demonic powers confronted. Because of this, the people groaned and travailed to do their part in helping to bring to pass what God had said.

I am convinced that the Church today will be led by the Holy Spirit more than ever to yield to the second level travail and pray and pray and pray! Let Him pray through you in this level to give birth and life to God's will and plan, and to break through the hindrances and bondages in your life, city, and nation.

I Travail Again

In the New Testament, Paul gives us several glimpses into his own prayer life. He says in Galatians 4:19, "My little children, for whom I labor in birth again until Christ is formed in you." Paul, as a New Covenant believer, *travailed* in prayer.

"I'm travailing in birth again for you," he told these Galatian believers. Notice he said that he was doing it *again*, which means he had prayed this way more than once on their behalf. Perhaps he did it regularly. We don't really know, but it was more than once.

The first time Paul travailed in prayer for them was for their salvation. There was travail through him that they might be born spiritually. The second time was after they had been saved and had come under religious bondage.

Paul said, "I travail *again* for you," because there was freedom and life that was necessary to come forth on their behalf. They had submitted to deception, seduction, and witchcraft, and that demonic power had to be broken with authority so deliverance and subsequent maturity could come to them, and they could walk where God wanted them to walk.

Paul travailed, he said, that Christ would be formed in them. Of course, travail is not the only way that Christ is formed in us, but it is a powerful weapon that will bring change to what is hindering Christ from being formed in a person's life, or in the situation for which we are praying. Travail will push out the powers of darkness with authority, and will bring to reality the will and plan of God.

God is looking for people who will travail in prayer; for those who will dare to give of themselves and to work, to labor with the Holy Spirit in this expression of the second level. He is ready — but are you willing? If you will yield to Him and let Him take hold with you in travail, you will discover a wonderful world of adventure and challenge that will change the destiny of people, churches, cities, and nations!

Weepings

The third type of groaning in the second level of the Holy Spirit's world is weeping. Throughout the Bible, weeping is used as a tool and expression of the Holy Spirit in prayer.

There are several reasons why weeping comes as an expression in this level. One of them is because the Holy Spirit within us can be grieved, saddened, or hurt when the will of God is hindered from being manifested in our lives or in the situations for which we are praying, since it is His primary job to bring the Father's will to pass.

Many people don't think of the Holy Spirit as a Person who weeps, but He is a divine personality, full of the heart and emotion of God. At times there is sadness in God's heart. It's not an oppression, but there can be a feeling of sadness, anguish, or compassion flowing from God's heart.

Ephesians 4:30 tells us, ". . . do not grieve the Holy Spirit." The Book of Psalms tells us that the children of Israel saddened or grieved the Holy Spirit; the heart of God was broken over the sin of the people and over their limiting God.

God wants to express His heart emotion through us in prayer so situations in people's lives can be conformed to His will. One of the ways He does this is through weepings expressed through us and our emotions.

When we come into these things of spirit life, we must be aware of the fact that spiritual emotion emenating from the Holy Spirit within us can be so real that it seems like an actual physical feeling we are experiencing. However, in reality, we are identifying with the heart of God.

Weeping is an expression of the Holy Spirit that begins in the spiritual world, is transferred to our inner man, and is then released and expressed in prayer. Although this type of prayer may affect our human emotions, it is not merely a soulish reaction to the affairs of life. The Holy Spirit is grieved, and we can experience or sense that sadness, grieving, or weeping in His heart. It does not start with our own mind or emotions; it starts deep in our spirits by the Holy Spirit Himself.

It's not just a matter of deciding to start weeping. Remember, in the second level of groanings, it's the Holy Spirit who initiates the various sounds or expressions, and we are working closely with Him. Weeping in prayer is not human sympathy; it's the expression, the feeling, and the heart of the Holy Spirit flowing through us in prayer. Our part is to simply yield to that expression when it is there.

Jeremiah, the Weeping Prophet

A good example in the Old Testament of weeping in prayer is found in the life of Jeremiah. As a matter of fact, he was *known* as the weeping prophet. He would see the sins and backslidden condition of the people and feel the heart, the love, and the desire of

God to set them free from their sins and have them turn back to their love relationship with Him. Many times the prophet said that his own heart was broken and full of tears as a result.

In Jeremiah 9:1, he said: "Oh, that my head were waters, And my eyes a fountain of tears." He was weeping for the sins of the people, for their backslidden state, and for feeling the hurt of the Israelites being under the enemy's bondage. He was overflowing with compassion for the people and feeling God's heart and jealous love toward them. He was also feeling the severity of their rebellion which had taken them out of God's will, and the urgency for them to repent and get it right! In verses 17-21 of Jeremiah 9, he continues:

> Thus says the Lord of hosts: "Consider and call for the mourning women, That they may come; And send for the skillful wailing women, That they may come.
>
> "Let them make haste and take up a wailing for us, That our eyes may run with tears, And our eyelids gush with water.
>
> "For a voice of wailing is heard from Zion: 'How we are plundered! We are greatly ashamed, Because we have forsaken the land. Because we have been cast out of our dwellings.'"
>
> Yet hear the word of the Lord, O women, And let your ear receive the word of His mouth; Teach your daughters wailing, and everyone her neighbor a lamentation.
>
> For death has come through our windows, Has entered our palaces, To kill off the children — no longer to be outside! And the young men — no longer on the streets.

Not only was Jeremiah weeping, but he also called for the people to come into intercession and to weep before the Lord as well. God's children had cut themselves off from Him because of their sin; they were not walking in fellowship, or in the fullness of God.

If you read the whole Book of Jeremiah, you'll discover that there was hardness in their hearts. This rebellion against God's ways and authority produced death; not only physical death, but spiritual death as well. To change that condition, the Holy Spirit called for weeping and mourning. He called for repentance and wailing over the spiritual state of His people. He called for a humbling before the God of heaven and earth, their covenant Father, that there could be a forgiveness of sin, and healing of the land.

The Holy Spirit is still calling for men and women to come and humble themselves, weep, and be broken before the Lord, exemplifying a tenderness in heart before God. God wants this kind of intercession, not just from women, but from the whole Body of Christ.

In the world, it's negative for a man to weep, because the world thinks it shows weakness. However, weeping in the Holy Spirit in the presence of the Lord is something that God counts as precious and powerful. God does not look at weepings as weakness, because they are an expression of His emotion and nature.

Breaking Up Hard Ground

Not only does weeping serve as a cleansing from sin and a breaking of death and hard heartedness; it serves as the Holy Spirit's "plow" that breaks up hard ground in our personal lives (see Jeremiah 4:3, Hosea 10:12). If there is hardness in an area of our hearts, it's difficult to express emotion or be vulnerable to God or man in that area. Usually, such callousness produces walls and rebellion that isolate and protect the area so no one dares to touch it; especially God. Weeping has the supernatural ability to break down that hardness of heart; it breaks down hard ground.

Many times the Holy Spirit has come over me and shown me my heart, or dealt with me in an area of my own life that was hard, closed, hurt or rebellious, and the response that would flow out of my spirit in prayer was weepings.

The Holy Spirit in me was longing to break up that hard ground — to help be break it up. He was grieving because my sin, disobedience, or whatever the case, had cut Him off from being the Lord of my life there. I was lord of my life and needed to break! There was an anguish in the heart of God to see me free and walking in His will.

Groanings expressed as weepings is not simply an expression of sympathy and feeling sorry for yourself. True weeping in prayer doesn't originate from your emotions or mind. It starts from your spirit, which is in deep contact with the heart of God.

Sometimes when you weep in prayer, you cry with actual tears, and sometimes you don't, but in either case you can sense and feel the crying of the Holy Spirit — first, to break down hardness and, second, to release the compassion, cleansing, and tenderness of the Lord.

God calls for His people to come weep before Him and to turn their hearts to Him. He calls for rending your *heart* and not your garments and for coming close to Him (Joel 2:13). He wants you to be released in the weepings of the Spirit of the Lord and, as Jeremiah 9 says, "wail!"

As you come into this prayer, you will sense sadness in your spirit and sometimes in your emotions, but always remember, we don't depend on our own emotions to carry us, nor do we allow a fleshly melancholy to grab us. Even though there is a feeling of seriousness, we flow *out* of the expression of the Holy Spirit through us.

When we talk about weepings, it doesn't mean we walk around depressed, sad, and heavy all day because we sense that God is sad and grieved. We have to carry it and pray it through, and not take it to a mere human emotion that is empty and powerless.

Sometimes spiritual things seem so real, they can affect us in the natural, but we can learn to be skillful in bearing spiritual things. Remember, Jeremiah said to call for the *skillful* women. There is a skill that can be developed in prayer where we can function in our everyday life, but still be carrying and expressing the heart of the Holy Spirit in and through us.

One of the ways to develop this skillfulness is to understand that you can yield to the Holy Spirit in prayer and release to this prayer, but always remember to *protect your joy*, no matter how serious or sad the case may be. Granted, it sounds contradictory to be grieved, weeping, repentant, tender, and open before the Lord, experiencing the feeling in His heart, yet at the same time to be joyful — but that's the way the Kingdom of God is.

We bear the things of God within — we give expression to the heart of God — and at times we *do* feel sad and serious in a real and practical sense, but we always maintain a strong element of joy.

Prayer is never melancholy. If it comes into melancholy, awareness of oneself, depression, or pressure that is regularly pushing down on you so it is hard or impossible for you to function in everyday life, it means you've taken it out of the realm of the Holy Spirit and you're carrying it in your soul. You can't win the battle in your soul, so acknowledge the Holy Spirit, and ask Him to help you take it back into the spirit in prayer. Then pray until you are released, and rejoice!

Learning To Be Sensitive

When I first started coming into intercession, my heart began to be sensitive to the Spirit of God, and I would know that the Holy Spirit was grieved about different situations. I would be grieved all the time, sad, and depressed.

Most of the time, depression is an attack of the devil from the outside against you, but there will be times as you grow in the spirit that you'll learn to recognize the spirit of prayer — that your spirit is grieved and that the Holy Spirit is grieved within you.

You ask, "How do I learn the difference?" Through practice. But whatever the case, you should pray. If you're being attacked, pray through the attack. Ask the Holy Spirit, "What is this?" You'll begin to learn the difference as you grow in the Lord.

When I first learned how to pray, I would talk to one of my friends on the phone. She'd say, "Everything's fine. It's all right," but I would know by the Spirit of the Lord and by my own spirit that everything wasn't fine.

This wasn't spooky — we don't walk like that — for that's not the Holy Spirit. The Holy Spirit works in peace and in knowledge, and He will reveal the truth about people and their situations to you. He is never eerie or vague. When He gives you something, you've got to go by what you *know* in your heart, and if you don't know anything, let it go, and don't search, question, or try to dig things up.

The Holy Spirit will give revelation to you only if it's needed, and if you have the authority and the anointing to set the person free. Whenever He gives understanding, there is a peace within you, even if He reveals things that are ugly, fleshly, or demonic, and He will always draw you to pray. But never pray just out of feelings; pray instead out of heart knowing and revelation. Then you will stay on safe ground. Test the spirits. If it's from the Holy Spirit, it will lead to setting people free and to lifting up Jesus, and you will be able to keep your joy, even if it is serious.

So I would know in my heart that everything was not right. I would be happy when I talked to my friend, but when I hung up the phone, I felt, "Oooh, what *is* this feeling of sadness and emptiness?" So I asked the Lord, "What is this?"

"*Pray,*" the Holy Spirit taught me. "I want to use you to pray for that person. What you're sensing are the needs in his life. That's why you feel this way, because I'm in you, and I want to meet his need, but I need someone to intercede for him. So just pray for him."

I would get on my knees, yield to the Holy Spirit, and pray, many times with weepings. When I'd prayed through, the feeling of heaviness would leave just as fast as it had come.

Sometimes when you are praying, led by the Spirit, you will know exact details about who and what you're praying for, and sometimes you won't. It's none of your business. The Holy Spirit just needs you to pray, so receive it as a natural part of your Christian life and obey God!

Don't make some big emotional or religious spectacle, "Oh, I prayed yesterday because I felt your needs." Stop all that fleshly action and talk, and work with God in the secret place of prayer.

Protect and keep your joy and victory, and develop a relationship with the Intercessor, the Holy Spirit, who wants to use you to pray for the needs of others and also help you to pray for yourself. When the weepings are there, yield to them. Pray through to victory — and joy.

There Will Always Be a Harvest

Psalms 126:5,6, tells us more about this expression of the Holy Spirit:

They who sow in tears shall reap in joy and singing.

He who goes forth bearing seed and weeping . . . shall doubtless come again with rejoicing, bringing his sheaves with him. (Amplified)

Weeping in the spirit in prayer is a form of sowing. As we're weeping, the scripture says we are going forth bearing seed. That spiritual seed, the Bible says, will always produce a harvest. God's Word tells us that if we sow in tears, we *will* reap joy and singing. It also says that we will return, bringing our sheaves, or our harvest, with us. Weeping and praying as the Holy Spirit wills, not by our own limited plans and methods, will always produce a harvest.

A good example of this happened several years ago while I was praying one afternoon with a friend. I thought we were done praying, but she said, "I feel we need to pray for your brother." I didn't really feel anything, but out of obedience to God and submission to my friend, I began to pray.

The Holy Spirit began to take hold with me strongly, much more so than He did with my friend. I started praying, and immediately I was carried from a feeling of emptiness to the second level of weeping and groaning. The prayer was so strong, I felt like my insides were going to explode! I was *groaning* and *travailing* in the spirit of prayer. Prayer came over me, flowed out of me, and then the weepings started. I was groaning and travailing and weeping all at once, on and on.

I sensed so clearly that the Holy Spirit was working something powerful into my brother's life, and what the Lord needed me to do was to pray for him to help bring it forth. So I prayed through to victory until it lifted — and a short time after it was over, I actually forgot about it.

A few weeks later, however, my brother and I were in a Gospel meeting, and the Holy Spirit began to minister to him in a special way. He called him into the ministry, and lifted him into a whole new level in his walk with God. It was wonderful to see what God did in his life.

I realized later that the intercession that had gone forth those weeks before — that groaning, travail, and weeping — had helped pave the way for God's plan to be brought to pass that night. The Holy Spirit knows best, and He knows how!

When we yield to the Holy Spirit and pray the way He wants us to, through whatever expressions He desires for that situation, it will produce His purposes, in His timing. One of the expressions the Holy Spirit chose to bring the Father's plan to birth for my brother was weepings. We don't always pray this way, but we are open to it; and when the way *is* open and we yield to whatever prayer expression it may be, it will produce a wonderful harvest.

Crying Out

We come now to the last expression of the Second Level — Groanings, which I call crying out. There are many different occasions in the Bible where people cried out to God, but this particular expression is a strong, deep, loud cry like the *roar* of a lion.

The *American Heritage Dictionary* reveals the similarity between roaring and crying out in its definition of these words: *roar* — "to utter a loud, deep, prolonged sound in distress, rage or excitement, to make a loud noise, to breath with rasping sound" and *cry* — "to make inarticulate sobbing sounds, to call loudly; shout."

Isaiah 42:13 in the *King James Version* actually ties the two words together:

The Lord shall go forth as a mighty man, he shall stir up jealousy like a man of war: he shall *cry*, yea, *roar*; he shall prevail against his enemies.

This scripture describes our Lord as a mighty man; as a man of war. A warrior is a soldier, a fighter who never accepts the presence, tactics, or works of an enemy. This quality is in the character of God: He is a Warrior by nature. There is something in Him that rebels against His enemies with fury, rage, and anger. He even stirs up His zeal and expresses this zeal with *shouts* of war and a battle cry! He loves to march out into battle and then demonstrate His victory by *showing* His power against His enemies.

Another description which identifies Jesus as a man of authority, ferocity, and prestige is in Revelation 5:5, where He is called the Lion of the Tribe of Judah. As a lion, He roars against His enemies, against what is contrary to His will, and against what makes Him angry (see Jeremiah 25:30,31 and Amos 1:2). He hates that which is evil (Hebrews 1:9), and He was on the earth to *destroy* the works of the devil (1 John 3:8).

This roaring nature of God even prevails in heaven and has penetrated His servants, the angels. For example, an angel came down from heaven and "cried with a loud voice, as when a lion roars" (Revelation 10:3).

If there is a roar in God's heart, and in eternity, there must be a roar in your heart as well, since you are God's child! You have the very same nature as your Father God. The Holy Spirit in you wants to express Jesus the Lion through you as a weapon that is powerful to pull down demonic strongholds, destroy the works of the devil, break down enemy presence and resistance, and lift up God's standard of righteousness over darkness and sin. You can proclaim God's victory with a roar!

Remember, in this chapter we are discussing utterances or sounds the Holy Spirit gives through you in prayer. This expression is not found in a natural word, or one that comes from your emotions, like we talked about with Bartimaeus (see Chapter 5); but this prayer comes from deep inside you as a cry and a lion's roar. When you dare to think of it as a roar, then you can get a sense of how this expression sounds and feels when it is prayed through you.

Your inner man is the reservoir where the stream of life from heaven meets you. When heaven is reacting to life on earth with a roar (and it does sometimes!), you will also experience that cry in your spirit. Your spirit is not dead! It's alive and will roar against the nature of hell and proclaim God's victory, but you must let that roar *out* so that it can do the work God intends for it to do in the spirit world. You can release it *in* prayer and as a form *of* prayer.

To yield to this prayer is not difficult when you understand that the spirit of might and the nature of God as a Warrior are within you and will be expressed through you by the Holy Spirit.

The best way to explain the operation of this expression is to look back at the meanings of the words "roar" and "cry out," and then to take them literally, because this prayer sounds and feels exactly like its name.

As with the other prayers, you don't have to behave in a strange or bizarre way when you pray in this fashion. If we do not permit this utterance, we limit the weapons that God has given us to be effective.

There are times in prayer when you will cry out from your heart, releasing and demonstrating the authority of God. The Hebrew word used in Isaiah 42 for "cry out" explains that the cry can be as loud as an ear-splitting sound. It is actually a sound that pierces — a sound we need to pierce the heavens and any spiritual darkness in the earth today! Its meaning also reveals that we cry out from within as a shout of joy, to sound an alarm, and to declare triumph! (see *Strong's Concordance*)

If you have never experienced this work of the Holy Spirit, it will seem strange at first, but as you continue to yield to it, you will become stronger and stronger in it.

The Roar That Shakes!

Joel 3:9-11,16 explains this principle of prayer:

Proclaim this among the nations; "Prepare for war! Wake up the mighty men. Let all the men of war draw near. Let them come up.

"Beat your plowshares into swords And your pruning hooks into spears; Let the weak say, 'I am strong.'"

Assemble and come, all you nations, And gather together all around. Cause Your mighty ones to go down there, O Lord.

The Lord also will roar from Zion And utter His voice from Jerusalem; The heavens and earth will shake; But the Lord will be a shelter for His people, And the strength of the children of Israel.

Verse 16 clearly states that the Lord will roar and speak from His dwelling place. The result is that the heavens and the earth will shake. This ties in with Hebrews 12:25-28, which reveals that now in the last days everything that is contrary to the kingdom of God will be shaken, so only what is of the kingdom of God may remain.

One of the ways God speaks today is through the prayers of His people. When we cry out and roar in prayer, it will shake the principalities and powers in heavenly places that wage war against the Church and against the anointing and will of God that is being revealed to this generation.

It is obvious that many individuals, churches, and nations need to be shaken by the Holy Spirit and revival. Some must be shaken first, so revival can come. Included in the shaking is a cleansing process which is a necessary part of revival. God can't pour His glory over flesh and sin, so He wants to confront it first in every area of international, national, and personal life, then fill it and shape it to His plan and glory! We are to be a part of that with our prayers so the kingdom of God may come on earth as it is in heaven (Matthew 6:10).

Satan and all His works *are* defeated. We have the joy of manifesting that defeat by working with God in prayer until He comes again to finally establish His reign on earth.

Because crying out causes a shaking, you need to be prepared and know that once you begin to pray this way in your personal life and your church, anything that is not anchored in the Solid Rock — anything that is of the flesh, worldliness, sin, and demonic influence — will start to react and be revealed.

Of course, the Lord is a shelter and a strength for us (verse 16), but Jesus said that anything that is not on the good foundation will be shaken and fall in a storm. When the rain of the Spirit falls and God's wind blows from heaven as the alarm of revival is sounded, ungodliness and darkness will be uprooted.

I say this to prepare and encourage you to let God clean out and purge your life and church. Be ready to set people free from areas in their lives where they have given up ground (knowingly or unknowingly) to the enemy and to help them walk in the spirit, because God will start dealing with *all* areas of life as the heavenly and earthly realms start shaking.

Naturally, if you begin praying against demonic strongholds in your city, if there are the same strongholds or related forces operating in your life or the lives of those who are praying with you, then those strongholds will also shake. God will require that you deal with those areas of your life; and that is good because He is cleaning up His Church!

Because we are positive people, we usually don't dare to talk or think like this. It is not natural for the flesh to be confrontive, but it's a mandatory step in revival. In revival time, our prayers will confront. In revival time, we will be personally confronted and changed to be clean and powerful vessels for the Lord.

Jesus Cried Out

In Hebrews 5:7, Jesus, our standard, prayed with strong crying and tears.

> . . . in the days of His flesh, when He had offered up prayers and supplications, with vehement cries and tears to Him who was able to save Him from death, and was heard because of His godly fear.

The Greek word for "cry" comes from a word that means "to croak as a raven, to scream, to call aloud, to shriek, exclaim and entreat (see *Strong's Concordance*). Jesus is our example in prayer, and we are to do the same things He did and He is doing now! Jesus cried out and made these sounds in prayer.

In the Temple, by the spirit of might, He confronted His enemies and knocked over their tables. He dared to shake and destroy the work place of the enemy! So can you with your prayers! Let the spirit of might flow through you as a roar in prayer. The Holy Spirit will manifest Himself through you as He helps you pray for your weaknesses and against your enemies. He will also declare and express victory through you in prayer as a battle cry and a shout of triumph!

In this expression, as in the others, there can be extremes. The roar I am referring to is not a cry against people where you vent your anger or frustration. It's not where you put on some kind of show and start barking like a dog or trying in the flesh to sound like a lion when you pray! You don't have to force this expression, or try to make it happen. Because the Holy Spirit is within you, you can't help but cry out and roar against God's enemies, which have also become your enemies because you belong to Him!

Let God arise in you and let His enemies be scattered (Psalm 68:1). There is a true, spiritual roar, cry, and shout that will come through you as a mighty weapon and be used to accomplish God's purposes in the earth. Draw from deep within and let it out! The Lord is storming forth in this generation through the roars and cries of His people; His warriors are raising the battle cry and marching to victory!

Pay the Price

Remember, roaring is only a part of what the Bible teaches as crying out to God. There are many different types of cries, both with the understanding and by the Spirit. Crying out to God is a type of prayer that is foundational in the Bible. Interestingly enough, one of the first references to prayer in God's Word is when men "began to call upon the name of the Lord" (Genesis 4:26 *King James Version*).

Jeremiah 33:3 invites you to call out to the Lord. The result will be revelation of mighty, hidden, and humanly inaccessible things. Calling out can be categorized by a wide variety of applications, but whatever the case, whoever calls, cries, invites, mentions, or proclaims the Name of the Lord *will be saved*. The redemptive process, revival, and restoration at any level *begins* by calling out and *continues* by calling out to the Lord. God is waiting for you and me to cry out to Him!

Let your heart reach out and call upon your God. Call with boldness, faith, and expectancy. He's waiting for you! Shout and pray *until* you see victories! Take time to be on your face, or walk the floor and call on Him to the point of knowing you have reached heaven and plundered hell! Jesus loves faith that will pay that kind of price. Sometimes that's what it takes to see results! Do it, regularly and consistently, and you will see the reward.

Giving Birth to a Miracle

In summary, let's go back to John 11 again and review how the spirit of prayer was used as a mighty weapon to change the spiritual atmosphere and give birth to a miracle. One thing to remember here is that Jesus did not have to yield or give to the Holy Spirit any more than we do. He *chose* to give Himself to the Spirit of God and flow in whatever expression was needed to bring about God's will.

As you remember from the Bible account, Lazarus had become sick, died, and been buried four days when Jesus arrived in Bethany. Lazarus' sisters were grieving, as were the friends who'd come to console and mourn with them. The atmosphere was filled with unbelief, confusion, and grief. The situation was certainly not conducive for a miracle.

The Jews were also there, and I imagine there was a strong reaction in them when they realized that Jesus had come to town. Many of the Pharisees and Sadducees hated and were, in fact, Jesus' most vicious enemies. They didn't understand Him, and I'm sure they were very surprised when He showed up that day.

Can you imagine the feelings that would have come up in them? "What are *you* doing here?" The thoughts that were in their hearts were ugly, though on their faces, of course, would have been a smile of sorts, because they were hypocrites.

Jesus arrived in an atmosphere charged with religion, tension, unbelief, hatred, and confusion. Verse 33, as we saw earlier in the chapter, tells us how Jesus responded:

When Jesus saw her [Mary] weeping and the Jews who came with her weeping, He groaned in the spirit and was troubled.

Jesus began to groan. He yielded to the Holy Spirit and the expression that flowed out of His spirit was groanings. He was stirred, disturbed by the spiritual atmosphere, and He *groaned*. The Holy Spirit through Him was beginning to break down the darkness and change that situation.

Then Jesus began to weep. But why was He crying? Jesus never walked by soulish dictates or in the flesh — He always walked in the spirit; so what He was doing here was in the spirit. The people all saw Him because Jesus was weeping and groaning publicly. People were watching Him, but they didn't understand what was going on. They were living on a strictly soulish level, and they understood His action purely in the soulish realm. "Oh," they said, "look how much He loved him." And Jesus did love Lazarus, but He was responding supernaturally, not just humanly.

Some of the Jews then began to openly mock and speak bitterly against Jesus. That hatred inside them toward the anointing was manifested. "Well, if He's so anointed, why couldn't He prevent this one from dying?" All the unbelief, the mockery, the hatred, the bitterness, and the grief came gushing out. Does it look like a miracle? No! But Jesus kept praying.

It says that Jesus again groaned, sighed, deep from inside, as He approached the tomb. He was walking, weeping, and groaning, and sighing deeply. Then, to everyone's amazement, He told them to take away the stone from in front of the tomb.

Martha's spiritual eyes were still not open; she was still in the natural. Jesus was working a miracle, but she just didn't see it. "Lord," she said, "he stinks by now." "If you believe," Jesus told her, "you'll see the glory of God!" But how was He bringing the glory of God into this situation? Through prayer — second level groanings and weepings. The glory of God was going to come even in this seemingly impossible circumstance.

Jesus, now standing before the open tomb, switched to a different type of prayer. He'd been groaning and weeping, and now He says, "Father, I thank You that You have heard Me." He prays the prayer of thanksgiving — right in the middle of groaning and weeping. "You always hear Me Father," He said, "I know You."

The more you know God and practice prayer, the stronger your prayer life is going to be, and the more sensitive you'll be to the moving of the Spirit and what He desires to do and say in each moment in prayer.

Then Jesus uses another expression of the second level — crying out. He *shouted* with a *loud* voice for the dead man Lazarus to come out. Just imagine this: He's been groaning and weeping, the anointing is over Him, strength is over Him, He prays the prayer of thanksgiving bold and strong and, at the height of that prayer, He cries out with a loud voice: "Lazarus, come out!"

The spiritual atmosphere has been completely changed by Jesus' prayers. Spiritual utterances as weapons have altered the spiritual climate, pushed back the darkness, and as Jesus cries out "Lazarus, come out!" A miracle happens. Death loses its grip, and *life* explodes on the scene. Lazarus is raised from the dead! A miracle has been done through the power of the Holy Spirit in prayer — through groanings, weepings, and crying out.

To see miracles today, we *must* boldly, with aggressive force and authority, use these weapons in this last-days war without compromise or fear. If we don't, we risk a brazen heaven, closed to the revival God wants to bring into the earth.

The Second Level — Groanings with its diversities of utterances is wonderful and powerful — and it's available for *you*! You can come into these prayers. Ask the Holy Spirit for them. You can be easily given to them. It's not just for Jesus. It's for *you*!

Turn This Loose On The Nations!

Friends, we are in desperate need of this kind of prayer in our churches! We *need* this kind of prayer in our cities! Weepings, travail, groanings, and crying out by the Holy Spirit will bring life where there is spiritual death. This kind of praying is powerful, effective, and has its place in the last-days revival.

Many believers don't understand it, or don't *want* to understand it. They don't like it, because it's uncomfortable for flesh and for natural reputation. In fact, it is foreign to the natural man; but when it's done by the Holy Spirit, it will work miracles, and result in a blessing for thousands who will reap the benefits of your yielding to the Spirit of God!

If it's radical, great! Be radical for God! Put action to your faith through prayer, and pray until you actually see miracles — miracles in *any* impossible situation: miracles in your life, miracles in our cities, and miracles in our nations.

People are hungry for miracles, and you can work them, but it takes *work*. People want to see with their own eyes what they see in the Bible: both the prayers and the results. So let's pray like the Word teaches us, and let's see revival and the glory of God that has been promised to our generation!

Chapter 14
The Prayer of Intercession

Greater love," the Bible declares in John 15:13, "has no one than this, than to lay down one's life for his friends." In God's kingdom, there are many ways to lay down your life for others. One of them is to pray; and when we pray for others, it is called the Prayer of Intercession.

Intercession is born out of the heart of God — it is born out of love. With this kind of prayer, there is a sacrifice of our very being; our lifestyle, time, and energy. There is a giving of ourselves to pray for other people, and for God's will, plan, and purpose to be done in the earth.

God is looking for people who care enough to pray, for people who love enough to give of themselves to Him and to the needs of others in the Prayer of Intercession.

Let's begin the study of intercessory prayer by looking at Jesus, whose life is our best example of an intercessor in action. Hebrews 7:24,25, referring to Jesus, says:

> But He, because He continues forever, has an unchangeable priesthood.
>
> Therefore He is also able to save to the uttermost those who come to God through Him, since He ever lives to make intercession for them.

Jesus as an unchangeable Priest is functioning right now in priestly ministry before the Father, making intercession. Jesus is praying for us!

Not only does Jesus have a priestly ministry, but the Bible declares that *we* have one as well. Revelation 1:6 tells us that you and I have been made kings and priests unto God because of the New Birth. In our kingly ministry, we walk in and use our God-given authority, and in our priestly ministry, we minister unto and before the Lord, with the sacrifice of praise and worship, the fruit of our lips giving him pleasure.

As part of our priestly ministry we also, like Jesus, make intercession. God has called us to be intercessors. Jesus is the Intercessor in heaven; we, by the Holy Spirit, are the intercessors in the earth. Jesus' prayers are ringing out in heaven; our prayers are ringing out in the earth. We join together with His will and His plan as we intercede.

Jesus Gives to the Uttermost

Matthew 6:10 says, "Your kingdom come. Your will be done on earth as it is in heaven." How does that happen? It has to be *born* into the earth; it has to be spoken and released into the earth through the faithful, continual intercession of the saints, agreeing with the intercession of Jesus in heaven. This will cause God's will to be seen and done on the earth.

The scripture says in Hebrews 7:25 that Jesus is able to save to the uttermost. Jesus as an Intercessor gives us much as He has and goes as far as He can to save and help people in the earth. This is part of the heart of an intercessor: giving and praying no matter what the cost — no matter what it takes — to see salvation; to see the fullness of the work of the cross and the resurrection in the earth today.

We know the work is finished, for the price was paid when Jesus died, but at the same time we join in and reinforce that work, so that everything God has planned and ordained might be a reality in the earth. By the grace of God through intercessory prayer, the Holy Spirit moves on the wings of our prayers to make God's will, plan, and purpose manifest in this natural realm.

Hebrews 7:25 also states that Jesus "always lives" to make intercession for us. Jesus is the greatest Prayer Warrior there is. He always lives to make intercession, and so can we, because our lives are in Him. One of our purposes for living is to pray — we *live* to make intercession!

Every believer is appointed to the work of intercessory prayer. We are all called to be like Jesus and function strongly in this ministry. Your lifestyle can be trained to be a lifestyle of an intercessor. You can be trained and taught by the Holy Spirit and by the Word of God to make intercession effectively, like Jesus did, and like He is doing right now.

When I teach about the ministry of intercession, I don't want to imply that intercession is a specialty ministry, that intercessors proudly wear a badge on their shirts, showing that they pray, or that intercessors have a special spiritual look on their faces because they are intercessors. No, every believer who prays is just acting like and obeying Jesus.

Jesus' Mighty Act of Intercession

In its simplest form, what it means to intercede is to *take the place of another; to stand on someone else's behalf.* Jesus performed the greatest act of intercession, or standing in the gap, that has ever occurred when He died on the cross and took our place. He didn't have to die on the cross for you and me, but He wanted to.

In my unsaved state my sins separated me from the Father. But there came One who was willing to give His life in my place because He was full of love, full of mercy, and obedient to the will of His Father. Jesus took my place, and His blood was enough to pay the price for my sin.

Jesus stood where I couldn't stand myself. My works could never have won peace with God. But Jesus' sacrifice was enough; His blood was enough — and He gave it, and it paid the price for me and for you. Jesus took our place on the cross. He brought us together and connected us with the Father when we couldn't do it ourselves. It was a tremendously powerful act of intercession; He literally took our place!

The offering of the sacrifice of Jesus' blood was enough to pay the price for sin. No man or woman will ever have to die on the cross again to obtain salvation. The price has already been paid. No one can add to it, and no one needs to; nor can anyone take away from it. It is forever settled in heaven. The sacrifice has been eternally paid.

Although the price has already been paid, there is one thing we can do: stand for others on *behalf* of the sacrifice Jesus made for them. We never have to die on the cross, but we give of our time and our love. We sacrifice our strength and prayers on behalf of others so the fullness of what Jesus did might come into their lives like God intends.

In intercessory prayer, we stand in the gap on their behalf and for their needs. We take it upon ourselves to pray for them; to stand, speak the Word of God, and fight for them, that God's will might be done to its fullest in their lives.

God always honors that kind of sacrifice. He looks over the whole earth for intercessors — those who will stand in prayer; those who will stand in the gap on behalf of the needs of mankind.

In intercession, we reinforce and stand for what Jesus has already done. This type of prayer involves work and sacrifice, love and time — but it's one of the most rewarding kinds of work you can ever do. Every believer should take that place of priestly ministry before the Lord as an intercessor!

People Today Need Intercessors!

Just as we needed Jesus to be an Intercessor for us in our desperate situation in life, people need intercessors to support them today. Humanity has needs, desires, and weaknesses that only God can help them with. Many are living in total darkness, and God wants to satisfy their hearts and bring victory to their lives.

The Lord has many plans He has ordained from heaven to bless and help them. Those plans are available in the spiritual realm, but they must be brought into this natural world. There are ways to get them from the invisible, or spiritual world, as a visible reality in the natural world. One of those ways is through the Prayer of Intercession.

God is looking for intercessors — and so is the human race. People desperately need intercession! There are churches that are in need *today* of someone to make intercession for them and stand against the onslaught of the powers of darkness released against their callings and anointing.

There are cities and nations that are on the verge of collapse today if people don't make intercession for them by standing in the gap and praying for God's will to come forth from heaven.

A godly man or woman needs to identify with the sins of the people by praying for the convicting power of the Holy Spirit to be upon them and for God to forgive them of their sin. There are individuals whose lives depend, right now, on the availability of an intercessor — someone who will pray and break through for them. God is looking, but will you respond?

Again, intercession means to take the place of another, but it also means *to bring together*. When we intercede, the result of our prayer is to join cities, nations, and individuals with the will and plan God has for them. That's what Jesus did when He died on the cross: He brought us together with the Father.

In intercession, we help bring God and man together (see Job 9:33). Our prayers work powerfully in the spirit world, and if we don't give up, but persevere, we will see the results of our prayers with our own eyes!

Stand in the Gap

Just imagine a person who needs in some way to contact God. For some reason he can't reach God Himself, or he simply needs help to obtain what God has for his life. As we intercede, we're connecting, or bringing the two of them together.

When we go to the throne of the Father in prayer, it's as if we literally take hold of God with one hand and we take hold of that person with the other hand. We don't see it physically, but this is what happens. We are being used to bring the two together; we are standing in the gap between them.

The Bible talks about this in Ezekiel 22:30:

> So I sought for a man among them who would make a wall, and stand in the gap before Me on behalf of the land, that I should not destroy it; but I found no one.

God is looking for people who will *stand* in the gap! I have noticed that most people are good at finding gaps. Many Christians, in fact, are what I call professional gap finders! They find all the problems (gaps) with everything everywhere. Then they analyze and criticize the gaps — but they never take the time to *stand* in them and pray!

God is looking for someone — just one person — to stand in the gap, to pray for His will to be done, and to pray for the Holy Spirit to bring the answer to the problem. He is waiting for Christians to use their God-given authority to break the powers of darkness that torment, harass, and hinder in the situation for which they are praying.

If we will do this, we can be used through prayer for God's life, will, and plan to flow to people in need. God will honor intercessors' identification with the needs of people as if the persons were actually praying for themselves!

Not only do we bring together, or stand in the gap, in intercessory prayer, but in the spiritual warfare side of intercession, we also *make* gaps between the powers of darkness and those for whom we pray.

Imagine believers who are being attacked by the devil. Their prayer request can be likened to a wall that is broken down because a demonic, destructive force is aggressively advancing toward them to steal their property. Immediate and defensive help is required!

So we, through the power of intercession, go in, use our spiritual weapons, and create a gap, not allowing the enemy to gain any foothold. We don't bring the two together; we stand there as a protective wall, as one who would dare to stand, guard, protect, and maintain the ground we've taken.

We make a gap *between the subject and the enemy* which can then be a starting point for building the wall back up to its rightful place and function. If the enemy tries to come back, we are in our place, standing in the gap. We intercede, we fight for our subject, and we keep the enemy away.

In Chapter 2, Effective Prayer, I mentioned that one of the kinds of prayer is the Prayer of Binding and Loosing, Spiritual Warfare and Authority. I have not taken this subject as a separate chapter, but as you have seen, it has been woven throughout the teaching in this book.

Jesus referred to binding and loosing in Matthew 16:18,19 and Matthew 18:18. In both places He describes to the Church how we are to use our authority in the spiritual world. He said, "I will give you [the Church] the keys of the kingdom of heaven." We have authority to lock up or bind principalities and powers in the spiritual world and to unlock or loose the will and power of God through our prayers that flow from the earthly realm.

Notice that heaven, or the heavenly realm, and earth are closely tied together, and that they have a *direct* effect on one another.

The word "bind" means "to forbid, to prohibit, to stop, and to declare unlawful and improper." You have the right to bind the power of the enemy in your life and in other people's lives as well, but you must pray and declare them bound in Jesus' Name. Remember, the words of your mouth in prayer are powerful if you mix faith in God with them when you pray. Bind up Satan, in Jesus' Name!

The word "loose" means "to release, to fire, to give free movement, unfettered, lack of restraint, and to declare lawful." We also have the right with our prayers and words to release the fullness of God, His ways, the Holy Spirit, goodness, righteousness, and justice into the spiritual world. When we pray and loose these things with boldness and faith, our prayers will have a direct effect in the heavenlies and will reap great results on earth.

Speak words of loosing to people who are in bondage. Pray for the will of God to be loosed over you, your family, city, and nation in Jesus' Name. The Church must take her place in the spiritual world and use the weapons that Jesus has given her to be powerful, mighty, and effective.

A Lawyer at God's Throne

Another aspect of the work of an intercessor is *to act as a lawyer in a courtroom*, or *to plead the case of another*. Let's look at Job 9:32,33. We see here that Job was looking for someone who would stand for him. Listen to Job as he speaks:

> For He is not a man, as I am, That I may answer Him, And that we should go to court together.
>
> Nor is there any mediator between us, Who may lay his hand on us both.

This is a prophetic scripture pointing to Jesus. At the same time, we can see the cry of Job's heart for someone who would know how to stand in the court of God and plead his case. He did not know how to do it for himself, and there was a cry in his heart: "Is there someone who can stand for me? Is there someone who can put his hands on both of us and bring us together?"

Job was looking for someone who knew what God's will was, who knew what God's law was, and who could go before God, stand as a lawyer, and present his case before Him. He wanted someone who knew about the higher law and could put a good case out in the spirit realm in his stead.

That's what we do in the work of intercessory prayer. We stand on the Word of God, speak the Word of God, take His Word into difficult and challenging situations, and it gives God something He can work with in the earth. God's highest and best is to work with men and women in the earth. When they are basing their prayers on the law of His Word, He has obligated Himself to honor His Word.

So to intercede means to plead the case of another. It means to be as a lawyer in a court room and to defend or vindicate others, even if they're guilty. Do you know that you and I were guilty of breaking God's law? Yes, we were found guilty, but Jesus stood in for us in spite of our criminal act, and God's grace was poured over us. Thank God, Jesus stood for us, brought us together with the Father, and plead our case!

Today there are Christians and non-Christians alike who have made a case for themselves because of their actions; they are guilty of violating the laws of God. They seem far from God, and it seems sometimes as if they don't even want anything to do with Him. However, the power of intercession released on their behalf can turn their situation around!

It may take some time, but if you and I will stand strong on the promises of God and plead the case for people, the situation will change. I can think of people who were backslidden for years, but someone wouldn't let go of God's promise — they *refused* to back away from the truth — and the backslider returned to the Lord.

Hang Onto the Lifeline

When we start praying for someone or something, God does not want us to turn loose or give up on what we are praying for until we see results. I have heard this compared to astronauts working together in a spaceship. They're all together, doing what they're supposed to do, but one of them decides to go exploring out into space. He puts on his space suit, hooks up to the oxygen supply, and ventures out on a space walk.

He tells everyone, "I'm going to come back soon. I just want to go out and have a look around."

"Well," his fellow astronauts say, "don't go too far. Remember, we have boundaries and limits on how far we can go."

"Oh, don't worry about it," he replies, "I'll be fine."

And out he goes. It's so interesting out there in space! He begins to have such a good time! Then he goes a bit too far, forgets what time it is, and gets out in territory where he's not supposed to be. Trouble comes to the once-joyous space walker.

Sometimes we have friends, family, and acquaintances who are in the same position in their life circumstances on this earth. They are walking around in a land where they're not supposed to be.

In dealing with such a case, do you know what the temptation would be? If you were in the spaceship, the temptation, if you stayed in the flesh, would be to take a big pair of scissors, open the hatch of the spaceship, and cut the lifeline so the rebellious astronaut would drift away. "Away with that problem! He was strange anyway. He deserves to be cut off. After all, we warned him!"

That lifeline has everything the person needs to survive, even when he's in territory where he's not supposed to be. In the spiritual sense, we are to hold onto people walking in dangerous territory; we are to hold the lifeline until the Holy Spirit can work with them and draw them back into the right way.

What we should do instead of *cutting* the lifeline is to open the door and use all our strength to pull the lifeline back into the ship and rescue the space walker. It is not God's will to cut humanity's lifeline!

God is full of mercy and longsuffering. He has much patience with people — and so can we by the Holy Spirit. We must refuse to cut people's lifelines! We must hold onto people in prayer and not let go until we see God's victory in their lives. We are led by the Holy Spirit, led by the truth, led by the higher law, and we keep praying, standing, and pleading their case so the Word of God can prevail in their situation. If the Holy Spirit releases us, then we go on; but until there *is* a release, we must stand fast!

Pray Through to Victory

Intercession is not a one-time prayer. It is not like the Prayer of Faith, where we pray once, believe we receive, and stand in faith until we see the manifestation.

There are some subjects of intercession that will lift off you and be prayed through in one time of prayer, and you won't need to pray for that subject again. Other issues, however, may need to be carried in the spirit, or in your heart, for days or weeks until you sense you have prayed through to victory, or until you see results.

Every prayer time should end in a note of victory, but to pray through in some situations takes time, and we must continue to pray for weeks, months, or even years until we see the break-through.

I remember one situation where the Lord prompted me to give a strong prophetic word to someone. Remember this: When you have the word of the Lord to give to someone, God will usually give you the responsibility to help pray that word to completion!

Many people want to be prophets, but they don't understand the responsibility that is required to stand in that place of ministry.

When we counsel people, not as prophets, but simply as believers, we should pray that God would work with them, not just through our counseling, but also through the Holy Spirit working with them as *we* intercede for them.

I gave that person the counsel of God, and for four days, the spirit of prayer was upon me concerning that situation. Every time I came into prayer, I had trouble praying for other things. Every time I prayed, groanings, weepings, and travailings would come over me as the Holy Spirit held me responsible to pray for that person.

Of course, with intercession it's important that you know how to handle spiritual matters with wisdom and godly order, so I went through everyday life doing what I was supposed to do. But the spirit of prayer was on me, and when I had free time, I'd get on my knees and pray and pray and pray until I had to go back to work.

It took four days to pray that particular case through. In the night I would wake up and weep and pray and weep and pray and then go back to sleep. I would get up in the morning and it would start all over again. It seemed as if I prayed all day. After four days, the Holy Spirit released me, and I knew I'd prayed it through. God had done what He needed to do with that case.

In intercession, we keep praying and praying until we sense the victory, until the breakthrough comes, or until the Holy Spirit discharges us from the case.

Intercession Begins in God's Heart

The burden for intercession begins in *God's heart.* People may be guilty of sin and trespasses, Satan may be accusing or attacking them, or perhaps they just need our help in prayer. It doesn't matter what the circumstance is; God loves and cares for people. He has a plan for their lives.

We don't pray just because we think it's a good deed to pray for people; we pray because people are in God's heart. Why do we pray for the nations? Because God has a plan for them; they are in His heart. Why do we pray for our families? Because God loves them and has a plan for them.

It's important that you understand this as an intercessor: All intercession begins in God's heart. We are simply working with Him. We can be bold as we declare His will, but we must always remember that intercession begins and ends in Him. We get no glory for our prayers; they begin in His heart — and He'll give *us* His heart by the Holy Spirit. God *wants* us to have His heart for nations, cities, and people around us. We must be sensitive to the Holy Spirit's leading us to pray for these things.

God doesn't want your motivation in intercession to spring from religious works or selfish desire, but from His heart within you. He wants His compassion, His will, and His desire to be birthed and recognized inside you.

The Holy Spirit wants to work in you, transforming your motives and desires in prayer to the point where your heart beats with the very heartbeat of God Himself. He wants to change you until you want what He wants, you're moved by what He's moved by, you long for what He longs for; until He truly has your heart — and you have His!

God is looking for people who are sensitive and tender like this. He's looking for people who *want* His heart, who *desire* what He desires, and who will dare to *feel* as He feels. He's looking for people who will work with Him, praying out His heart and will into the earth with the fervency, love, and fire that comes from an innermost being that is in contact with the loving God. Will *you* be one of these people?

Where Is an Intercessor?

In Isaiah 59 we find that the Israelites were severed from their relationship with God because of their sin. There was no justice or truth in the land. The people were in a compromised and backslidden condition. In verse 15 it says:

> **So truth fails, And he who departs from evil makes himself a prey. Then the Lord saw it and it displeased Him That there was no justice.**

Notice that the Bible tells us that the Lord saw the situation. God sees *everything* going on in the earth and in your personal life. When the Lord saw what was happening, their unrighteous actions displeased Him.

People say, "Then why doesn't God do something about it?" The answer is found in verse 16: "He saw that there was no man, And wondered that there was no intercessor."

God saw the situation, was moved to judgment by their behavior, and His first course of action was to look for an intercessor. But the sad thing is, He found none! He wondered why there was no intercessor, because the power of intercession could have served justice and satisfied the claim of guilt against them, thus reversing the charge and, in God's eyes, changing the spiritual position of the people.

The story here, of course, points to Jesus, who became the Intercessor for the sins and the judgment of mankind. It also points prophetically to our being intercessors in our day.

The state of affairs for the Israelites was not positive. There was no peace, and the will of God wasn't regarded or established as final law. Often when we start in intercession, that's the way it is with the people or situation we pray for. The will of God isn't seen or known, but God is looking for someone who will stand in that place before Him. He is looking for someone who will pray, intercede, and ask to see His will established.

God is searching the earth everywhere for intercessors. His heart is *longing* for people who will work with Him so His will might be released into the earth. In these verses, it is clear that the scripture is pointing prophetically to the intercessory work of Jesus, but we also know that the same principles carry over into intercessory prayer. God is looking . . . He is looking today. All it takes is one man. God said, "I looked for one man who would stand."

Old Testament Insights

In the Old Testament, we encounter an interesting Hebrew word, *paga*, which means "to intercede, to come between, to cause to extend, to fall upon, to make intercession, intercessor, entreat, to light upon, to meet together, to pray."

As we investigate the various passages where that word is used, we can understand more about the nature of intercession and some of its intricate qualities. One of the meanings of intercession, as revealed in the use of *paga*, in Joshua 19:10,11, is "to reach out, to extend, and to establish to the full inheritance."

In these verses, the land of Israel was being divided between the various tribes. God was giving the people specific details about how far their borders were to reach. Everyone knew where their inheritance was to begin and end, but they had to reach out, to extend to those borders, and take possession of their land. They had to actually *take* the inheritance that had been given to them.

One of the purposes of intercession is to reach out, take, and establish what God has given us. The Israelites were to establish their property and their rights, and were reaching out to take what was theirs. This is what we do in intercession.

If they did not take their inheritance, it would not have been God's fault; it would have been their own fault, because the Lord gave them exact directions about how far they were supposed to go. They were then responsible to reach out and take that land.

Take It All!

Every believer has an inheritance that belongs to him or her in Jesus Christ. Likewise, every church has an inheritance or a destiny in the form of a vision and a calling that belongs to it in Christ. How much a church has of its divine destiny is not dependent on God, although it comes from Him, but on *believing* that God has given it and on how much they actually *possess* in prayer.

Every time we intercede, we are establishing what God has given to us; we are making it stronger; we are praying out the specific details and direction for it; and the roots of our real purpose in life are going deeper in God and in us.

There is a reaching out, establishing, and extending to the fullness of the will of God that takes place in intercession. We reach out or stretch to the borders God has given us; we extend out to receive *all* our inheritance in Christ. We must learn to intercede and establish the will of God.

Another characteristic of intercession that can be ascertained from the use of the Hebrew word *paga*, as found in First Samuel 22:18, is that intercession involves attacking enemies. In intercession, we aggressively fall upon or launch a violent assault upon our "foes." This is a part of intercessory prayer — not the only part, but a powerful and important part.

You wonder why we do spiritual warfare? Because it's the part of intercession that attacks, possesses, overcomes, rises above, conquers, takes by force, subdues opposition, defeats, and overwhelms the enemy with victory. God has given intercession this quality within itself, just as much as He has put genes and chromosomes in a human being.

Now let me explain what was happening in First Samuel. David was running from King Saul, because Saul's bitterness had become so deep he was out for David's blood. Instead of killing only David, he looked for someone who would respond to his command to kill *all* the priests of the Lord, hoping that David might be killed along with them. Saul wanted a servant who would react immediately to kill the priests.

This is not a positive story from the standpoint that the priests were killed, but it reveals the fact that assailing enemies is involved in intercession *(paga)*.

Obedience to the King's Command

Notice the servant's response to Saul. The command came, "Kill the enemies," and without question, he jumped on them immediately.

The Holy Spirit wants to show us from this story that you and I are under the command of a King. His name is Jesus! He has given us weapons that are mighty to pull down strongholds, and as soon as He commands us by the Holy Spirit to attack the enemy, we are to respond like the servant Doeg did.

We don't question God. We don't run and hide; we respond *immediately* to our King's commands. We turn with our weapons and aggressively plunder the enemy. Where do we do that? In intercessory prayer!

Look at Psalm 149:5-9:

Let the saints be joyful in glory; Let them sing aloud on their beds.

Let the high praises of God be in their mouth, And a two-edged sword in their hand,

To execute vengeance on the nations, And punishments on the peoples;

> To bind their kings with chains, And their nobles with fetters of iron;
>
> To execute on them the written judgement — This honor have all His saints.

This passage refers to our spiritual battle. The high praises of God in our mouths and a two-edged sword in our hands both pertain to the weapons of our warfare.

We, the saints of God, execute God's vengeance on the nations through intercession and by praying for repentance, forgiveness, and mercy for the sins of the nations, which often are connected to the ruling demonic powers.

Verse 9 gives us a further picture of intercession. We are *enforcing, executing,* and *activating* the power of the Spirit of God over what is written in the Word.

We do not participate in warfare because we think it's fun to do. There is a purpose in it: to enforce what has been written and to fight for the nations of the world.

The Church is to bind the strong man and principalities and powers through the power of intercession. You have this honor — take it!

Meeting God — By Accident!

A third quality of the Prayer of Intercession that we find in the use of the word *paga* is revealed in Genesis 28:10. Here, *paga* means an accidental meeting place; to come on something by chance, to come to a place by chance, and to discover that God is there.

In Genesis, we find that Jacob chose a sleeping place for the night. He was not expecting anything out of the ordinary to happen there; it was simply a good place to rest. That night, however, heaven came down to earth and transformed that ordinary place into a place where a life-changing encounter occurred with God.

How often have you had a thought about someone or something that wouldn't go away? You kept thinking about that person, even though you had no reason in the natural to do so. Often, the Holy Spirit will come to you through simple thoughts. Those thoughts must be weighed in your spirit and mind in line with the Word so you learn the difference between your thoughts and God's thoughts.

If you'll take your simple thought and begin to pray about it, often the Holy Spirit will take hold with you, and what you thought was a coincidence or an accident turns into a place that God wants to make Himself or His will known to you through intercession. He wants to use you to help that person or situation through the Prayer of Intercession.

Your experience with God comes, in a sense, as an accidental meeting — but God really shows up! What a wonderful side of intercession this is when the Holy Spirit shows you who or what to pray for when He knows it's needed.

Paul said to pray always, to be easily given to prayer — all kinds of prayer — and that includes intercession. Be easily given to intercession! God is looking for people to stand for and with Him. He is looking for those who will fight in the warfare that is going on in the heavenlies, and for those who will pray for His will to be established on earth as in heaven in the lives of individuals, cities, and nations.

Are you willing to take the challenge? Are you willing to "pray the price"? Then God wants *you*. He'll flow from you to bring blessing and change to this generation through the power of intercessory prayer.

I have not taken the time in this chapter to explain the details of *how to* intercede. My purpose here has been to give a basic, simple, and elementary understanding of what intercessory prayer is. The lesson is in no way complete, because the subject is worthy of a book all its own.

Because intercessory prayer is so close to my heart, and because I learned so much about prayer in intercession, I am prayerfully considering doing that as a future project. But for now I feel what I have written in this chapter, together with the principles of other chapters — i.e., Praying With the Understanding (Chapter 4), The World of Tongues (Chapter 11), Simple Tongues (Chapter 12), Second Level — Groanings (Chapter 13) — is sufficient for the intercessory prayer teaching in this book.

Ask God to make you an intercessor for Him, and you will be surprised how much the Holy Spirit will teach you and help you to become a powerful intercessor for the nations and for the last-day revival in the earth. Ask Him now, and start praying today!

Chapter 15
The Prayer of Forgiveness

And whenever you stand praying, if you have anything against anyone, forgive him, that your Father in heaven may also forgive you your trespasses (Mark 11:25).

The Prayer of Forgiveness helps us deal with the condition of our hearts in our everyday relationships with other people. Jesus is so practical, He knew we would have these relationships and we would often need the help of this type of prayer.

The Prayer of Forgiveness allows us to stay free from bitterness, unforgiveness, and resentment that can result from our dealings with those around us. It is so important that much is said about forgiveness throughout the Bible, and Jesus often spoke about it Himself.

The Prayer of Forgiveness is vital in keeping our relationships pure. A lack of forgiveness will quench our faith. In fact, in the above scripture, Jesus tied the Prayer of Forgiveness with the Prayer of Faith.

Unforgiveness is a killer of faith. It will cause your faith not to work. When we are harboring unforgiveness, we are not walking in love, and Galatians 5:6 says that "faith works by love." No love, no working faith!

That's why Jesus said, that when you stand praying in faith, praying the Prayer of Faith, if you have anything against anyone, you must forgive him; you must be sure you have nothing against anyone.

Forgiveness is a key to the working of your faith. It is a beautiful trait that should characterize our lifestyle.

Let me share a story with you about how forgiveness caused faith for healing. I was in a meeting with another minister and a woman who had severe arthritis came up for prayer. It was so bad, she had to use a walker to get around.

We were about to pray for her when my friend said, "The Holy Spirit tells me that you have unforgiveness in your life, and before we pray for you, we need to deal with it." (Not every sickness is caused by unforgiveness, but it can open the door to it.)

"That's right," the woman said, "I *hate* my husband! He's dead now, but he treated me like dirt all my life, and I hate him."

Imagine — her husband was dead, but she was still full of hatred, unforgiveness, bitterness, and resentment toward him. Her life was depressing and defeated because she was so angry.

"Well, are you ready to get that out of your life?"

"Yes," she said, "I'm ready." The Holy Spirit had been preparing her. She began to cry, to repent, and to forgive. She prayed the Prayer of Forgiveness, we laid hands on her and prayed for her to be healed — and *nothing* happened. She walked away exactly the same way she'd come.

The next night, the pastor said, "If God has done something good for you in these meetings, I want you to testify." 'Way in the back, a woman lifted her hand and began to shout, "I have a testimony!" She stood up. It was the woman we'd prayed for the night before!

"I have a great testimony," she said. "I've been taking many aspirins every day for years because of my arthritis. I walked with a walker for years because of this arthritis." She walked out in the aisle; no walker.

She was shouting again. "Today, for the first time in many years, I don't have my walker, and for the first time in many years I haven't taken any aspirins, and I'm not going to take any, because I'm completely healed. I don't have any more arthritis in my body, glory be to God!"

The whole church went wild, screaming and shouting praises to God. It was a *tremendous* testimony, not only because she was healed in her body, but because she was happy and free because of the Prayer of Forgiveness.

We Are Commanded To Forgive

Paul knew this, and in Ephesians 4:32 he actually *commanded* Christians to be forgiving with one another: "And be kind to one another, tenderhearted, forgiving one another, just as God in Christ also forgave you."

Christ has forgiven *you*. When you were a mess and did all kinds of crazy, detestable things — when you were against God, bound in sin — God in His love and mercy totally and completely forgave you. You didn't deserve it, but because of His grace, His love, and His mercy He completely forgave you.

God loves you so much that every thought, every word, and every action that opposed Him, He forgave. And if you ask Him about them, He doesn't even *remember* them, because His blood washed away your sin as far as the East is from the West.

So Paul said, "You *must* be kind to one another, tenderhearted and *forgiving* one another even as God in Christ forgave you." Just think about how much God has forgiven you!

God wants you, as His child, to forgive others just as He has forgiven you. It's not impossible, although sometimes it may seem so. What the Word of God tells us to do, we *can* do. God Himself will help us.

Let me explain something about unforgiveness. You don't have to dig around and wonder if there's unforgiveness in your life. If you have an open and honest heart, you will *know* if it's in you. If your heart is open, God will show you. He will reveal it to you by the Holy Spirit.

The Holy Spirit shines the light on your words, attitudes, thoughts, and actions, and it will be clear. You don't have to be confused and soulishly groping in a quest to find unforgiveness.

"Oh, I wonder if I've forgiven. I wonder if I have unforgiveness in my heart?" Trust the Holy Spirit to show you. Ask Him to show you, and when He does, accept it and pray the Prayer of Forgiveness. Get rid of it! It's *dangerous* to let bitterness and unforgiveness take root in our hearts. In fact, it's a sin.

If there is a root of bitterness in your heart, let the power of God through the Prayer of Forgiveness help root it out. God wants you to be clean and pure, full of mercy and forgiveness in all your relationships. It may seem impossible, but Jesus will help you do it, if you are open and willing to change.

Protection for Our Heart

Because the Prayer of Forgiveness deals with our heart, one of the effects of walking in the power of this prayer is a heart that is guarded and protected from unwanted enemies. It *protects* us from hatred, bitterness, resentment, and strife.

Because we all have relationships with others, there are opportunities for all of us to let these negative things come into our lives. The Prayer of Forgiveness keeps our heart protected so they can't get in and take root.

When we pray the Prayer of Forgiveness, it is an act of love and faith that puts mercy into motion: God's mercy and our mercy. It is a way to release the love of God to other people and to come into peace and security in our own mind toward people, even in negative situations.

I heard someone say this once: When someone sins against you, when someone speaks evil against you, when there is confusion and unforgiveness in a relationship, the way you should react is to consider that the person is turning in a prayer request for himself to you.

So instead of responding the way the world does — to hit back, be angry, bitter, hard, and unforgiving — we can realize, by the love of God, that he is asking you to pray for him. This person needs help. He is saying by persecuting you, by being in strife with you, by hitting you with his words, "I need prayer. I need prayer." If we will respond with prayer for those who curse us (see Matthew 5:44), it will protect our hearts.

You can make forgiveness a lifestyle. When people come against you and sin against you, just remember they are turning in a request for prayer. They're asking you to pray for them. If you do that, it will help you walk in love, forgiveness, and understanding in every relationship you have.

One of the greatest dangers of unforgiveness in a Christian's life is that it can become bitterness and hardness toward God. Many times bitterness goes hand in hand with rebellion, because one of the definitions of rebellion is bitterness.

For example, in Isaiah 1:2, God says the children of Israel were rebellious, and in verse 6 the fruit of the rebellion was wounds, bruises, and sores.

Many people say, "Oh, it's my personality; I'm just so easily hurt and rejected." They allow self-pity, unforgiveness, and so forth to operate in their lives. Others think it is the right response, even the legal response, but that is self-deception.

I'm not saying that hurt is not real. Hurt is a very real thing that must be dealt with, but the healing for any hurt is found in Jesus Christ.

There are people who actually *worship* their hurts; they worship rejection, and use it as an excuse to do their own thing or blame others. "Well, I am so rejected. Please pray for my rejection."

Rebellion And Hardness Must Go!

If there is no change, the root of bitterness turns into rebellion, and this rebellion toward God and people must go!

There can come a point with wounds that if they are not dealt with by the Prayer of Forgiveness, by repentance, and by praying about the relationship, they turn into walls of isolation and hardness of heart in a person's life. Then they become calloused in their heart - hard toward other people, hard toward their family, hardened in their emotions, and hard toward God.

"No one's going to hurt me again. I've been hurt too much in the past. You don't know how I've been mistreated. You don't know what's been said, or how those words have hurt me!"

That hurt causes walls of independence to go up that protect the self-life of the person. Sometimes it is not easy to see those walls — they wear many masks — but the hurt has turned into hidden independence and rebellion, most likely toward people and often toward God.

Jesus wants you to be free from hurt, rejection, rebellion, and every negative word that's been spoken into your life! He wants you to be delivered from that pattern in your life. It has *no right* to harbor inside you unless you let it.

Hatred, rejection, walls, and bitterness — these all have to come down. *Every* wall must come down in Jesus' Name. All the hurt has to go. Stop accepting it and enjoying the self-pity, and begin to rise up against this stronghold!

"But I've been hurt, and I'm going to protect myself." *Any protection of self is rebellion.* The minute you try to protect yourself, it's rebellion, because rebellion is simply independence from God and dependence on self. Any way you look at it, it is rebellion.

"Well, it's just my *personality* to be hurt and rejected all the time." No it's not. You have accepted a lie, and that hurt and that rebellion toward God and man have to go! We are created to be vulnerable to God and to one another; not to the wrong spirit of coming under another's control, but to true, pure love, tenderness, and openness.

If bitterness and hurt are not dealt with, they turn into hardness, walls, rebellion, protection of self, independence from others and, most dangerous of all, from God. He can't deal with us if we won't let the walls down. Others can't help us, if we won't let the walls down. We are closed to God's Spirit, and it can affect every part of our life if we are not careful.

Bitterness, hurt, and rebellion are dangerous things. But, thank God, there's forgiveness and true healing in the Lord. You have a choice to make: You can choose either forgiveness or bitterness, hurt, and a lifestyle of rejection. It's better to choose forgiveness than bitterness. Choose to be better, not bitter.

Choose to forgive. It's not the choice of the flesh, the world, or the way we've been trained, but it *is* the way of the Spirit. Choose *now* to forgive! If these patterns have an uncontrollable grip on you, cry out to God to set you free, and He will help you! Press in for your freedom. Jesus is the Healer and Deliverer!

Walking Continually in Forgiveness

In the New Testament, we find that Peter had questions about this area of forgiveness. In Matthew 18:21, he asks Jesus:

> Lord, how many times may my brother sin against me and I forgive him and let it go? [As many as] up to seven times?

> Jesus answered him, I tell you, not up to seven times, but seventy times seven! Matthew 18:21,22 (*Amplified*)

Peter thought forgiving seven times was enough. "How many times do I have to deal with this," he asked, "seven times?" "No," Jesus responded, "Forgiveness is so vital to you, it's not just seven times; you must be willing to forgive 490 times!"

That's how Jesus looked at it and how He wants us to look at it. That's the importance He placed on forgiveness. I don't believe He was referring to praying the Prayer of Forgiveness over and over again; we can pray the Prayer of Forgiveness and know it was worked by faith.

I believe Jesus is talking about the fact that there will always be opportunities to forgive, and no matter how many times we have to do it, we've got to continually walk with forgiveness in our lives and purity toward others in our hearts.

God looks seriously at how you and I deal with our relationships with other people. He looks at bitterness and unforgiveness very seriously. Of course, the easiest thing for us to do, and the thing many people do, is to put the blame on other people for all their problems.

However, when dealing with forgiveness and our attitudes, motives, and thoughts, the Holy Spirit always points the finger directly at *us*. He says, in effect, "It isn't important what someone else is doing — what about *you*? How are *you* reacting?"

This is exactly what Peter brought up: his own responsibility in relationships. He asked, "How many times, when my brother sins against me, must *I* forgive him?"

We Must Let the Debt Go

In Peter's question we discover the first step in the Prayer of Forgiveness: *You* must forgive the person who has wronged you. What did Peter say? "How many times must *I* forgive him?" You must, from your heart, forgive.

This doesn't have anything to do with feelings, because our feelings may want to punch the person in the nose and never see his face again!

But when you and I choose to do it God's way and work with the Holy Spirit, we must do what verse 35 of Matthew 18 says: From our hearts we must freely forgive. *You* must, in front of God, with a confession of your mouth, openly *forgive* that person.

What does it mean to forgive? Look again at how *The Amplified Bible* reads: "Lord, how many times may my brother sin against me and I forgive him and let it go?" What does it mean to forgive? It means to *let it go!*

Jesus let go, for us, of everything we did wrong. Every debt we had, He let go. Every sin we ever sinned, He forgave. He released us from it and let it go.

How many times do I have to let this go? Don't bother to count, Jesus was saying; just keep walking in forgiveness.

We can see this principle again in Matthew 6:12, in The Lord's Prayer: "And forgive us our debts, As we forgive our debtors."

Notice it says, "Lord, *You* forgive us as *we* forgive those who have sinned against us." *The Amplified Bible* says:

> And forgive us our debts, as we also have forgiven (left, remitted, and let go of the debts, and have given up resentment against) our debtors.

I like that. As we have left, as we have let go, of the debt. It's so easy to want to hold onto the debt. "Well, I'll forgive, but . . . " No, you have to let go of the debt. You must choose to let go of what that person owes. You must pay their bill with your forgiveness. You must clean the bill! Don't try to figure out how to get back at them, how much they owe, or how much they've hurt you. You must, from your heart, forgive them.

Do Not Charge Them, Father

The second step in the Prayer of Forgiveness is to ask God to forgive your debtor. The story of Stephen in Acts 7 is a good example of this second step.

Stephen was preaching under the anointing of the Holy Spirit, but the religious people of that day could not stand the power, wisdom, and authority of God that was coming out of him as he spoke. They put their hands in their ears and ran toward him to kill him! In verses 59 and 60, we read:

> And they stoned Stephen as he was calling on God and saying, "Lord Jesus, receive my spirit."

> Then he knelt down and cried out with a loud voice, "Lord, do not charge them with this sin." And when he had said this, he fell asleep.

What did Stephen pray here? He cried out in the Prayer of Forgiveness, "Father, forgive them!" He prayed on their behalf that God would not charge them with the evil they were doing.

Jesus prayed exactly the same way. Do you remember what some of His last words were when He was on the cross? "Father, forgive them." He was saying, "I forgive them and, Father, I ask You to forgive them and not to put this on their charge." He was crying out that they would be released; that God would forgive them.

There is a side to the Prayer of Forgiveness that is a form of intercession; a side where we stand in the gap, that God would not remember the sin of the person who has sinned against us. That's how much *love* there is in this prayer. It doesn't have anything to do with our feelings, good or bad.

Remember, it's a *choice* we make. We *choose* to pray the Prayer of Forgiveness, and when we believe when we pray, it works. God hears and answers this kind of prayer. He loves it!

Did You Enter In?

In the Prayer of Forgiveness we have: step one, *you* must forgive them; step two: ask *God* to forgive them; and step three, ask God to forgive *you*.

If you have entered into the battle through complaining, ugly thoughts, ugly words, feelings of hatred, and so forth, you have given place to unforgiveness, and you need to ask God to forgive you for your attitude, thoughts, and words.

You need to call it what it is: sin. Just ask God to forgive you. Pray, "Father, first of all, I thank You that You showed me that this attitude was in my heart. I thank You, Father, that You love me and You showed me this. Father, I ask You to forgive So-and-so for what he did and said and for how he acted, and for all the others who have been involved in this situation.

"I ask in faith, out of the love of my heart, and with all the sincerity of my heart. I ask You, Father, to forgive them and, Father, I forgive them. I *forgive* all those words they said that hurt me and are not right. I forgive them, I ask You to forgive them, and together we let that go from their case.

"And Father, I ask You to forgive me. I came into this and I thought negatively about it. I have been angry about it, and I have spoken angry words. I've harbored bitterness in my heart toward this, and I don't want it to go any farther. I don't want a root of bitterness to be in me.

"Father, I ask You to forgive me. I know that I've said things in a wrong spirit and a wrong attitude about this person and about these people and, Father, I ask You to forgive me. I call it sin. I have sinned against You and against them. I confess it, and I thank You that when I confess my sin, You are faithful and just to forgive me and restore me. I thank You, Father, for the purity and the cleansing of the Holy Spirit over my heart and mind and this relationship."

You don't have to be religious. Just pray out of the sincerity in your heart and in faith. Call it sin, and ask God to forgive you.

Release the Hurt

Now, step four: Release the emotion of the situation and the relationship to the Lord. Pray about the hurt and the rejection and release it in the presence of the Lord. Choose to let the rejection, feelings, and hurt go when you pray.

It's very simple. Pray, "Father, I also ask You and I thank You that You have healed me right now of those words and the hurt. I don't want to come to You with self-pity, pride, or hardness toward You or anyone.

"Father, I ask You to touch my heart. As an act of my will, I choose not to be hurt. I release the hurt, the rejection, and the emotion in this relationship. Father, I bless those who curse me.

"Thank You, Father, for your power in my heart and mind that takes away hurt, rejection, and bad feelings. I receive your power now. I have it now, and I thank You for it in Jesus' Name. The feelings, the hurt, the emotion is touched right now by the Holy Spirit. I thank you for it. I receive it in Jesus' Name. I *refuse* to accept hurt, anger, isolation, frustration, or rejection.

"Thank You, Father, for the freedom and the flow of the Holy Spirit touching my heart and mind right now. I take it by faith, and I'm *healed* in my heart, my mind, and my soul. I look to You, Holy Spirit, as my Comforter."

Sometimes, as the Holy Spirit heals, there are tears of cleansing and release. Let those tears flow. The Holy Spirit will help you. Be sure not to cry simply because you feel sorry for yourself, but from your heart rivers of healing can flow.

Many people pray to forgive, but they never release the emotion that goes with it. As an act of your faith, by the words of your mouth, release the emotion, the anger, the hurt, and the pain. When you release it, the power of the Holy Spirit, if you believe, will comfort and fill you with the mercy, grace, and healing you need.

Choose To Forget

The fifth and last step is: Forget it! Right there in your prayer, just forget it. Again, this is something you have to *choose* to do. Many people *want* to remember it, think about it, talk about it, and remember it some more. No! Forget it! If you'll do that in your prayer, the Holy Spirit will help you.

This doesn't mean the relationship is automatically going to change; you have to understand that. There may still be things that have to be dealt with, but what you're dealing with in this prayer is *your* heart and keeping it clean and pure. When the Holy Spirit leads you to pray this way, *do it!* There's power in this kind of prayer.

If you have to pray in tongues, you can add that in here, too. It's no problem. Pray in the Spirit if you want to, and then say, "Father, now that I've prayed about this, I leave it here in your presence. I choose not to remember it. Holy Spirit, help me not to remember this. I leave it in your presence. It is finished. It is done. I *forget* it because of the blood; because of love, in Jesus' Name.

"Holy Spirit, help me to walk this out. Help me, Father, because I still have to deal with these people; but now I can deal in purity and love, and I don't have to deal out of hurt, bitterness, unforgiveness, or hardness. I can walk in your wisdom, purity, and love and walk through this relationship victoriously, with your power.

"I thank You, Father, for your help in this relationship. In Jesus' Name, I will keep my heart right. Thank You, Father, that now I can walk in forgiveness. Let forgiveness flow from my life. I thank You for it.

"Satan, I rebuke you and your hold on my life. You can't bind me in this situation, in Jesus' Name. I break the power of all rejection and every evil force released against me, in Jesus' Name. Thank You, Jesus, for victory. In Jesus' Name, Amen."

The ultimate goal is for you to develop a lifestyle of forgiveness. When you need to pray this prayer to cleanse your heart and to release others, you have it. You can have a lifestyle where you forgive easily and quickly, and you walk in the spirit of forgiveness.

You can be totally delivered from every bondage in human relationships and be happy, pure, and free before God and man. It's so wonderful to get unforgiveness, bitterness, and resentment out of your life and to keep them out — forever!

Chapter 16
Group Prayer

The Early Church was born on the Day of Pentecost, when the disciples were all filled with the Holy Spirit and began to speak in other tongues. The Church was literally born in prayer! One of the first things they did was pray. And the spirit of prayer that came over them and into them that day became an absolute in every aspect of the life of the Early Church.

The first believers not only began in prayer, but the Bible says they *continued* daily in prayer (see Acts 2:42). The entire Book of Acts describes the supernatural life and order that was found in the Early Church. Both the universal church and the local church today can and should maintain that same standard.

Just as the Body of Christ was originated in prayer, so must the end-time Church be a strong, praying Church to be original!

Before discussing some of the principles of corporate prayer, I would like to clarify the kind of prayer groups I am referring to when I talk about group prayer. I am convinced that in these last days, God is going to do mighty things in and through the local church. Therefore, the prayer I am referring to in this chapter primarily deals with groups within the local church authority structure.

I am aware that there are group settings other than the local church. Some of them are rare, like groups praying under evangelistic ministries. This is fine as long as there is a ministry representative present with authority and responsibility for the prayers and actions of the group.

It has been my experience that prayer groups outside of proper biblical order and some kind of local church or pastoral authority are usually weak and open targets. The devil attacks them through members' carnal or spiritual problems that are not being dealt with through proper authority and counsel.

Remember, when you are under authority, you have authority. You can use that authority powerfully in prayer!

Another aspect of corporate prayer to consider is what actually constitutes a prayer group. With the prayer habits of the Early Church described in the Book of Acts as our guideline for principles on group prayer, we can ascertain that most of the prayer in Acts was done by *the complete church unit*, not just small, special groups.

It would be foolish to assume that we wouldn't have small groups that pray within the church, but the first and foremost prayer group in the church is the corporate local body itself.

The power and privilege of prayer has been given to the local church as a whole, not just to the pastor or the intercessors. Jesus wants *everyone* in your local church family to be a strong prayer warrior! The Early Church gathered all who believed together and they prayed (Acts 2:42,44).

The Church Has the Keys

God has given local bodies of believers tremendous authority in the spiritual realm. Matthew 16:18,19 tells us:

And I also say to you that you are Peter, and on this rock I will build My church, and the gates of Hades shall not prevail against it.

And I will give you the keys of the kingdom of heaven, and whatever you bind on earth will be bound in heaven, and whatever you loose on earth will be loosed in heaven.

Jesus says here that He gave these keys to the Church. The more believers in the local church we can get together to pray, the better. Local churches in the last days need to be trained to take hold of the keys Jesus gave them — and to grab them *together*. Then whatever the church binds on earth will be bound in heaven.

Tremendous power is released when local churches use part of their meeting or one particular meeting to pray together. Of course, there has been a fight over this in the past, because it makes the devil nervous to think that 50, 200, 500, 1,000, or 2,000 believers could actually get together and pray strongly together!

For this to happen, we must change our thinking. In fact, this may already be new thinking for you, but I am convinced that God wants to do a miracle in your church by developing the men, women, boys, and girls into a strong praying body. Then out from that body come the various smaller groups.

One of several corporate prayer meetings found in the Bible is described in Acts 4:23-31:

> And being let go, they went to their own companions and reported all that the chief priests and elders had said to them.
>
> So when they heard that, they raised their voice to God with one accord and said: "Lord, You are God, who made heaven and earth and the sea, and all that is in them,
>
> "who by the mouth of Your servant David have said: 'Why did the nations rage, And the people plot vain things?
>
> The kings of the earth took their stand, And the rulers were gathered together Against the Lord and against His Christ.'
>
> "For truly against Your holy Servant Jesus, whom You anointed, both Herod and Pontius Pilate, with the Gentiles and the people of Israel, were gathered together
>
> "to do whatever Your hand and Your purpose determined before to be done.
>
> "Now, Lord, look on their threats, and grant to Your servants that with all boldness they may speak Your word,
>
> "by stretching out Your hand to heal, and that signs and wonders may be done through the name of Your holy Servant Jesus."
>
> And when they had prayed, the place where they were assembled together was shaken; and they were all filled with the Holy Spirit, and they spoke the word of God with boldness.

Unity in Prayer

In these verses lies one of the keys to success in group prayer. It says, "they raised their voice to God with one accord." They were in one accord; or in unity. This unity is a key to group prayer. It is not everyone in the group doing his own thing his own way.

Group prayer is one mind, one spirit, one direction, one purpose, and one heart. Therein is true unity — not soulish unity — but unity created by the Holy Spirit. To be successful in group prayer, this kind of unity must be developed in the group and in the prayer time. It is vital in the production of Bible results when you pray together.

In the prayer school I currently direct, I demand that the intercessors exercise the discipline of being in unity in prayer. One person isn't on one side of the room praying for his grandmother, while someone else is trying to stay awake, another person on the other side of the room is thinking about what time it is, someone else is wondering what he's going to have for lunch and, in the middle of it all, another person is groaning, travailing, and weeping in intercession for a lost and dying world. That is not effective!

We all come together with the leadership, and we flow together in unity — in one mind, one spirit, and one accord. Sometimes we pray on our own, but we know what we are praying for. We all pray for that subject in the same direction. That's what made their prayers so powerful in the Book of Acts.

It is also important not to neglect the fact that they lifted up their voices to God. These people were not quiet, shy, or intimidated about praying! They were not whispering, and they were not in silent prayer. There is a time to be still before the Lord; however, subdued prayer was not the normal pattern in the Early Church — intense prayer was!

For example, when Peter was in prison, "constant prayer was offered to God for him by the church" (Acts 12:5). The word "constant" here also means "regularly, persistently, and earnestly (with sincerity and seriousness)." Other translations say that "long and *fervent* prayer was offered" *(Weymouth)* and "there was a *continual stream* of prayer going up to God from the church on his behalf" *(Knox)*. I heard another minister say once that the Greek words here imply that the church was actually "stretched out intensely" in prayer for Peter.

It certainly doesn't sound like a dry, boring prayer meeting to me! Together these believers were in united, intense prayer, *lifting up* their voices to God.

Ingredients for Unity

There were several ingredients that produced this powerful unity. First, they were *together in mind*. In other words, they were all thinking the same way and about the same thing.

They took the thoughts of their minds captive — and sometimes you have to do that in prayer, because your mind will want to wander. You can't be thinking about everything and everyone when you come into prayer.

194

You have to take hold of your thoughts, come into the mind of the Spirit, and put your attention on what you're praying for. Demand that your mind concentrate! There's strength when we come together in one mind!

Being of one mind also means that there is knowledge and understanding in the prayer group about what is being prayed for. Be as specific as possible to avoid the "just-praying" syndrome. This will make people secure and stable in the group, and will put a stop to the idea that being vague is somehow spiritual.

Second, they were *together in purpose.* They all had made the same decision: "We're here together to break down this resistance and do the work of God." They were there to pray. In group prayer, the purpose is to *pray.* They weren't there to build their ministries, reputations, or to gain personally; they were there to meet with God and pray!

You have not come to the prayer meeting to teach, talk, gossip, drink coffee, or personally minister to everyone present — you have come to pray! That is a decision every member of the group needs to understand and make individually: "We have come here to pray."

The flesh, even the enemy, can trick you and water down your prayer time if you don't make that decision. You must make a disciplined choice that you're not going to sing or do something else the whole time, but you're going to pray — to give yourself to the Holy Spirit and the work of God in the spiritual world.

Remember also that the purpose for prayer is not to "feel good." Feelings are often a cover for the flesh. A successful outcome in prayer is not judged by anyone's feelings. Prayer is not based on how we feel, or whether we feel like we've prayed well or not.

We're led by the Spirit of God. We pray by faith and flow in the Spirit. Whether we feel good or not, we're there to pray. When everyone has that same purpose, it will help keep the group in true spiritual unity.

They were also *together in vision.* The Bible tells us in Proverbs 29:18 that without a vision, people perish, or go in a wrong way. Having the same vision gives you purpose and direction. If you know what God has said, you know where you're going.

When everyone in the group lays down his or her own ideas and visions and comes into the same vision — whether the vision of the church, of the ministry, etc. — it produces strength that the devil hates but God loves! When all take up God's heart and goals — what God has said and longs to see manifested in and through the church — it's powerful!

Not only were they together in mind, in purpose, and in vision, they were also *together in spirit*. They were all of the same flavor and the same heart. Remember what it said in Acts 4:23? That the disciples being let go, "went to their own companions." They went back to their own company, to the people with whom they had a covenant, to the ones who thought, prayed, and believed like they did.

Being together in spirit is vital if the group is to function effectively in prayer and have the powerful results God desires. You must find the people who have the same spiritual attitude and climate you have. Find your own company; find those who have the same heart you do — and then *pray* together!

Give Focus to Your Prayer Time

They also had the *same prayer request*. They were all praying for the same thing; in the same direction. When we're praying together, it's important that everyone knows what we're praying for and hooks up with that direction or prayer request and goes with it. The Holy Spirit may impress people to pray about different things in that one area, but we are all to go in the same direction.

For example, the leader could say, "Let's pray for Czechoslovakia," and within the group someone may pray for revival in Czechoslovakia, and someone else may pray for something else in Czechoslovakia, and so on. Although each is praying about a different aspect of the topic at hand, everyone is praying for the same prayer request — Czechoslovakia.

When everyone knows what the group is to pray for, it gives focus in prayer. You can pray directly with the leader, and afterwards you can pray by yourselves under that specific subject. The leader should decide what specific topics and areas to pray for. Naturally, we don't want to limit the Holy Spirit and what He wants to pray through us, but He does work with us, and He will honor our faith. We can decide what we're going to pray for.

What I usually do is ask the Holy Spirit, "What do You want us to pray for today?" Or I take a specific need we can pray for, or areas I feel as the leader, that the group needs to cover and keep covered in the Spirit by prayer. Having a topic to pray for gives focus in your prayers.

Some days I say, "Let's just pray and find out what the Holy Spirit wants us to pray for." We don't do that every day, because it can be ineffective and rigid, but some days we do, and it's very powerful. My usual practice is that I decide what we will pray for. Be led by the Spirit of God when you pick a topic. He'll tell you what He wants prayed for that day, and He will acknowledge your sensible choices.

How Do We Pray?

You may be asking, "How often do you pray for a certain topic?" It depends on what you're praying for. Sometimes you only pray once for a particular area, but you can also take prayer projects — outreaches in the church or ministry, different departments, the pastor, and so forth — that you pray for over and over again.

Remember, intercessory prayer is not just praying one time. It's praying over and over and giving birth to the will of God for what you're praying for.

You can also take special things that will be happening in the church weeks before they come and spend many hours praying for them. Pray the Word for them; pray what's in your heart; pray by the Holy Spirit, doing spiritual warfare for those situations, and you'll see tremendous results because of it.

Of course, you can also pray for emergencies that come up, but you can't live on just needs and emergencies you see around you. To be effective in prayer, you need to have a focus.

When there is an emergency, be ready to pray — to take it in the Spirit, find out what God says about it, and then pray for it. You can and should be able to be flexible and flow in all different kinds and ways of prayer.

Sometimes you may pray the whole time about one prayer request. Can you imagine that — a whole hour spent praying for one subject because that was what was required that day? Be led by the Spirit and find where the flow of life is for each request.

That doesn't necessarily mean you'll always be in strong warfare. You're open to strong warfare, but you're also open to go down any other avenue the Holy Spirit wants to take. Give as much time as necessary to that particular subject and then go on.

Sometimes I don't necessarily feel the Holy Spirit is saying something special, so I tell the prayer warriors, "We've prayed enough for this now. Let's change to another subject." At other times, I sense the Holy Spirit leading a certain direction or grabbing hold with us to pray, and I say, "All right, this is where the flow of life is. Let's pray this way. Let's pray over this for a while!"

When it lifts — when the Holy Spirit has used us as vessels and I know by the Spirit that it's time to go on to something else — I let it get quiet, and I begin to lead the people into praise. After a rest and an acknowledgement of the note of victory for a moment, we change to another subject; another area.

You'll learn as you mature in prayer how to flow in this as a group. Just remember that everyone needs to know what you're praying for, and you all need to keep together on the request so you'll have a focus and be more effective.

In Group Prayer — Pray!

We've seen that the key to group prayer is having one mind, one spirit, one vision, one direction, one purpose, and one heart. Now let's look at the different functions of the prayer group.

Of course, the first and the foremost reason your group exists is *to pray*. You must diligently guard this purpose, because one of the things people's flesh would like to do is to get away from prayer and turn the prayer group into a meeting, a teaching session, a social time, or a "Bless-Me Club."

The purpose, however, of your coming together is none of these things. You are meeting together as a group to pray! You've come to pray and to be trained to pray. That's why we call one of our groups "prayer school" — it's a school of prayer.

Always keep in mind that the number one purpose for gathering is for prayer.

The second purpose of corporate prayer is teaching. Although it may not seem significant in the light of the power of prayer, imparting knowledge is important for effective prayer. No prayer warrior will grow beyond his knowledge of the Word of God.

Teaching keeps prayer warriors healthy and instructed, and allows their faith to continue to expand as they hear the Word. Colossians 1:28 tells us to teach and admonish every man so we can present them complete in Christ. Let's build complete prayer warriors!

Always remember this: In spite of its importance, teaching is the second purpose of your prayer group. It must not be allowed to take the place of prayer.

Third, the purpose for group prayer is demonstration. Paul said in First Corinthians 2:4 that he had not come just in preaching and in teaching, but in demonstration of the Spirit. There were manifestations of the proof and evidence of God's power when Paul ministered. Paul went to Corinth, but he was not just preaching; the people saw and felt the power of the Holy Spirit through his ministry.

In prayer, the Holy Spirit teaches and demonstrates prayer through the leader and through the intercessors themselves. You experience and feel what it is like to pray in different ways. You develop a relationship with the Person of the Holy Spirit. It's important to learn to flow with the Holy Spirit in prayer, to demonstrate the power of God, and to flow in the gifts of the Spirit.

You learn in prayer to move with God in actual practice and demonstration. For example, the atmosphere in a prayer meeting will feel different in worship, as you experience the holiness of God, from when you are entering into second level groanings (see Chapter 13). It is a living and a powerful experience when the intercessors develop sensitivity to how different prayers operate and how they actually feel in and around you when you pray.

Last, the fourth purpose for group prayer is ministry to those who come. It's not a good practice in a prayer meeting to consistently make it a time of personal ministry for everyone. Some prayer groups turn into just that, where everyone comes to the prayer group simply to be ministered to, but that is not what your prayer group is for. *You're there to pray for others!*

There are rare times when there are people who need personal ministry, so we are open to pray for them. The leader and other group members can be aware of the needs of people who are present; however, our personal needs don't have first place. In our prayer school there are times, and they are few, when we minister to each other; but the most important function of our group is praying for others.

I believe that the needs of group members should primarily be met in other spiritual settings in the church, and that the group leaders can help see to it that those needs get met outside the actual prayer meeting. Remember what happened to Job:

> . . . the Lord restored Job's losses when he prayed for his friends. Indeed the Lord gave Job twice as much as he had before. (Job 42:10)

Allow for Variety

As you come into corporate prayer, you'll discover that each time your prayer group meets it will be different. Of course, you'll have some of the same patterns and principles you follow each time, and that is good. God will bless an outline and a structure, because He is a God of order, and He has designated courses and boundaries that He uses to release His power. Yet, at the same time, it's good to have as much variety and freedom as possible.

I'm not encouraging so much openness that every day the people wonder what's going to happen. Do not give in to the fleshly desire in people who want prayer to be something spectacular or soulishly thrilling, although it *is* exciting.

Prayer is not to be fleshly entertainment. Of course, you should have a variety of ways to pray; otherwise, when you pray every day, it could get boring. Keep your standards, principles,and disciplines high, and then be open to variety and to flowing with the Holy Spirit.

In Appendices 1 and 2 you will find spiritual exercises you can use in your prayer group. They will help bring scriptural variety and growth to the group members. They include things that will enable you to learn how to pray different kinds of prayer. I believe the program will be a blessing to you if you incorporate it in your prayer group to promote spiritual growth. Don't let it take the place of prayer.

Different prayer groups have different personalities, but we want to use all kinds of prayer with structure and order, led by the Holy Spirit in the fervency of the Spirit of God.

Faithful to Prayer

It's important for your prayer group to have as many people present on a regular basis as possible. Some prayer groups are weak because they have people coming in and out all the time. People come one week and don't come the next.

It's important that you as a prayer warrior make a decision to be with your group as much as possible. Don't let things distract you. Remember, the devil never wants you to pray, but he is defeated.

People are at different levels in prayer, but if they'll come every time, and if you can get a group of people who are committed to praying, it will cause depth and strength to develop in that prayer group.

End in Victory!

The right way to end a prayer meeting is with victory! Philippians 4:6 states:

Be anxious for nothing, but in everything by prayer and supplication, with thanksgiving, let your requests be made know to God.

The scriptural way a prayer meeting should conclude is by everyone in the group giving thanks for that particular request, or for everything you've prayed for that day.

Let the rejoicing, the joy, and the thanksgiving flow by faith, knowing that God has heard your prayers; that He's working at that moment in all that you have prayed for.

Rejoice before the Lord. Sometimes you may even dance before the Lord before you leave. Spend some time in the spirit of joy because your prayers are working and because joy is your strength.

God's Word declares that we can and should pray — and one of the ways we can do that and see great results is in a group. God intends for your prayer group to be mighty and powerful, sensitive, and skillful in the Spirit of God.

Your group can change your city and nation and reach to the ends of the earth, touching many people. By the power of God you can pray effective, fervent prayers together and see tremendous power released to establish God's will on earth.

Chapter 17
Leadership in Church Prayer Groups

Now that we've talked about group prayer as a whole, plus its place in and through the local church, we will discuss in this chapter a vital aspect of group prayer — its leadership.

It is clear as we continue our teaching on corporate prayer that prayer groups will have many different sizes and styles. Just as each church will have its own flavor, given by the Lord and formed by the territory and work the Lord has called it to, so will prayer groups be unique.

I like to draw a parallel between churches and families. Going into different churches is like going into different family settings. You experience different tastes and smell different smells, but the household is still a real home and family unit.

You don't say that another family is not a family because the house doesn't look the same, have the same rules, or function like yours does. The family is free to be who they are. And when you go into that house, you must eventually become like them to be in harmony there.

Prayer groups should also be free to be who they are in Christ and to operate as God has called them to function. Then they can be their best and produce everlasting fruit.

Even though the group is free, it is freest when it is submitted under the authority of a pastor or ministry. From that point, there should be established order and authority within the group itself. To maintain the peace and freedom when others come into the praying "family," they must follow the family rules, become a part of the family, or go somewhere else where they can fit in.

I have found that no matter how big the group is, or what its style is, to maintain order and be effective, there should be one person who leads the group and is responsible to the head pastor or minister for the group. Sometimes choosing the leader is difficult, but the pastor and group members can settle this with maturity and humility toward God and one another.

My recommendation for a prayer group leader begins with someone who qualifies under the biblical standards for the helps ministry. First, the leader must be one who recognizes and understands God-given authority and how to obey that authority. The leader should be humble, teachable, and in harmony with the pastor, and keep the prayer meetings within the boundaries of the vision, calling, and principles of the Word of God and the church.

Second, a God-given leader should be one who shows fruits of faithfulness — dedication to the Word, to God, and to the church. A faithful leader is dependable, and by the fruit of the Spirit able to be steadfast under all circumstances. Paul said it is best to commit revelation to faithful men (not just those with education or reputation), and it is these men and women who will be able to teach others (see Second Timothy 2:2).

Third, leaders must have a good testimony and strong character qualities in their personal life. A good checklist in the Word of God is in First Timothy 3:8-13, which teaches about the qualifications of workers and helpers in the church.

A leader should have these qualities, or should be openly working on the development of them before God and the pastor. People who are living in known sin, or who are hard and stubborn toward change in fleshly and carnal habits in their lives should not hold a position of leadership.

Finally, Acts 6:3 declares that helps ministries, servants, should come out of the church itself (not be hired or borrowed from the world or another church except in a training situation). They should be full of the Holy Spirit, faith, and wisdom. It is people like this that God is developing in the local church to be placed over the business of the prayer work in the church!

Prayer — A Helps Ministry

Notice that I have called the business of prayer in the church a part of the helps ministry. An intercessory prayer group always comes under the category of the helps ministry, and it is never to be considered a fivefold ministry gift in position, authority, or anointing. Every fivefold minister should be an intercessor, but not every intercessor is a pulpit fivefold minister.

What I have seen in the past is intercessors overstepping their God-given realm of authority and sometimes going into realms they have no right or anointing to be in.

For example, as a believer-intercessor works with the Holy Spirit in intercession on the level of John 16:13,14, the Holy Spirit will show him things to come. Sometimes an intercessor will also come under a prophetic anointing in prayer to see and hear what God wants to do on the subject the group is praying for. But a believer-intercessor is never a prophet!

Prayer warriors stand without "glasses." God has given "glasses" to fivefold office prophets to see more clearly and much further than those without these God-given glasses. Some prayer warriors try to wear prophet glasses, but become confused and fall into ditches because they can't see straight. They walk on ground they are not equipped for, and they end up attacked and killed because they knowingly or unknowingly overstepped their area in God.

The devil likes to attack intercessory prayer groups with lies that they are prophets, and they have control over the pastor and the order and decisions of the church. Some are deceived into believing they are the only ones who hear from God. Directions for life and ministry are never predetermined by an intercessor or anyone else, for that matter. They are determined by God and God alone.

Anytime we pray, force, or manipulate our own ideas, plans, and will on someone else, it is witchcraft. If a believer is overstepping his boundaries, that's an open door for Satan to release control and manipulation against members, families, the pastor, the church, or the Body of Christ.

Be sure you are in the right position, praying out of true, sound revelation from the Word and the Spirit, and be sure your motives are pure love and the promotion of the kingdom of God.

Every Believer, An Intercessor

Another attack on prayer groups can be super-spirituality, pride, and exclusiveness. One of the best ways I have found to overcome this is to lay this foundation in your whole church: *Every believer is called to do the works of Jesus* (John 14:12).

The works of Jesus are teaching, preaching, healing, casting out demons, and praying. Therefore, *every believer* is called to do these same things, one of them being to intercede.

All believers are intercessors. All must press in to pray like Jesus did. All can be mighty in prayer!

When this foundation and standard is established, it must be walked out. The pastor and leadership can't be prayerless or afraid of prayer. They must be the first, the wildest, the loudest, and the freest! The people will do as the leadership does. The people then must be encouraged, trained, and practicing prayer.

When believers know that everyone is called to pray, and all are doing it, or growing in it — when it is a *common* goal for the whole church — no one feels intimidated or superior, because the church does not accept that kind of mentality or talk.

No one wears an "intercessor badge" on his shirt; no one is special — all pray. Some obviously have more time than others to pray; some have more experience, but that's all they have. Those with experience should openly teach the others, be willing to learn more, and never think they have all, know all, or do all!

When this principle is established and lived out, everyone can feel safe and secure in prayer, knowing the boundaries and guidelines the church has established in the Lord.

The Pastor and the Prayer Group

If you are a pastor, there is no need for you to be afraid of prayer or strong intercessors in your church. If you are afraid of prayer, your hands are tied and you can't do anything.

A wise pastor knows there is a place for everything in the Bible and all operations and manifestations of the Holy Spirit within the local church. There is room for everything in a local church!

God can and will anoint you to help and guide all the groups in your church. He will teach and show you what is right! Trust Him to do that, and don't get intimidated or throw prayer out because of strong prayer warriors or past bad experiences with prayer warriors. If you fear this, ask Jesus to set you free.

If you are afraid of offending people with prayer, ask Jesus to set you free from fear of man. Your church is called to be a strong, bold, fervently praying church. Be open and public about it!

There are several ways to overcome problem prayer groups in your church. First, you should pray and hear from God the calling and specific directions for your church. Be firm with it. Don't compromise with people who want to manipulate you by their rebellion.

Second, communicate this plan with the church and the prayer leaders. They can be the best support you have; and, as in a marriage, communication is a key. Openness is vital in your relationship with your prayer leaders. Listen to what they have to say on some areas, but remember that *you* must make the final decision.

Most good prayer workers can accept that; especially if you allow them to share with you what they think the Lord is saying — even if they are wrong! Listening and respect is vital from both parties.

Third, learn as much about prayer as possible. You may not be the expert or pro, but be open and teach the people by precept and example. If someone knows more than you, use them to your own benefit, at the same time being secure in your calling and position as the pastor.

Last, be open with your people about your prayer life. Let them know you pray and let them see you at the prayer meetings. A pastor can never expect a prayer group to do all the praying for the work, or have all the responsibility to carry the work. Pray, lead, and feed!

Prayer has an important role in the life of the local church. It is not something we can ignore, throw out or, on the other hand, become exclusive with. A pastor once told me that his church wasn't called to pray, so they don't really do it much. I thought, "Poor man and poor church!" Then I prayed, "Lord, help them see and come boldly and strongly into what You have for them!"

Establish an Authority Structure

Once a leader has been chosen, it is important that he or she understands how to be the leader of the prayer group. The leader is established by the authority and is then given the responsibility to actually take charge, manage, and direct the prayer time. Again, it is best to have one leader, because "anything that has two heads is a monster," and anything with no head will walk into a ditch!

Just as there is an authority structure in the local church, so there should be an authority order in a prayer meeting. The leader is neither a dictator nor the expert intercessor, but the one who is under the pastor and the Holy Spirit to take the group into God's plan for the prayer meeting.

Group prayer should be free to flow in the spirit, but if there's no structure and no channel for the Holy Spirit to flow through, it makes it difficult to maintain the strength, purpose, and focus of the group. The leader serves this purpose.

Often people don't have the knowledge or ability, as a group, to come together and take themselves into the presence of God and flow in the spirit as a corporate body. They become so disorganized with everyone trying to do his own thing that nothing really gets accomplished. That's why it's important to establish a leader.

The leader should be someone who knows about prayer and is submitted to and working closely with the pastor. However, if no one knows anything about prayer — if you're faced with a simple beginning, which is the best place to start — you can use the teachings in this book to help you. The Holy Spirit will train, teach, and help you to be a leader in prayer if you have been given that responsibility. God is with you! Believe it!

Communication Is Vital

It's important that the leader of the prayer group have the heart, calling, vision, and purpose of the ministry in his or her own heart. He should know what the heart of the leadership of the church is. His job is to take that heart and vision, and what he knows about the natural needs and circumstances, and begin to take it into prayer with the group to see the results of the vision come to pass.

Not only is it important for the leader to have the heart and the vision of the ministry in his own heart and mind; it is also important for him to have contact with the authority — the pastor or the ministry he works with — so he can have some knowledge of what specific needs are to be prayed for, where God is leading, what the enemy is doing, and where the ministry is going.

It's vital that there be communication between the leader of the prayer group and the work itself; especially if the pastor is not leading the group personally. This communication also shuts the door for misunderstanding in the future between the pastor and the prayer group. If we are wise, we can keep the door closed on the devil and his tricks with prayer groups!

The leader of the group represents God's authority in and for the prayer group. Some people don't like the word "authority," and many really don't understand it, but it's necessary that there be an authority structure. Remember that group prayer is different from individual prayer, because you are not alone, and you must be willing to sacrifice your opinions, ideas, and position to be in God's order in the group. You must be willing to respect, recognize, and submit to the chosen leader.

Many people's attitudes and motives must be dealt with immediately, because jealousy, fear of submission, rebellion, and private ambitions will destroy any prayer group. You must be willing to flow in the direction the leader takes the group by the Holy Spirit, and give up your own individual ways and personal desires. God will bless this, and the group will be strong.

Because you are not at home praying with the freedom of being alone, group prayer is a discipline. In group prayer, every member must submit to the direction of the leader. The goal is for each person to come into the flow of the *group*. It's important that you discipline yourself when you come to group prayer to go the way the group is going and not the way your flesh and mind want to go.

Group members should keep one ear, as it were, on the voice of their inner man and one on the leader, and they should try to pray the same way the leader is praying; to follow the leader. You have to practice this technique to actually get it to work for you. But there is strength when everyone is going in the same direction, praying the same way in submission to the leader. Again, independence and rebellion have no place in group prayer.

If travail comes over you, but not the leader or the rest of the group, just put your head down and quietly yield to the Holy Spirit, all the while checking to make sure that it *is* on you. Even though the Holy Spirit may lead you a little bit differently in the prayer, your attitude is not to be an island to yourself, or to draw attention to yourself.

Discipline yourself to work as closely with the leader as possible. Learn to listen to the Holy Spirit and find where the flow of life is and the kind of prayer the Holy Spirit desires there — and go that way together. If there is a discrepancy, the leader's way prevails! Discipline yourselves to all flow in the same direction.

Take the People Into Prayer

The primary job of the leader is to take the people into prayer. As we saw in the last chapter, the key to success in group prayer is one mind, one spirit, one accord, and one vision. The leader's job is to bring the people into that place of unity.

You say, "Well, that seems impossible," but it's not impossible if you realize that as the leader, you represent authority, and the people will do what you do. The people will follow what you do as a leader. So lead!

You must establish your authority in your prayer group by taking it. That is not to say you walk around controlling, dominating, or ruling the whole meeting. However, for a structure and a flow of life, people must know that they should submit themselves and follow you as the leader.

If there is a problem with this, it may be necessary to confront any rebellion in the group or have the pastor reiterate who the leader is. Of course, there are times in the prayer meeting when we pray alone or in smaller groups, but when the people know there is a leader present in the room, it brings security and strength to the meeting.

As a leader, your function is to lead people into prayer, to help them in all kinds of prayer, and to teach them how the Holy Spirit is directing to pray for a particular situation.

It's important in the prayer group that the leader be open and sensitive to God; that he knows the different kinds of prayer himself, and he is ready to go in the direction the Holy Spirit leads. When you are open and obedient to God, you will find that the Holy Spirit will give a God-ordained variety and freshness to the group.

Group prayer will become boring if you fall into religious, monotonous routine. That is not to say, of course, that you won't have standards and patterns that you adhere to, but you will lose people if you pray exactly the same way about everything all the time. That's why it is good for you to know and practice different kinds of prayer, as led by the Holy Spirit. And, of course, you are also more effective that way.

Be Aware of the Spiritual Climate

When the group actually comes into the time of prayer, the leader has three purposes. First of all, the leader must be aware of the spiritual climate surrounding the situation being prayed about. You will notice that usually each subject you pray about in your prayer group has a different "feeling," so to speak, in the spirit.

For example, when we pray for our pastor, there are some days when the spiritual climate around that situation is quite open, and there is a tremendous sense of ease in praying for him. On other days, if the persecution has been strong, or if there are other attacks concerning his life and work, the climate is very hard; so as a leader, I must be sensitive and be able to help the group come through in that climate.

On days when it is hard, I just keep praying and carry it through. If the group wants to quit, I don't allow them to stop until we pray through to a note of victory. I am careful to communicate to them what the Holy Spirit is showing me so they don't feel lost or weighed down and not know why.

Second, the leader must be aware of where the group members are as a whole. The group will increase in knowledge the more you practice, and the more you pray. The more the people learn to pray and work with the leader, the stronger the group will become.

The leader, however, needs to be aware that there can be different attacks, cares, or thoughts in the minds of the intercessors, so it's important to bring them all together by encouraging them to take their thoughts captive, cast their cares on the Lord, and keep on praying. Sometimes people come to the group who are not at the same skill level as the others, and that can make it harder to pull everyone together — but it can be done!

The job of the leader is to hold onto the spiritual climate, to know where the people in the group are and, third, to work with the Holy Spirit and carry the prayer need, the prayer request, all the way through until you get the answer.

The leader must be sensitive to the Holy Spirit, because each day, and for each prayer need, He will flow in different ways. The leader must be aware of this and work with the Holy Spirit. It may sound like a lot, but it really will flow and work as you grow.

I've had people ask if the leader can stop the prayer in the middle of praying. Yes — absolutely — if the prayer is not working, or if the Holy Spirit is leading another way. The leader should stop the prayer if the group needs correction or direction, if they're not praying the right way, or if the leader feels there needs to be a change, an explanation, or an encouragement.

I stop the prayer many times and say, "This is what the Holy Spirit is saying. This is where we need to go." I encourage the prayer group, "Come on, keep praying, keep praying. We're going to stay with this now." Communication is important in your prayer group, so don't be afraid to communicate what the Holy Spirit may be saying and the direction you should pray.

Developing Warriors

Now let's consider the prayer warriors themselves from a leadership perspective. First, any believer can be trained to pray, so the prayer group can and should consist of different kinds and ages of people. I really believe it's important for the group to have a variety of people participating.

When you plan this way, you can break any spirit of exclusivity that would try to come over your groups. Even if the group is small and doesn't have much knowledge about prayer, they can be trained in group prayer and be disciplined if the leader will teach, lead, and encourage, and if they'll pray together regularly.

Another thing I have found about prayer groups is that any group that is really serious about prayer usually is "tough" or strong spiritually, and can be developed into a mighty powerhouse for God!

Some days it seems exceedingly hard to pray, and I wonder how the group is going to handle it — if they'll be worn out, or want to give up. Most groups, I've found, can take a lot more than your carnal mind thinks they can handle. The tendency of the flesh is for comfort and ease, but if you purpose to break through these things and train them to pray in hard times, they will succeed and be strong.

If you will train the prayer warriors, lead them, and all go into prayer as one person, each helping to pull the load, you can accomplish more than you think. The group can pray strong, loud, and for a long period of time and not be stressed out or worn out spiritually. This doesn't come overnight, but if you want it and ask God for it, He will give it to you.

I remember a prayer group I was in once that helped me grow tremendously. One time when we were praying, I wanted to quit. My mind was wandering, and maybe I was tired or hungry. The prayer group leader said, "Somebody here is not praying."

I thought, "Oh no, I don't want her to find out that it's me," so even though I was tired, I put my head down and kept praying and giving what I had. God honored it, and its fruit was endurance and strength in my prayer life.

Prayer warriors can take more than you think. Don't be afraid to work and get stronger in the spirit. Press in a little. It may hurt your flesh or your spiritual muscles, but I have never had one prayer warrior die from working a bit. They only get stronger. Sometimes prayer will be work and require rigorous and even tedious action because the ground you are walking on spiritually will often be of different terrain.

Teaching Is Important

In a prayer group, it's a good practice to take a limited amount of time to teach scriptural principles about prayer. During this time, the leader's primary purpose is to instruct the group in all kinds of prayer and what the Bible says about the prayer life.

Be careful when it comes to the teaching time not to waste valuable prayer time by teaching too long. It's easier on the flesh to teach than it is to pray. It's important that you as a group not lose your purpose or let anything steal your prayer time. To do this, teaching must be kept to a minimum.

When you do give instruction, provide knowledge about different kinds of prayer and about the spiritual world and how it functions. Share your own experiences with the Lord. Teach on the lifestyle of a prayer warrior, the Christian life, biblical principles about prayer and God, or anything else that could be related to the prayer life.

After the teaching, it is time to enter into prayer. The biblical way to enter in is through praise and worship. This time should be kept short, because the purpose of the group is to pray, not just to worship God, although worship has its place. In church prayer groups, I keep praise and worship to a minimum unless the Holy Spirit strongly leads us to worship, because worship is a kind of prayer (see Chapter 8).

Sometimes people get tired and need to be refreshed, so you may worship for a longer time; but usually it's best to devote a short time to sing, rejoice, get the heart and mind on God, and set the atmosphere. I always say that prayer begins with worship and praise. People should enter in then, not when there is prayer in tongues or in the understanding. Spend some time worshipping the Lord. Then, from that point, go right into praying.

Another way the Holy Spirit may periodically lead your group is to have members deal with their hearts before the throne of God. Praise and worship leads us into fellowship and communion with the Father.

Because of that, prayer warriors need to learn how to spend time with God in the secret place, how to be quiet with God, how to cry out to God for themselves, how to break up hard ground in their own hearts, how to confess sin if they need to, and how to rejoice before the Lord by themselves in a group.

As you bow in worship at the throne of God, the fire of God will burn away chaff and expose the heart. At the throne, God wants to speak, and impart His nature, and intimate secrets to His people.

When your group is in that place, take a few minutes, depending on how the Spirit of God leads, and let them find the place in their hearts where the flow, the river of the Holy Spirit, is located. Have them pray in the spirit and listen on the inside. Then let them be alone with God, and encourage them to allow God to deal with their heart before Him. Encourage them to feel and experience the presence and holiness of God.

The leader must be sure at these times that the prayer warriors don't come into a melancholy spirit or dig into their self-consciousness, causing a fleshly sadness, depression, and isolation. Make sure, when they're reaching out to God, loving Him, or confessing sin, that they're always in a flow of *life* — even though it may be serious. You are always to come out and up to God, not be pushed back and down into yourself.

The prayer warriors are now ready to go into strong battle. They've dealt with their hearts before the Lord, and they have worked together with Him. They're sensitive and ready to go wherever the Holy Spirit leads.

Flowing with the Spirit in group prayer, you will discover that you go through different times and seasons in prayer. All of them are a vital part of your prayer group and are important if the group is to maintain its strength and an exciting, fresh atmosphere.

People should love to pray. They love to pray because of the tone and attitude the leader creates. Create an environment that considers prayer a joy. Prayer *is* a joy; it's not a burden or obligation. Have fun when you pray! Meet God!

Break Through Resistance

When you pray, you will find that the atmosphere, or the spiritual climate, can be different every day. As you pray on a regular basis, you will also find that when you come into the door of the spirit, the environment will feel different, depending on what you're praying about. There are times when prayer will seem like it is a burden.

An example of this is found in Daniel 10. Daniel was praying about God's will for the children of Israel. The first day he decided to pray, his prayer was heard before God, but because there was warfare in the heavenlies, the angel could not come through that warfare in one day.

It took 21 days for the angel to break through with the answer! When Daniel was praying, there was much resistance around him, and the spiritual atmosphere was hard, yet he continued to persevere, and the answer came.

Sometimes when you come into the prayer meeting, you sense that there is much resistance or spiritual heaviness around you. It's not because something is wrong with you, but because the "temperature" around different subjects varies. Because of what may be happening in the ministry at the time, or because of the subject you're praying about, you can experience resistance and, like Daniel, you've got to keep praying.

When you experience resistance in the spiritual climate, it's not a time to sing; it's a time to keep praying. It's not a time to try to force your prayers out; it's a time when the prayer warriors should draw from their inner man and really press in and press through the resistance.

You have to be willing to pray for more than two minutes! Go as long as it takes to sense a breakthrough and victory. This takes some practice, but the more you pray and work with the Holy Spirit, the stronger you'll become.

Because of a lack of knowledge about the spiritual world and how it works, many prayer groups go down in the initial resistance.

There are many examples of men and women in the Bible who faced opposition, but they did not quit. Actually, the opposition encouraged them to go harder, stronger, and bolder. For example, when the early believers were threatened not to continue (and that's what the devil wants you to do) preaching the Gospel, they went home and asked for *more* boldness (see Acts 4:29)!

They didn't think something was wrong with them, and they didn't get discouraged. They knew God was with them, even in opposition, persecution, and hard times. They had obeyed God and hit the enemy in the face — and he had simply reacted. Now they needed to keep going!

There are tasks and assignments that God will give you and your prayer group to pray through until you see results. God knows that you can carry it, and that with Him you can solve every problem. The Holy Spirit will show you the keys of how to break through in prayer, and how to actually see results in the natural; but we must determine to come up higher in God and to stand firm in His will.

There is a temptation daily in the work of prayer and in the Lord's work in general to give up. Remember, God is with you. God wants to conquer through you and take territory from the devil.

You will be attacked, but God will create in you an aggressive, fighting spirit. He wants you to take the initiative, gain knowledge and experience, and be a good soldier; not a lazy, undisciplined soldier!

God wants you to react in the spirit like David did toward Goliath, and run *toward* the enemy to take him. He doesn't want you to run *away* from problems, or any kind of opposition through intimidation, fear, and defeat!

Keep on the Right Track

When you renew your mind and accept the fact that there has *always* been resistance to the Gospel and that you will also experience some when you start following the plan of God, you will be able to go on when the dust is flying everywhere! God will give you a revelation in your spirit to *live* as a warrior, and not just think or sing about it.

God will see to it that you become strong and free to stand as a mighty warrior. It will take some changes on your part — stronger dedication, holiness, discipline, and deliverance. It will take more Word in you, and a retraining of your thinking and actions, but if you want this with all your heart, God will give it to you! Be open to Him, and let Him do it in you however He wants to — whatever the cost!

The Body of Christ must realize that one of our promises and blessings in Jesus Christ is that we are over, and not under (see Deuteronomy 28:13). When that is a revelation to you, you can use resistance to push you up in the spirit instead of letting it push you down.

I always tell prayer warriors that when we sense resistance in prayer, we're on the right track! You're not going to experience resistance every day, and you shouldn't look for it every day, but when it's there — and you'll *know* when it's there — let it lift you up.

Train yourself to enjoy it. Make up your mind to *like* resistance. I teach our prayer warriors that we are created for hard times, so keep praying. I also tell them that even when you have some resistance, eventually it has to break down and back off, if you don't first! It will come down. You and your group are stronger than any resistance that can come against you in the spirit, or any persecution that can come against you in the natural.

One thing that can create resistance is natural circumstances. For example, a church on the cutting edge of what God is doing in its city and nation may sometimes receive unfavorable publicity, or unbelievers and believers alike may say negative things that can create a strong feeling of opposition, isolation, and resistance.

Of course, we never need to fight our battle against people in the natural, but because we understand where the battle is coming from, we can continue to break through into victory through prayer.

Sometimes resistance comes from people in the prayer meeting. Their minds, flesh, or carnal ideas can cause resistance or pressure in the spiritual atmosphere. Submitting the flesh to the Holy Spirit is a decision, and that decision can create an atmosphere for breakthrough in a prayer meeting. That's why dealing with our hearts, as we mentioned earlier, is so important.

Be Ready for Battle

There are many factors that can make a spiritual climate difficult to penetrate, so remember: Every prayer meeting is a battle. Train yourselves as a prayer group that even though there may be some form of resistance, you have weapons you were created to use, and they do pull down strongholds. You will pray through!

Another type of resistance you will encounter as you pray is an unplowed area; new ground that has not been worked before. It could involve a new revelation or a work God wants to do in your church, your city, believers there, yourself, or the ministry you're part of. When you start to pray about that area, you realize it's like trying to open the gate to a field where no one has been for many years.

The gate is very squeaky; perhaps even rusted shut. In the spirit, it seems like you're pulling that gate open through your prayers. The Holy Spirit will help you. It's hard work, and often there is resistance.

Sometimes it seems like you have to stay in there and *pull* that gate open — or perhaps it would be more accurate to say it seems like you have to go in and *kick* the gate down! But, praise the Lord, the Holy Spirit is with you, and He'll help you.

Praying for an unplowed area can also be compared with walking through a swamp. There are weeds, trees, muck, and obstacles everywhere. You've purposed in your heart to go to the other side, to get through the swamp, but it's hard work just pulling your feet out of the mucky water at times. It takes effort to keep going.

However it seems as you pray, do keep going, keep pressing in. Kick open the gate, go in there, pull out the weeds, knock down the trees, clear out the obstacles, and come through the swamp. Pave the way for what God desires to do in that area. This is what prayer does. It takes some work, but it's exciting!

You will experience resistance in different ways and different forms, but you will always win if you don't quit. You will always prevail with the Word, with the Spirit of God, and with the anointing that's over you to pray. You will get stronger and better at prayer as you continue to pray.

These are just a few guidelines for you as a prayer group leader. There is more material in Appendices 1 and 2 that will help you develop a strong prayer department in your church and ministry.

Every prayer group is called and equipped as God sees fit — there are no two that are the same. I pray that you will find a group or start one that is based on biblical principles, has a pure and right spirit, is bold and mighty, and gets powerful results to God's glory!

God bless you as you begin to pray effective, fervent prayers!

Appendix 1
Spiritual Exercises

To grow in any area of life, we must put into practice, or exercise, that specific area. People do not get stronger physically without exercise. People do not get stronger spiritually without spiritual exercise.

Exercise is defined as "the act of bringing into play or realizing in action, regular or repeated use of a faculty or bodily organ, something performed or practiced in order to develop, improve or display a specific skill or power, a drill carried out for training and discipline" (Webster's).

Prayer is the heart of Christian living. In practicing prayer, or exercising prayer principles, skill can and will be produced. A team does not grow, improve, or win unless they work out.

Your prayer group can periodically practice the following drills so that they can grow, improve, develop, and become skillful in prayer. It may take discipline, training, and working on "untrained muscles," but do not hold back; go for it!

Remember, growth calls for extended periods of time devoted to the mastery of certain skills. Growth is not simply the acceptance of an interesting idea.

1. Present a topic that needs to be prayed over. Pick three people to share scriptures on that topic. This helps to renew our minds concerning what God says about situations and gives a foundation for faith.

2. At times when you pray in the understanding, have new and different people in the group, not always the leader, take the lead in prayer.

3. Have each person practice praying in tongues and then interpreting their tongues. You could also have them practice

singing spontaneous love songs to the Lord in the spirit and in the understanding.

4. Practice different tongues and dialects.

5. Have each member of the group pray in tongues for personal edification only, not intercession, for 30 minutes before you begin to intercede.

6. Have each member speak to God for five minutes in the understanding only.

7. Find something Paul prayed for people and have your group pray it over each other, your congregation, or your ministry.

8. Break into smaller groups periodically.

9. Spend one prayer time just thanking God for all your requests. Minister to the Lord. Wait on Him.

10. Spend a prayer time praying only for the traveling ministries your church loves and supports. Pray also for other churches.

11. Always encourage a periodic sharing of praise reports and answered prayers.

12. Spend 30 minutes just praying for the government on all levels.

13. After a special meeting at your church, pray over everything that was said and done, and pray over any "word of the Lord" that came forth in prophecy or in the Word. (Daniel did this over Jeremiah's word.)

14. Spend 30 minutes praying for the lost and for other countries.

15. Pray for the pastor and staff weekly, with or without their being present. Pastors could have trusted intercessors pray for them, their families, and church leadership regularly. Periodically, the pastor or group leader should lay hands on and minister to the intercessors. All this helps prevent "battle fatigue" and promotes unity in the spirit.

16. Periodically, have a special speaker just for the prayer group.

17. Have a question-and-answer session prior to praying.

18. Do not be afraid to experiment and try new things that work for your prayer group.

These can be used if your group is young, or to promote freedom in the spirit. Use these exercises if you need them.

Each group is different. Follow after what God has for you. The highest compliment to a strong leader is when the intercessors say after a prayer meeting, "We did it ourselves."

Appendix 2

Guidelines for Prayer Group Leaders To Develop Mature Prayer Warriors

Over a period of many years, I have been involved with several different prayer groups. For the most part, my experience has been blessed by the Lord.

I have learned a variety of things directly from God, some things from other people's experiences with prayer groups, and yet other things from working with prayer groups and prayer schools intimately and regularly.

I want to share these thoughts with you to help you as you press on to know the Lord in corporate prayer. It is possible to have strong, stable, mature groups that will be a blessing in your church or ministry.

These suggestions are in no way all inclusive: I am sure you can add to the list yourself, but I know these notes can be a start in the right direction for your group.

1. People will learn by watching and listening to the leader pray. They will do what you do. Be sure to be yourself with the Father and with others. Do not be afraid to let them hear you pray, to ask for forgiveness, to ask for help, and to be honest before God.

2. Do not pressure intercessors to be spiritual or to grow. Let God develop them. Be an inspiration, not a pressure.

3. Be sure to keep yourself built up so intercessors can draw on you. They need to be ministered to at times so they don't develop battle fatigue. You also need to be "prayed up," so if God wants to use them in a prayer meeting, you will need to be sensitive to His hand on them.

4. Be sensitive to the appropriate time when intercessors can share what the Lord is teaching, saying, or revealing to them personally about prayer subjects, or about life with God.

5. Teach intercessors all kinds of prayer. Practice all kinds of prayer.

6. Be interested in their personal lives, and encourage them to go on with God and grow in their faith. Defeats and victories in the personal areas in your prayer group's lives can affect the overall atmosphere of the prayer group. Pray for the group members in your own prayer time.

One thing I have noticed is that when prayer groups start to enter into higher levels of intercession, the Holy Spirit will begin to deal with and reveal different areas *in their own lives* that need to be corrected or changed.

It is true that when you walk in the light, all forms of darkness are exposed, including those that may be working in and against the prayer warriors.

Purity, holiness, and deliverance are required to walk in high and strong levels with God. God will speak about this and bring you into the cleansing process so the devil doesn't hit your group members as you begin to hit his kingdom! Trust God to do this and to help you when His dealings start to flow. The Lord wants the intercessors to be strong and free!

7. Have the group pray Paul's prayers regularly.

8. Teach intercessors always to be worshippers of God, teachable, and respectful to people, to God's orders, and to positions in the Body of Christ.

9. Be sure to be specific, not general, in prayer.

10. Do not necessarily teach travail first. Let the intercessors learn to develop confidence in working with the Holy Spirit. Build a solid foundation. Yet be sure to teach travail, so they are skillful and strong in it.

11. Be sure to stay in the Word, and when you pray, be sure to set guidelines according to scriptural principles. Have the group members look in the Word for themselves and practice finding specific scriptures to stand on for specific prayer requests. Equip and train them spiritually. Have them look over their weapons and know how to use them effectively. Some weapons include the Name, the Word of God, tongues, and groanings.

12. Be available for questions, but if you do not know the answer, be honest and say so.

13. Always be open for new people to join the group. If you encourage them and train them, they will learn with time and be a blessing, especially if they have a right heart.

14. Put something into your intercessors. Tell them you love them. Pray for them. Allow the nucleus of the group to carry the group through. Do not be concerned about numbers. Be led by the Spirit on how your group is to operate, because every group is different.

15. Be sure to accomplish your purpose — no gossip or unnecessary ministry to individual group members.

16. Teach the prayer group members to keep guard over their mouth. That which is discussed and prayed about stays within the group. What God reveals is not grounds for personal pride, or to build someone's spiritual reputation or career.

Unnecessary talk can minimize the power of your prayers, especially if you pray one way and talk another! A prayer warrior's mouth is one of the greatest weapons he or she has. It should stay clean and full of faith!

17. Give intercessors freedom to grow and develop in their personal prayer lives. Do not control them, yet keep a watch on them in the Spirit. Never lose touch with where they are with God, so they will not get flaky. Remember, sometimes people just grow out of things spiritually — God helps them.

18. To avoid exclusiveness and pride in the group, always encourage the members to be involved with other activities within the local church. Intercessors are not exclusive or special — they are believers!

19. There may be group members you must be willing to confront, correct, or report to the pastor, if necessary. These are the tendencies to be aware of and watch closely. A person who:

   a. regularly prays louder and out of harmony with the group
   b. talks and acts more "spiritual" than the others, and regularly seems to have some kind of exotic spiritual experience
   c. always wants to be in control and have personal power
   d. seldom is in church services; neglects practical obligations with family, home, and work
   e. exhibits no desire to have God deal with character in their life

f. talks against authority, including yours or any other leadership, especially the pastor's; always knows better and has a better opinion of how things should be done in the group or the church

g. regularly has guidelines, advice, or prophecies for someone else's life and ministry, and these guidelines are the "law" — these guidelines can be especially dangerous if they are the "do-or-die" type

h. suffers severe bouts of bitterness, rejection, and rebellion from being corrected

i. always wants a title

The Holy Spirit will help you and show you the group members' hearts and motives and how and when to deal with them in love. He will also show you who fits and where they fit in your group and in the overall work of the church.

Go for it! Take ground for God! Have *mighty* victories!

To receive our free newsletter,
or for ministry information, contact:

Mary Alice Isleib Ministries
P.O. Box 46105
Minneapolis, MN 55446

Feel free to include your prayer requests
and comments when you write.

For further education and instruction by precept and example on Group Prayer, Mary Alice Isleib Ministries offers a three-tape video series and teaching manual called "God's Warriors — Prayer in the Local Church." For ordering information, please contact our office at the above address.